Two Wheels Around New Zealand

A Bicycle Journey on Friendly Roads

by
Scott Bischke

Ecopress
Corvallis, Oregon

Ecopress

"Books and art that enhance environmental awareness"

1029 NE Kirsten Place
Corvallis, Oregon 97330
Telephone: 1-800-326-9272
SAN: 298-1238
Email: Ecopress@compuserve.com
World Wide Web: http://www.peak.org /~ecopress/

Back cover photos (clockwise from top): Milford Sound, New Zealand Kiwi, North Island biking in the rain, Urewara National Park creek crossing.

Photos by Scott Bischke and Katie Gibson

Printed on 100% recycled paper (>20% post-consumer)
ISBN: 0-9639705-1-8
LCCC: 89-35041

Printed in the United States of America
10 9 8 7 6 5 4 3 2 1

for Kate

CONTENTS

Chapter	Page

ACKNOWLEDGMENTS

This book exists because of the support and encouragement of friends and family. Foremost, of course, are the myriad of Kiwis (and Aussies) who unselfishly shared their homes and lives with us. Your numbers are boundless and the story might never be told if I stopped to name each of you individually. I have endeavored to capture you faithfully in the pages that follow. Hopefully you will see yourselves, laugh, and remember. Possibly that can serve as my thanks. Also, there is this–wherever Kate and I land, our home and hearts will always hold a place for you.

Yanks have also done their share. First, thanks to Chris Beatty and **Ecopress** for creating the opportunity to share our story, for their enthusiasm, and for their spirit of environmental awareness. Thanks also to the many unofficial editors who helped improve the book along the way. Thanks to friends Bob and Mary Parham, who labored through the earliest addition. Special recognition to Bev Louie and Ron Finch for the use of their computer, without which this book would have remained a wild musing of the mind. Bev's editing suggestions were sometimes radical, yet always filled with wisdom. Much of the book's layout is directly creditable to her

And family.... Thanks to my folks and Susie and Dennis for believing in our dreams—first the journey, then the book. Heartfelt thanks to Ellen and Giff Gibson for their continuous support. Ellen's comments provided much help (and a few chuckles). Giff's limitless knowledge was only matched by his unending willingness to help correct my bumblings. I can only hope to someday be as worthy a writer as he.

Finally, my thanks and love to Kate. Without you, this would mean nothing. You are, now more than ever, my inspiration.

Scott Bischke

New Zealand

OF EELS AND POSSUMS

Chapter 1

"Eels have sharp teeth," Russell was saying as we rattled down the road towards the start of the track. We sat three-abreast in the dusty front seat of his truck; the packs bounced along in back. "Eels chase trout sometimes," Russell continued. "Consider 'em good tucker, I reckon."

"They don't bother fishermen, do they?" I asked, leaning forward and looking past Kate to Russell.

"Most eels won't worry you, you'll be 'right." Then, as kind of an afterthought, he added, "They do get mighty big, though."

How big, I wondered.

We pulled in at Ngamuriwai Flat and unloaded the packs. Russell slid back his terry cloth hat and then started to roll a cigarette.

"You're likely to run into a possum or two," he said without looking up. "Pesky lil' buggers. Kiwi possums have a sort of pig-like snout and make a gruntin' noise. Not like the possums you Yanks are used to. They're nocturnal and damn me hide if they don't get into everythin'."

We pulled on our backpacks, bid Russell farewell, and started walking. Kate and I were tramping to the junction of the Wairoa and Waiau Rivers on New Zealand's North Island. It was

December 29th. We'd been in New Zealand exactly two weeks.

For the first couple miles we tramped through hills stripped bare by lumbering. Then we crossed into the Urewara National Park and, simultaneously, heavy bush. The track dropped into the deep recess of a valley. Hungry hook grass tore at our legs; pigfern hindered our passage. At the valley floor the track zigzagged across a small stream a hundred times. Often the track simply was the stream. Six hours in from the road, Kate and I reached Parahaki Hut and unshouldered our packs. Thick bush bordered the hut on three sides, the Waiau River on the fourth. A wooden veranda ran along two walls of the hut. Inside we found chairs and a rickety table, an open fireplace, and old candle remnants. Twelve torn mattresses topped an equal number of bunks that stood three high against one wall.

We were alone.

Later, near dusk, I stood in thigh-deep water, fishing and shivering. I cast my fly to pass along an overhanging bush. Suddenly a four foot apparition slithered out of the black, opened a giant mouth to the fly, then pulled back. As quickly as it had come, the eel disappeared. I looked down at my bare legs, then eased myself out of the water—enough for tonight.

● ● ●

A couple days after we arrived at Parahaki Hut, a round bushman and his twelve year old daughter strolled in. The man wore a soiled shirt, soiled running shorts, and half-laced gumboots. He carried a scopeless rifle. His small compatriot was similarly stained and frequently pushed back her stringy blonde hair. She carried a hunting knife belted bandito-style around her middle.

The pair were deer hunting along the river and stopped by in hopes of finding a cup of tea. Earlier we had learned that bush etiquette states that the hosts provide a "hot cuppa." Soon the billy pot came alive with the smell of sweet tea. As the tea began to boil, I asked about eels.

"Oh I'm keen on eels," the man said as he sat down on the wooden veranda. "Beautiful piece of flesh to eat. Bit greasy, but nice white meat."

"You catch eels and eat them?" Kate asked, joining him.

"Dead right," the man returned. I poured the tea. The round man and the small girl wrapped their hands around the cups and felt the warmth. The girl blew the heat off the top of her cup. "Jus' find the stinkiest, rottenest, ol' piece of meat you can," the man continued, "and put it on a treble 'ook. Then find a dark looking log jam and drop it under. Wait 'til they swallow it 'ole or the 'ook will just pull right out." Kate and I exchanged looks.

The man sipped the tea and gave a sigh of satisfaction. "She caught an eel last night," he said, nodding to his daughter.

The girl smiled, eyes twinkling, and replied, "You helped, Dad."

He smiled back at her, like they were sharing a secret.

"We got it 'anging in a plastic bag back at our 'ut," he said. "We were going to leave today but, with the eel, we'll stay another day. If we're lucky enough to get a deer, we'll probably stay a few more."

The girl followed her Dad's words attentively. When it came time for her to talk, he didn't interrupt. She spoke with childish enthusiasm and often looked to her Dad with pride. "Dad used to hunt here when he was a lad. Back then there were heaps of deer and he could get all he wanted. Yesterday we almost shot one but Dad wasn't sure if it was a stag or a hind."

"How do you pack a deer out of the bush?" I asked.

"No worries, mate," the man responded. "Bone out the front, sack it, and put it in the small pack for 'er. I carry out the 'ind quarter on me back, rest me arms on the legs."

"What about storing the meat if you decide to stay?" Kate asked.

The man looked into his emptying cup and smiled. "Well, you can do a couple things. I might dig a 'ole in the river bank, bag it, and bury it. Or 'ang it in the fire 'til it gets all sooty and crusty. Even if it does get blown, don't matter."

"Blown?" I asked.

"Ya know, if the blow flies lay their eggs on the meat and maggots start eating away. Jus' cut the bad 'unk off."

I smiled. Kate turned green. The round man and the small girl lifted their cups high, thanked us for the tea, and moved on.

● ● ●

That evening Kate and I took turns reading aloud by firelight, then dozed off. Sometime in the middle of the night, long after the fire had died, we were awakened by a loud grating noise on the metal roof. "BANG, BANG, BANG" moved across the length of the hut, followed by a hurried, panicked scurrying, an agonizing slide, a brief moment of silence...and finally a deafening "CRASH!"

By this time Kate and I were both upright in our bunks. I crept to the door and peered out in time to see a chubby possum extracting his bruised ego from a pile of metal alongside the hut.

"It's just a possum," I reported with a sigh of relief.

"Great," agonized Kate. "I have to pee."

"Go on," I said, "it won't hurt you."

"There's no way I'm going out there," she replied, and with that returned uncomfortably to bed. Soon, however, Kate stood back at the door, timidly peeking out. As she stepped onto the porch, I heard a bloodcurdling scream. "Scott! He's right there!" WHAM!, the door slammed. Only the far wall of the hut stopped Kate's retreat.

Sure enough the possum sat three feet from the door, staring at us like a lost child. The possum was about the size of a big cat. Fat and fur lumped its belly. The possum's eyes looked like oversized marbles and glowed with the reflection of my flashlight. A long tail, curled at the end, stretched out behind it. We looked at each other for several moments and then the possum made its way slowly up a post and disappeared onto the roof. Kate, meanwhile, huddled behind me muttering articulate things like "Yuk" and "Gross."

As I closed the door, Kate crossed her legs; her face contorted in pain. "I gotta go so bad," she moaned.

"Then go! I'm going to bed."

"No, no, wait, wait. Please! You shine the light while I go. If he jumps on me I'm going to die." Kate walked hesitantly onto the veranda. At the edge she stopped.

"I am not stepping off this porch...ooo, no way! He's so uncoordinated he'll fall off the roof on me and bite my butt!"

"Good night, honey," I said. "I'm going to bed." I started to close the door.

"OK, OK. Just don't leave me!" And so Kate went, but not without yelling, "Shine the light over there, quick over there." As she sprinted back into the hut at the end of it all, Kate pronounced, "I WILL NOT go back out there tonight no matter how bad I have to go!" With that she zipped deeply into her sleeping bag, mummified for the night.

From above came the rattle of the possum moving precariously about, oblivious to the excitement it had caused.

North Island

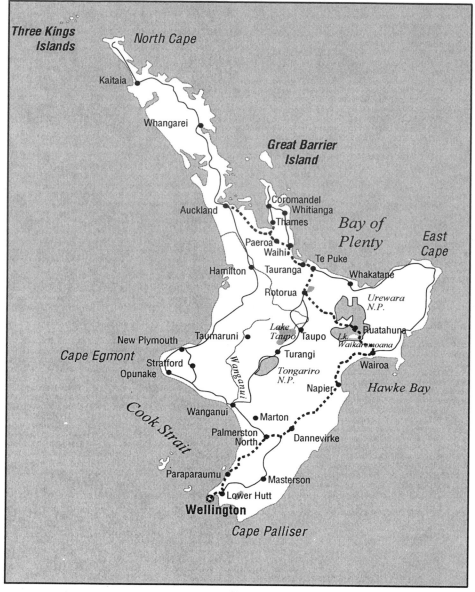

THE HOP, THE SKIP, AND THE JUMP

Chapter 2

Kate and I didn't even know what a Kiwi possum was the day we stepped onto our Air New Zealand flight. We did know that I was sick. Quitting "normal" life to become a traveling transient is sufficient cause for a queasy stomach. My stomach had treated me to spasms from the moment we checked the bikes through in Los Angeles.

Dinner helped quell my fever and quiet the fluttering butterflies. As the flight attendant cleared our trays away, Kate put her hand to my forehead, pronounced it cooler, then wrapped a blanket around me.

A moment later a Kiwi (maybe he was an Aussie—I couldn't tell at that point) stopped and said, "I heard them call for a doctor a while back, mate. Thought it was for you. Glad it wasn't. I've seen how sick you look, but the little lovely's doing a fine job caring for you." He tucked Kate's blanket around her shoulders, patted her head, and departed with a smiling, "Cheerio."

I reclined my seat and Kate leaned her head against my shoulder. The cabin lights dimmed. A few reading lights blinked on as folks rose to search for pillows and blankets. Kate, worn from a sleepless night, soon breathed heavily.

I couldn't sleep; thoughts of other days and other places tumbled in my mind like clothes in a dryer. Like the day Kate burst into our ninety year-old house in Longmont, Colorado, full of excitement. I had just returned from a cold, dreary run. It was icy outside and people in their cars looked at me like I was a fool. Returning to the dilapidated house that we shared with a dozen wild, fragrant cats didn't help my mood.

Kate was an electrical engineer in Fort Collins; I worked as a chemical engineer in Boulder. We were both in our first year of work following graduation from the University of Colorado in Boulder. The next day held the promise of another traffic-choked, smog-filled, horn-honking commute for each of us. And another day at work meant another day of phone calls and memos and paperwork that held little meaning for us. At twenty-two and twenty-five, Kate and I were being sucked into the lives we dreaded.

Then Kate burst through the door carrying a stack of library books and wearing a big smile. "You have to see these pictures of New Zealand!" she exclaimed. We crawled into our sleeping bags and laid the books out on the floor. The pictures were of towering mountains and rugged coastline, deep jungle bush and open tussock meadows. And the pictures carried with them the genesis of an idea, an idea for escape.

A year later we made our plane reservations. The seed that had been planted by a couple of coffee-table picture books took full bloom. We had absorbed anything and everything about New Zealand, questioned friends and friends of friends about their trips. Our plan to work and save five years for a journey to New Zealand had already been revised twice: first to three years, then to two years.

I stood up to stretch and take a walk around the plane. When I returned to my seat, Kate stirred but didn't wake. The past week had been hard on her, hard on us. Every day the tension grew. Everything that didn't fit in a five by five foot locker had been sold. Our jobs were gone. Our bank accounts, which had been carefully nurtured for two years, would grow no more. The going away party was done, the goodbyes said. My folks had arrived from Montana to pick up our car. The only thing left was to box the bikes and pray.

The night before departure we didn't sleep. Thoughts, mostly questions, raced through our minds. Leaving for a year, maybe more, maybe less, entailed so much uncertainty.   What lies ahead? What are we giving up? Are we nuts? Why do we have so damn much gear?   We felt hesitant yet eager, scared yet excited. But mostly we wondered about each other. For five years Kate and I had formed a happy, though not always perfect, partnership. What would a year of solid togetherness mean to us? Destruction or solidification?

Sometime in the middle of the night before our departure, Denver's yearly Thanksgiving snowstorm hit. We drove to the airport in glare ice conditions. At nine o'clock, departure time, Dad and I watched passing cars from our vantage point in a ditch. We were axle deep in snow. I stepped gingerly out of the car to push, dressed in premature Hawaiian shorts, and wondered if some ominous message about our journey was being relayed from the heavens.

The planes had their own problems with the weather. Ours took off at noon, with us aboard   Tears accompanied the goodbyes with our folks. What could happen in a year? To us? To them....

I reached into the seat pocket in front of me and pulled out an airline magazine, but couldn't concentrate long enough to read a page.   Finally, the cabin lights flickered on and the flight attendants came around with hot, lemon-scented towels. Kate never stirred, just continued her open-mouth, closed-eye gaze at the ceiling. Twenty minutes later the big jet's tires screeched on the tarmac.

"C'mon Kate, time to get up."

"Huh," she mumbled in a stupor. Then, sitting up and rubbing her eyes, "Where are we anyway?"

"Honolulu. C'mon, we have to get off here. Remember? We're spending a week in Hawaii."

"Hawaii?" Kate fell back and pulled the blanket over her head.

"Wake me up when we get to New Zealand."

● ● ●

We landed at Honolulu International Airport at two a.m., December 1, unboxed the bikes, then slept on the floor next to the revolving luggage carousel. Six or eight other travelers slept nearby. Most of them looked unsettled and I guessed that we weren't the only ones starting a journey.

The bikes had really been an afterthought. Six months before our departure for New Zealand, Kate immersed herself in biking, quite separate from our travel plans. It didn't take long for the two ideas to mesh.

We took few training rides in the months before our departure, instead jealousy guarding our weekends for backpacking. A year was plenty of time to learn how to bike tour, we reasoned. Training didn't seem imperative.

Pain is my most vivid memory of the training rides we did take. On our first stab at long distance pedaling, we progressed at a snail's pace and our legs quickly turned rubbery. Ravens circled overhead like vultures. In the end we made twenty miles—half of that was downhill.

Our lack of training showed as we loaded the bikes and wobbled uncertainly into Honolulu. I started off by putting my panniers on the wrong sides. Within two hours we had an angry islander shake his fist at us, rode illegally on a four lane highway, and got lost three times. Our butts ached, our skin burned from the heat, and I'd pretty much had my fill of biking.

The solution, it seemed, was to escape the congestion of the city for the tranquility of the country. Unbeknownst to us, however, gale force winds were forecast. The winds greeted us just after we passed the protective shadow of Diamond Head. We pedaled hard but made agonizingly slow progress. It was like swimming upstream against a heavy current.

The wind intensified at the coast. Gravel and stones sandblasted our skin. Short rails and steep cliffs bordered the road; an angry ocean crashed directly below.

"Scott!" I barely heard the scream over the roar of the wind, but turned in time to see Kate tossed from her bike.

"This is hopeless," I yelled as I helped her brush off and pick up the bike. Kate didn't reply, just struggled back into the saddle.

It got worse. We crossed a headland and pushed through an opening in the rocks. Wind rocketed through the gap. Cars coming up the back side of the headland had difficulty maintaining a straight line. The wind stopped Kate and I in our tracks. We tried to climb on the bikes again, but couldn't overcome the wind to get started. Defeated, we grabbed the handlebars, bent low, and pushed the bikes down the hill.

Beyond the gap, I stopped, dejected. We found a stone wall, anchored the bikes against it, and wedged ourselves in. Wind and sand roared overhead, but for a moment the wall protected us.

"What in the hell are we doing?" I yelled at Kate. "This is crazy!" Somehow Kate seemed responsible for our misery as she'd originated the asinine idea of traveling by bike.

"It's not my fault!" she screamed back, then turned away from me, head down, and said no more. I fell silent, too.

Dust swirled on the pavement in front of us. Thoughts—good thoughts—of work and home filled my mind. No one in Hawaii cared that we had quit our jobs, that we'd said goodbye to family and friends, that we'd given up everything. No one in Hawaii cared that we were pinned down in the middle of nowhere by a ferocious gale that wanted to toss us over a cliff.

I wondered how tough it would be to bike back to Honolulu and climb on board a plane for home. Sorry folks, we were just kidding...changed our minds...decided to come back....one day seemed like long enough to be away....

A year of bike travel looked like a very long time.

We eventually struggled on to Waimanalo Beach and set up camp in the token windblock of some shrubs. Later, in the tent, Kate pulled out the flashlight and a list of dangerous campgrounds we'd been told to avoid. Waimanalo stood at the top of the list with "robberies" scrawled next to it. It was dark; the wind continued to howl. We huddled into our sleeping bags and realized we had no place to go. The tent was to be our fortress.

• • •

All told, Kate and I spent a week in Hawaii. We moved up the coast in the days following the gale, but biked sparingly and spent much time considering the transgressions of our first day on the road. We also spent much of the week just getting to know our bikes. We played with truing the wheels and adjusting the derailleurs, with cleaning the drive trains and oiling the chains.

Kate pedaled a blue Raleigh Technium. The Technium, a sport touring bike, had a bonded aluminum frame and twelve speeds. Kate, who tends to comfort over speed, customized the Technium with upright handlebars, a soft seat, and inch and three-eighths tires. I rode a Specialized Rockhopper mountain bike which had fifteen speeds and inch and a half tires with a riding rim. I bought my Rockhopper four months before our departure; few scratches interrupted its smooth flow of red paint.

The bikes hustled us back to Honolulu at the end of the week. This time the wind allowed us unperturbed passage. Kate and I felt ready to start our journey in earnest. Hawaii provided a period of transition: a chance for us to sample our new-found freedom, to test the bikes and gear, to adjust to the road. We planned a week in Fiji to continue the transition, then the jump to New Zealand.

• • •

Air New Zealand deposited us in Nadi, Fiji, at four thirty a.m. We spent three hours clearing customs, stashing cold weather gear into a locker, and assembling the bikes. As fledgling bike mechanics, we needed over an hour to assemble or disassemble the bikes, a necessary task for boxing. Later, we learned that Air New Zealand accepts bikes unboxed, and we began simply wheeling the bikes to the check-in counter. Baggage handlers claimed they took better care of unboxed bikes. Our mutilated bike boxes corroborated their claims.

By seven thirty a.m. we stood at the door of the Nadi airport, drenched in sweat. We hadn't stepped out of the shade or climbed

Fijian family at a raadside fruitstand.

on the bikes, yet the early morning heat was stifling.

Yells of "Bula, bula!" began almost the moment we exited the airport. Every hundred meters or so were clumps of houses, often with thatched roofs, and always with women and small children sitting outside in the shade. The children raced to the road yelling "Bula, bula!" and waving madly. Kate and I laughed, waved back, and soon countered with our own yells of "Bula, bula!"

We biked into the center of Nadi. A wooden walk separated the dusty street from a myriad of dilapidated shops. A sign in front of a pub read "Public Welcome, Women Excepted." We stopped inside a nearby milk bar. Small lizards crawled along the wall. The glass counter was cracked and dusty. A young Fijian boy, barefoot, stood behind the counter. I ordered a hot cup of coffee, then wondered why as sweat from my nose dripped into the cup.

In the coming days we biked south and west along the coast of Viti Levu, Fiji's main island. Water-starved cows were tethered beside the road. Moms and kids waited at roadside stands to sell mangos. Men worked in the sugarcane fields that lined the roads and, as we passed, they stopped to yell "Bula" and wave. Most of the them worked barefoot, even though the cut cane was sharp. Their feet were huge, well-padded, and covered with thick skin.

It wasn't far into our first day in Fiji when Kate and I realized that biking between ten and three was suicidal. Fiji's sun stands straight overhead and its breeze has no cool. Our skin, even though prepared by a week in Hawaii, soon dried and cracked. We took to departing for our rides at five a.m., hoping to get a head start on the searing temperatures. Even at five, however, the sun held the promise of heat and power, revealing itself in the center of the horizon.

Likewise, nights in Fiji were warm and moist. We used our sleeping bags as pillows and woke sticky and uncomfortable. Frequent swims and briny showers left our hair stiff, our skin grimy, and our lips tasting of salt.

Fiji's heat acts as an omnipresent tranquilizer. Activities are slow and relaxed—witness the Great Fijian Bus Ride, an adventure worth the price of admission.

One morning Kate and I stood at the roadside and flagged down the first Suva-bound bus, a rusty, open-sided breadbox with bald tires. The smell of half-burnt fuel surrounded the old bus like bad perfume. The engine protested our start with a cough and whine and, ten minutes after we climbed aboard, the old bus sputtered to its death.

Shortly, another bus circled in and took us aboard. This bus worked after a fashion, though I felt sure we were going to have push on the hills. The bus stopped at every hut and village. Folks waved happily as we jolted up. Someone would emerge from a house down the road, saunter up and climb on, jabber with the driver, get off, then hand up two small kids or toss in a burlap sack of fruit or slide a crate of squawking chickens under a seat. Often the bus stopped so that one of the passengers could talk to someone along the road—without anyone getting on or off.

Four kilometers out of Navua both of the second bus's back tires blew out. The bus carried no spares, not even one. None of the locals were perturbed—much less surprised—and as Kate and

I weren't in any hurry, neither were we. An opportunistic Indian stopped and yelled out the window of his van, "One dollar to Navua. You get another ride there."

In Navua, a madman in an old Datsun pickup stopped for us. He drove with anger, passed with no concern for curves, and almost ran over a mongoose. The madman dropped us outside of Suva. Twenty-five cents and the city bus finally got us into town—three hours, five vehicles, and a hundred twenty kilometers from where we'd started.

After exploring Suva, Fiji's capitol, through the hot afternoon, Kate and I returned to the bus stop for the ride back to our camp. This time we took the Express Bus service. As near as I could tell, "Express" simply meant that the bus didn't break down.

● ● ●

Another morning, Kate and I walked into the fields near our campsite. Railroad carts, stacked high with sugarcane, waited to be hauled to market. A small diesel engine chugged out of the valley ahead and stopped in front of us. Two men leaned out of the engine and waved. The older man, a Fijian, had slim legs but a stomach that pushed against his shirt. He smoked. The younger man, an Indian, had flowing black hair. His shirt was buttoned down to the waist and rolled up above the elbow. Both men wore long pants and leather shoes.

"Where are you taking the sugarcane?" Kate asked.

"Lautoka, to the plant, then to Japan, Australia, and New Zealand," the older man answered.

"This must be a good job," I said, looking up and shielding my eyes from the sun. "Is it fun to drive that engine?"

The older one puffed up with pride. "You want to ride? Climb up to here."

The engine was old, squat, loud. Two rickety seats with torn pads were mounted in front of a cracked windshield. The controls were simple—forward, neutral, reverse, a hand brake—with an identical set on each side of the engine. We jolted through several exercises, removing the empty carts from the full, aligning the full carts for the haul to Lautoka. The older man drove; the younger man jumped out and threw the switches to move us between the narrow gauge tracks.

After the loaded carts were all arranged, the younger man detached the engine and we started off down a long straightaway. The older man pointed to the throttle on my side of the engine and yelled, "You, you drive." He dropped his throttle and the motor wound down.

I picked up the throttle, gingerly, and pushed it forward. The engine surged; I backed off. "More" he motioned with a snaggletoothed smile. I pushed the throttle forward to its limit and we banged across the field in a powerful clatter. I wondered about the curve ahead, but the older man only laughed and waved me on. At the edge of the field his smile straightened and he reached forward to grab the throttle.

I stepped back while the older man drove across the field to pick up the loaded carts. The Indian fellow, who stood silently next to Kate during my turn at the helm, reached down to a murky bowl of liquid sitting on a short stool. He used half of a cleaned out coconut shell to stir up the sludgy bottom. Next, he scooped some of the green-brown liquid into the shell and offered me a swallow.

"What is it, kava?" I asked. Kava, I knew, was made from the pulverized root of a pepper plant. The intoxicating drink, a mild narcotic, is highly revered in Fiji. Good joke, I thought to myself, this obviously isn't kava, it must be for cooling the brakes.

"Kava," he smiled back and continued to offer the shell.

Great, I thought, as a new member of the fraternity I'm duty bound to drink this stuff. The taste didn't differ from the appearance, roughly like dirty dishwater. I took three swallows in a show of good will.

Satisfied, the Indian turned to Kate, offered the shell, and said, "For you."

"No, that's OK," she replied, backing to the far corner of the locomotive, "I'm really not thirsty." With a little cajoling we convinced Kate to try some. Her post-drink smile was less than convincing.

● ● ●

At the end of our week in Fiji, we found ourselves along the Coral Coast enjoying a day of rest and relaxation. I took a long run to the interior of the island. The dirt road climbed straight up and away from the ocean. The sun hung high overhead, hot.

Six horses, untethered and unfenced, led me up through the hills. Every time I came around the corner, they were there. When I approached, they ambled ahead another hundred meters. The horses moved easily; I breathed hard and dripped with sweat. Atop the final hill, I stopped to survey the tropical scene inland. Sweat stung my eyes. The horses pawed the ground, waiting for my next move. A black horse, the apparent leader, soon lost patience and started nipping at its compatriots. The six circled past me, off the road, and galloped downhill through a pasture. A broken lead flapped in the wind behind one of the horses.

I watched them pass, then lifted my sights higher to the ocean and to the south. My thoughts weren't with the horses, or even with Fiji. My thoughts were on New Zealand.

● ● ●

We landed in Auckland on December 15th and moved outside to load the bikes. New Zealand felt immediately right. The sun shone brightly but without the stifling heat of Fiji. Everything radiated green. People stopped to talk and wish us well. Even the sight of cars driving on the wrong side of the road didn't confuse us after a week of pedaling in Fiji.

The area around our bikes looked like a battlefield. Six thousand pounds of gear blanketed the sidewalk. Unlike Hawaii and Fiji, none of our gear could go into storage. We'd already sent home ten pounds of "indispensibles," and quickly packaged up another ten for jettisoning. I'm not sure what I thought I was going to do with six books and an electric razor.

Another couple, from Bellingham, Washington, set up their bikes beside us. They looked over our mounds of gear and chuckled knowingly. They were just completing a thirteen month, twenty thousand mile, bike ride around the world.

We'd met seven bikers since departing Colorado. All of them were traveling, ho-hum, around the world. A year in

New Zealand was beginning to feel very tame and unadventurous. Yet we felt certain that our plan was a good one: to immerse ourselves in the Kiwi culture, to become a part of New Zealand, not just to pass through it.

The airport sits south of Auckland and is bordered by green paddocks and open country. We rode a euphoric high into the city. Auckland is big and sprawling, yet dotted by green hills which preserve a rural feel. The ocean is almost always in view; few high rises disturb the skyline.

We pedaled through town and found a crowded motor camp. A hundred tents and caravans squeezed into space better suited for twenty. It didn't matter. Kate and I were so ready to love New Zealand that we could have been robbed and mugged and still come up championing its virtues.

The following morning we biked into central Auckland. By noon, our euphoria subsided. Eight hundred thousand people were still eight hundred thousand people. It was time to get into the country.

● ● ●

We hoped to spend the Christmas holidays in Urewara National Park, a reportedly unpopulated and seldom-visited area. Then we planned to bike to the South Island for the warm summer months before returning to the North Island in the fall, perhaps April or May. (As New Zealand is in the Southern Hemisphere, the seasons are reversed; also, the farther south, generally, the colder.) Later, winter possibly, we would bike the Coromandel Peninsula and Northland, the northernmost, and hence, warmest sections of New Zealand.

Kate and I hopped a commuter train to Auckland's southernmost suburb, Papakura, to avoid the traffic of the city. A woman at a grocery shop in Papakura asked what we were up to. When she learned our plans, she exclaimed, "Push-bike around the country, luv? Oh my, you must be fit." We puffed up with hollow pride, realizing that we'd yet to do anything.

Kate and I pedaled off to nearby Ramarama and spent our second New Zealand night in another motor camp, this one empty and rural. We already appreciated the bounty of Kiwi motor camps, which offer hot showers, laundry machines, a common room, a light at night, and kitchens with hot water Zips, ranges, refrigerators, and sometimes even microwaves. The entire package cost about $7NZ($4US) for the two of us.

In the morning, Kate and I started south and east. Released from the influence of Auckland, the land becomes rolling and green. Lush fields, some close-cropped, are intermittently interrupted by shelterbelts and conservative farmhouses. Dark, dense foliage encroaches on the fields and overflows the gaps between the hills.

The fields are not empty. Seventy million sheep, more than twenty per head of human population, inhabit New Zealand. Merino, Cheviot, Perendale, Suffolk, Coopworth, Hampshire, Ryeland, Dorset Horn.... Each breed represents a special wool or hardiness or flavor.

Every patch of grass in New Zealand is fair game for sheep. It wasn't long before we spotted a rural golf course. A hundred sheep busily munched their way through a fairway. A short fence surrounded the green. Sheep, in turn, surrounded the fence, sticking their heads as far out onto the putting surface as possible. Approach shots must have required great care.

We landed in a small diner near Bombay for breakfast. I ordered baked beans on toast. Kate, who's tastes tend to be far less exotic and far more healthy than mine, ordered unbuttered toast. As we looked over our maps, an elderly fellow stood outside making all manner of funny faces over our bikes. He was tall, slim, and wore a white garden coat, shorts, black leather shoes, and knee-high socks. A moment later, the old gentleman approached our table. "And where, pray tell, do you keep the kitchen sink?" he asked.

"Well, in the side pocket, of course," Kate answered.

Our new friend chuckled and a big smile spread across his face. "My name's Mike," he said and stuck out his hand. His handshake was solid, his hand long and bony but with an unnatural lump. Mike's skin was pale, dry, and flecked with age spots. He wore glasses that emphasized the vitality of his eyes. Enormous eyebrows sprouted from his forehead; hairs hung over his glasses like vines falling over a window sill.

Mike pulled up a chair. "I always thought to myself how easy it is to be friendly and say hi," he said. "Easier to be friendly than the other way around, I'd say. Communication, that's what life's all about, isn't it?" He waved vigorously to Kate. She smiled back. "See there, we just communicated."

Mike paused just long enough for us get a swallow of tea, then took off on a new tangent. "Lived in Palestine for twelve years starting back in thirty-eight. Was part of the British policing units there. Bloody Jews shot me in the hand. Had to yank out one of my bones to get my fingers to work. Wrist's still stiff." Mike produced the hand; its misshapen form confirmed the story.

"Been to Disneyland six times." Mike didn't need any prompting to jump topics. "Last time I was there a family from San Francisco adopted me. Said why don't you spend the day with us."

The waitress arrived with our food. As she walked away, Mike sat back, pulled off his glasses, and started cleaning them with a napkin. "Got friends all over the world," he continued when he looked up again. "Lived in Palestine, born in Toronto. I'm a citizen of Western Australia now—had a wife there but turned out she was a hussy, so I got rid of her. Got a wife in the Philippines now with four adopted kids."

About then the waitress returned, glanced at our untouched food, and spoke sternly to Mike, "You detaining these two young people, you old coot?"

"Not a bit," I replied for him.

As she walked away, Mike slid his glasses back in place and grinned. "Diamond in the rough is what I'd call that one. Treats me very well here. I come down to do odd jobs three or four days a week. Take care of my house and goats, got three hundred trees to work on. People ask me if I ever get bored. 'Got no time to get bored,' I tell 'em. Wrote two hundred fifty-eight letters so far this year. Keep records of where, when, how much for post, everything. Every time I get a letter from overseas, I raise the flag of that country. Got one yesterday from Canada. Flag's still up today."

Mike started to rise. "You two come back through, I expect to see you. Course," he paused and pointed to the ground, "I may be down there."

"No way Mike, not you," Kate laughed. "You've got too much life still in you."

He smiled, moved to the door, and waved. "Well anyway, happy hunting. And by the way, a very Merry Christmas to the both of you."

We attended to our neglected food and shortly thereafter rode out. Mike stood in front of his house, a hundred meters up the road, trimming the trees. A Canadian flag flapped overhead.

● ● ●

Kate and I turned east at Pokeno and pedaled through rolling hills to the Firth of Thames. Ahead, the dark Coromandel Range rose skyward.

It was hot and we pedaled without our helmets on to better feel the cooling breeze. The breeze carried with it two divergent smells: the salty odor of the sea and the stench of blood and decay. Duck feathers and entrails matted the road every fifty meters. The highway looked like a war zone.

Ahead, two mallards popped out of the grass from a roadside swamp. From behind came the sound of a fast approaching semi-truck. The road was narrow and Kate and I moved far to the left.

"Look out you ducks!" I yelled.

The ducks waddled happily across the road, unaware of the big truck bearing down on them. At the last moment the ducks looked up, terrified, and lifted their wings for escape. They never got airborne; the big truck turned them to mush just as it passed us. One second there were two ducks, the next feathers, ribs, and webbed feet spread in a red streak over thirty feet of asphalt.

The truck thundered on without pause. We pedaled quietly for a while, both nearly sick to our stomachs. Then Kate stopped and said that she wanted to put her helmet on. The helmets were futile against a twenty ton truck, yet we never biked without them again.

● ● ●

We camped near Thames, then turned south in the morning and pedaled over small hills to Paeroa. The Coromandel Range, near at hand now, loomed tall and densely vegetated to our left. We turned east at Paeroa, up the bush-lined Karangahake River, and pushed across the Coromandel Range to Waihi. The locals there pointed us towards the Athenree Gorge for camping. We pedaled on for twelve kilometers, then called it an evening at a roadside picnic area. We both hurt. Seventy-nine kilometers rated our highest output of the trip.

Since neither Kate nor I had bicycle toured a lick, we expected the first couple weeks on the bikes to be tough. Our expectations did not prove false. My butt ached constantly from the unaccustomed abuse of the bike saddle. Kate dragged from muscle fatigue. When I asked where she hurt, Kate replied, "Everywhere." My answer to the question was equally simple, though not so eloquent.

To appease our aching muscles, we rode only twenty kilometers the next day, to Katikati. The following morning we pushed on for Tauranga. The road rolled and pitched like one standing wave after another. Every downhill brought with it another agonizing wall to climb. Our bodies fought us every pedal of the way.

After lunch in Tauranga, we pedaled wearily on to Te Puke. A sign at the edge of town announced: "Te Puke—Kiwifruit Capitol of the World." They could keep the kiwifruit, all we wanted was a beer. The street was quiet except for one pub. Twenty motorcycles and some surly looking characters in torn black leather sat out front. "Mongrel Mob," the man at the British Petroleum station explained. "Walk in there looking like push-bikers, mate, and you won't walk out lookin' the same." All things considered, we opted for a bottle of wine in the tent.

A light rain began at midnight and continued til morning. The clouds broke long enough for us to pack and depart Te Puke for Rotorua, but soon the rains started again, this time heavily. Water hindered our vision; small rivulets ran down our bare legs.

Then the hill started. Not hills. "Hills" would imply an up and down style of travel. This hill simply stretched on and on and up and up. We'd fight for twenty minutes to reach a corner and round it, only to find another upward stretch. The skyline never appeared. Cars flew by, dousing us in spray; the comfortable occupants often waved.

Kate sagged and fell far back. When I waited, she always approached, pedaling slowly but without fail.

I had three advantages over Kate in the hill climbs: monster thighs, lots of hill running experience, and last, but far from least, a Granny gear. The Granny, a third chainring, effectively gave me four or five gears lower than Kate. Thus, while I dropped to lower and lower gears to meet an increasing incline, Kate struggled, having long since reached her bottom gear.

The improper gearing of Kate's bike reflected our initial lack of understanding about the demands of bike travel. Somewhere in our pre-trip planning the question of gearing ratios came up, but we blissfully pushed it aside. Kate's off the rack gearing rendered a smallest equivalent wheel (easiest pedaling) of 39 inches. My Rockhopper, by virtue of being a mountain bike and not of my forethought, had a lowest equivalent wheel of 21 inches. We discussed switching bikes in those early days, but to Kate, who had a near-religious love of her bike, the idea was preposterous.

From the top of the monster hill, we descended to Lake Rotorua just as the clouds released their full reserves. Sheets of water pounded the road. We considered taking shelter, but then opted to race for Rotorua as we already dripped. I bent low to protect my eyes from the rain and squeezed my handlebar grips to battle the downpour's onslaught. Water ran from the sodden grips as if they were two saturated sponges.

The sweet stench of sulfur greeted us just outside of Rotorua. Rotorua is a geothermal hotbed, with geysers and mudpots and steam flowing from every drain. We took a room for the night, poured the water out of our panniers, and collapsed into a searing mineral pool.

● ● ●

A backcountry road in Whakarewarewa State Park.

After a rest day in Rotorua, Kate and I were anxious to climb back on the bikes and continue plugging towards Urewara National Park. Glorious sunshine replaced the rain and muck of the previous days. Our muscles felt strong and rejuvenated.

The ride down Highway 5 wound through rolling hills. Traffic was moderate. Whakarewarewa State Forest Park, steeped in trees and tangles of bush, bordered the road to the north. Further along we turned east on Highway 38, towards Murapara and Urewara National Park. Farmhouses and sheep-filled paddocks became scarce. A hint of dark mountains showed briefly on the skyline before we passed into Kaingaroa Forest, one of the largest man-planted forests in the world.

Without warning, amid the endless rows of tall pines, everything came together in our biking. We put the hammer down and cruised effortlessly for the first time. Trees flashed past in a blur of green. Kate drafted me, our rhythms in perfect sync. Then the highway plummeted towards Murapara. The descent was beautiful—an endless glide with no traffic; nothing but open asphalt, warm sunshine, and twenty minutes of rounding corners and seeing the road always slanting away. Please God, let this go on forever, we thought. Maybe our muscles would recover, maybe biking was going to be OK.

New Zealand seemed very good at that moment. We were no longer pensive about bike travel, about being far from home. Our self-confidence was growing daily and we felt ready to meet adventure and adversity. Little did we know, both lie just ahead.

UREWARA COUNTRY

Chapter 3

Murapara is a small settlement, mainly Maori, on the edge of Urewara National Park. As we coasted into town, I was reminded of the Indian reservation villages of Montana. The town is not wealthy. Locals, with seemingly little else to do, stared. Admittedly we posed an odd sight, two pakehas (the Maori term for white people) stuffing three hundred pounds of food into bike panniers.

The Maoris are New Zealand's indigenous population. They arrived by canoe around the fourteenth century, several hundred years before the first Europeans. In time, however, the Maoris, and New Zealand, fell under the influence of the English.

About one-tenth of the Kiwi population is considered to be Maori, though few pure-blooded Maoris exist today. While Maori-pakeha relations are better than most similar native-conqueror partnerships, Maoris still hold less than a proportionate part of New Zealand's wealth. And islands of bigotry remain. A silver-haired white woman spoke with great feeling when she told me, "Here it's so bad. I don't rightly know

Kiwi family trekking in the Urewara National Park.

what it will be like ten years from now. It gets worse every year. Why, we have a rape almost every weekend in Auckland. The whites and the Maoris don't get along. And the looks of the lot of them. My God, some of them are such a mess you can't believe it." Judging from Murapara, we agreed that Maoris could be a visually imposing lot: tattoos, big biceps, rough haircuts, torn clothing. We would quickly learn, however, that the rough look was the look of the Kiwi bushman, not the look of the Maori.

Kate and I were jamming food into the panniers because it appeared that Wairoa, a hundred sixty-six kilometers from Murapara, would be our next resupply point. In between we planned to spend a week tramping in Urewara National Park. The food didn't all fit in the end, so we slung the extra grocery sacks over our rear panniers like saddle bags.

We pedaled to the Urewara National Park office, just outside Murapara, to check on road conditions. National parks in New Zealand bear little resemblance to their counterparts in the United States. Entry is free and unrestricted, rangers are never present, the atmosphere is far less militaristic, and services are usually few. Of New Zealand's dozen or so national parks, Urewara is even more casual than most.

The park office echoed with emptiness, but Kate and I found the person in charge, a Maori woman, out back. She and several giggling friends welcomed us with big smiles and cheerful waves. "Ooo bikees!" the woman cried out as she rose to greet us. "I so love you bikees, you're all so fit."

Our new friend took us inside, gave us some maps, and told us that a hundred and thirty kilometers of rough metal road waited ahead.

"Metal road?" I asked with apparent confusion.

"Rightio," she returned. When our befuddled expressions didn't change, the woman explained, "Metal–you know, dirt and rocks...no seal."

"You mean a gravel road," Kate exclaimed as the idea made a connection. "There's no metal on it, certainly. Why on earth would you call it a 'metal road'?"

The woman got a puzzled look on her face. "I guess I really wouldn't have a clue."

Back out at the bikes I told Kate, "Metal road–no worries."

We should have worried.

Shortly, we pedaled off the tar seal and into the hills. Chunks of rock and washboard jolted and rattled us until we thought our arms would drop off at the shoulder. The few locals that passed left behind clouds of choking dust. We were tired and Kate's improper gearing forced her to walk on steep pitches.

The rough ride went on for an hour before darkness set in. We pulled off the road and set up camp on a logged-out hilltop. It had been a long day, over eighty kilometers, and the promise of the day to come was not good.

● ● ●

Dawn on December 24th arrived ominously. Clouds hung low and angry over the mountains in front of us. The road was heavily graveled, steep, and spoiling for a fight; the night had not changed its disposition. Three summits stood between us and Ruatahuna, a small town in the center of Urewara National Park

A three summit Christmas Eve Day in Urewara N.P.

where we planned to spend our Christmas Eve. The first summit fell quickly and our spirits lifted. For ten minutes Kate and I bounced through a downhill, wondering what was next.

As I led the way down the hill, my thoughts turned to Christmas Eve and home: Mom cooking clam chowder, Dad reading the Christmas story, sneaking downstairs to fill the stockings.... A lump formed in my throat but I successfully choked it down. A second lump, however, proved more wily, and I succumbed to my thoughts. I started crying.

Though I pedaled hard to stay away from her, Kate soon caught up, saw my predicament, and asked why I was sad. In heaving sobs I babbled, "I'm sorry I'm being a baby...guess I'm feeling bad about Christmas...I s'pose I'm just homesick."

We stopped in the middle of the road and stood astride the bikes. Kate reached out and hugged me. Our helmets bumped together and we laughed at how ridiculous it all seemed.

On we rode. Rough land, barren from lumbering, gave way to deep bush as we crossed into the park. I continued to struggle against homesickness, trying to console myself with the thought that at home, on the other side of the date line, it was really December 23rd and hence a day early to be sad about missing the holidays. My neurotic mind reminded me, however, that our December 26th would be Christmas Day at home; thus I really had three days to suffer. Never play mathematics with emotions.

A cold, steady drizzle began and the road quickly turned greasy. We started up a steep incline to the second summit. While I labored with homesickness, Kate labored with the hill and rocks and rain. Golf ball size gravel negated any chance of Kate and her skinny tires negotiating the climb. She dismounted to walk, angry and frustrated. I pedaled on, mired in my homesickness. Kate fell far behind and I soon lost sight of her.

After a long wait, I started back and found Kate sitting in the mud on the side of a steep embankment, crying. "I HATE THIS!" she screamed. "I'm wet and cold and tired and this hill just keeps going up and up. Why didn't we just take the bus?"

I said nothing, just sat down in the mud next to Kate and slipped deeper into my homesickness. The rain stepped up a notch. It was Christmas Eve Day and we were in a shambles.

Soon a car passed with the word that the summit was only a few kilometers away. We decided to continue. I began to ride my bike forward, then trot back and relieve Kate in her push up the hill. Moving like this we made the summit in forty minutes.

As we started down off the second summit, the drizzle ended and the downpour began. The downhill ride was slick and treacherous. At the bottom came another choice: camp now or attack our third, and highest, summit of the day. The road ahead wound steeply away and was quickly enveloped by thick,

Summits can be sweet!

uninviting bush.

Why quit when you're having fun? We charged the hill. Fifty meters up, the charge faltered as Kate was forced to dismount and push. For the next two hours we yo-yoed: me riding ahead, trotting back, and helping push. Kate slogged relentlessly upward, no tears now; this had become war. A scowl was all that belied her inner struggle.

The further we snaked up the hill, the less helpful I became. My body cried out for relief. Rather than lean my bike against a pole before jogging back to help, I began to throw it down beside the road. Christmas homesickness was long forgotten. Today was the monster in our closet, the one so easily ignored when planning a fun little bike trip.

Finally I spotted the opening where we would cross the watershed. I threw my bike down and ran, stiffly, back to Kate, whooping all the way. As we crested the hill the sun broke through...no kidding.

With hands glued to the brakes, we plunged off the summit.

The breeze from the downward coast iced our drenched bodies. We shivered, no longer creating heat, and stopped at the bottom of the descent to change into dry tops.

The rest of the ride to Ruatahuna was flat. The road broke out of the deep bush into an open valley of cool green meadows. A clear stream, with long, rippled runs and emerald pools, flowed through the bottom of the valley.

At Ruatahuna, population a little more than zero, we looked for a room. Christmas Eve, coupled with the tough ride, demanded the decadence of a hot shower. True to the script, however, the motel, which doubled as the gas station, grocery shop, tea room, and post office, was full. The proprietor directed us to a house around the corner to enquire about staying in a Forest Service hut. Neither the house nor the hut were far. The twenty or so buildings that made up town were within a broken-arm stone throw.

We found a shed, some rusted cars, a picnic table, and four beer drinking men outside the conservative clapboard house. Three of the men looked to be in their twenties and thirties. The conversation centered around the fourth, an older fellow. He was short with close-cropped grey hair; silver stubble highlighted his round, friendly face. Without a hint of surprise or so much as a hello, the older man looked up from under his terry cloth hat and asked, "You folks want a beer?"

"Yes!" I almost shouted back.

"Like a man who knows what he wants," the older man returned.

We bantered with the four fellows for a while about where we were from, our bike trip, and about the bad ride that day. Russell, the old fellow, waved the talk of our troubles aside with one brush of his hand. "You wouldn't want it easy. Need to put in a little work to get something worthwhile. You've made it to a beautiful spot, suns out, no worries. You can't expect to dot all your i's and cross all your t's."

Soon, inevitably, I asked if anyone did any fly fishing. Well old Russ perked up and gave a little grin; a twinkle came to his eye. The other Kiwis sat back with knowing glances.

"Done a bit, I reckon." Russell's mates giggled.

"Are the stories about New Zealand trout really true?" I asked. "Are they huge?"

Russell produced a picture of a happy young fellow holding a big brown trout. "Nine or ten pounds, that one will go," Russell offered when he saw my jaw lying on the table. "That couple stopped in here a year ago 'bout Christmas, same as you, looking for a place to fish. I sent them the same places I'm gonna to send you."

I looked closer at the picture and read the logo on the fisherman's hat–The River's Bend, Bozeman, MT. "He's from Montana!" I shouted.

"Nnn, nnn," Russell mumbled. He had a cigarette paper attached to his lip; in his hand he rolled tobacco. Russell was forever rolling his own. "Place called Buzzman, I think."

"Bozeman," I said. "I went to college there!"

"Montana must be a nice place, I reckon," Russell countered. He gave the cigarette a last roll and reached for his matches. "About two years ago this time, had a bloke stop through from a place called Great Falls. Was kind of wondering when you folks would show up this year."

• • •

We spent the night in the forestry hut, then rose and prepared for our first tramping trip into the bush. Both Kate and I biked with internal frame backpacks strapped to our rear racks. The backpacks had short stays and compacted to a reasonable size, and thus weren't terribly ungainly for bike touring. While we biked they served as oversized stuff sacks for our sleeping bags, pads, and the tent. Also, for the months while we were tramping, we carried two pairs of shoes: lightweight running shoes and low top hiking shoes.

As we rolled the bikes into the Forest Service shop to store them, Russell waved us over to his place. Russell, wearing his ever present terry cloth hat, wanted to show us a Maori hangi being built. A hangi is an earthen covered steamer; hot rocks and food are covered by wet cloths and steam-trapping dirt and allowed to sit for several hours. Russell's clan was cooking wild boar, eel, trout, beef, and mutton for their Christmas feast. Russell was a pakeha, but his strapping son-in-law, who did most of the shoveling, was a Maori.

Russell suggested we try tramping down the Whakatane River. He knew I desperately wanted to catch a big trout. As Andy, one of the beer drinking mates, rolled up in his four-wheel drive Jackeroo, Russell offered a last bit of advice. "With a bit of wit, a bit of luck, and a bit of persistence, you'll get your big fish." Russell had a way of biting off his t's that left them dangling from the end of his home-rolled cigarette.

We hopped into the Jackeroo and bounced down the rugged road to the start of the track. Andy arranged a time to pick us up four days later, then headed back for Ruatahuna.

Kate and I slipped our backpacks on and started down to the Whakatane. Before us stretched the largest expanse of native bush in New Zealand. We walked in awe. Everywhere was green, thick bush. The undergrowth precluded stepping off the trail. Actually "undergrowth" has little meaning in the New Zealand bush—there's simply a single continuum of green from ground to sky. The bush takes you in and swallows you whole. Clearings provide little relief, you're still surrounded.

A glance at a topo map showed that the northern half of Urewara National Park has two main ranges, the Huiaru and the Ikawhenua. Between them runs the Whakatane River, which we followed for four hours into our Christmas outpost, Tawhiwhi Hut.

Tawhiwhi Hut sits in a flat clearing above the river. The hut is green—meaning it matches everything around it—with corrugated metal sides and a dark metallic roof. A small wooden veranda sits outside the single door; pipes run from the hut's metallic roof to a rain catch alongside.

Inside are twenty musty bunks and a sooty fireplace. There are no tables or chairs, but on this day there was a half-eaten bag of rice, a box of kelp custard, an open jam tin, and a symphony of loud flies.

We were alone in the hut. Dusk settled; the air began to cool. Kate started a fire and its warmth felt good. After dinner we walked outside to watch the Southern Cross rise in the dark sky. The soft glow of our fire shown through the hut window. Deep bush and wonderful new sounds of the night surrounded us.

Back inside, we lit some candles and sat in front of the fire. Kate suggested we sing Christmas carols and so we did, every one we knew. Frequently we forgot the words and simply hummed. Other times we just kept repeating the words or phrases we did remember. It was quiet and peaceful. At last we sang "Silent Night", both lifting candles high in our own candlelight service. Later we lay close and fell asleep, our Christmas Day done.

● ● ●

Kate soon resigned herself to the fact that for the next couple of days I would be mentally incapacitated; my fly fishing gene kicked in and all hopes for intelligent conversation vanished.

I caught three nice trout in our first walk along the river. We kept the third, a two pound rainbow, for dinner. Its stomach was chock-full of dark nymphs, a green beetle, and a half digested grasshopper.

So inspired, I switched to a ratty grasshopper pattern on our next walk along the river. My first cast went to a deep pool sheltered by three large boulders. Out of the depth came an enormous open mouth, followed by a similarly proportioned body. ZIP! I set the hook prematurely and ended up with a pile of line in my face. I cast again and the 'hopper landed in the pool a microsecond later. Again the big fish rose. This time my patience held. Shortly the rod bent double under the marvelous pull of a strong trout.

There was a vicious splash as the fish charged out for fast water. The giant skipped across the surface and splashed down in the next pool below. For a moment we stalemated. The water was gin clear and I saw the big fish sitting three feet down, gathering strength. Our eyes locked; the fish was mad.

Suddenly the big trout charged up and out of the water, an angry slash of red hanging two feet in the air. For ten minutes the fight continued. At last the fish tired and I maneuvered it towards

A beautiful New Zealand rainbow trout.

shore and pounced, rod flying aside into the rocks. Nothing in life was as important as that giant fish.

"I got a hugey!" I screamed to Kate. Shortly, I slipped the giant back into the stream. As nine pounds of bruised ego and sore mouth melted into the darkness, I knew that the stories about Kiwi trout are true.

● ● ●

We'd been told to expect crowds as it was the holiday season. But for a couple days, Kate and I fished and tramped and spent the nights in Tawhiwhi Hut alone. If this was New Zealand's busy season, we were in hog heaven.

A few hardy trampers showed up as the days drew away from Christmas. One evening a family joined us. Ian, Wendy, Kerri, and little Max were the epitome of Kiwi trampers. They wore gumboots, carried Macpac backpacks, and wore plenty of sandfly-repelling Dimp. Among their staples were Vegemite, Continental instant meals, and a large supply of tea. The family's knowledge and appreciation of the bush seemed boundless. Ian and Wendy pointed out majestic totara and rimu trees, tasty pepper plants, low ferns, and sticky needle. Kerri and Max spotted a fantail, flightless wekas, and a melodious bellbird.

Another night Tam and Coreen, a couple of rock-hard Kiwis, shared the hut with us. Tam muscled seventy-five pounds of gear in a tattered canvas pack that had no belt and no padded shoulder straps. Coreen was outfitted in kind. The great American tradition of being more worried about the gear and the label than about the experience is not prevalent in New Zealand.

Much of the Kiwi bush is filled with wild boars and Tam was a pig hunter. Pig hunting is a team sport: the hunter and his dogs versus the pigs. The dogs track and corner a pig, then hold it by the ears. The hunter sticks the pig with a knife or flips it over to slit its throat. Dense bush generally precludes the luxury of a rifle kill. Killing is sweaty and noisy; the pungent smell of death stays close.

By firelight, Tam recited endless stories of pig hunting in the bush. On one hunt an enormous boar, one hundred ninety-eight pounds dressed, slashed the dogs with its tusks, then treed Tam and his mate. Pinned in the tree, Tam lashed his knife to a six foot branch and repeatedly stuck the crazed beast from above. The angry boar kept coming, but soon weakened enough for Tam to climb down and finish the job.

● ● ●

As we fixed a pot of tea one afternoon, the sound of pounding hooves and hard breathing animals shattered the quiet. A quick look out the window revealed six wild horses circling the hut at a full gallop. They stopped, rose on their hind legs, nipped each other, and kicked their heels to the sky. Then they raced off again, circling the hut three times.

Russell later told us that these were Maori horses. Private Maori lands dot the Urewaras and the horses are allowed to range in the park. They're collected once a year or so, depending on when they're needed. The horses learn to love their freedom and don't take to the saddle willingly.

Shortly, two rough hunters rode through the clearing, carrying rifles and scoping the hills. They wore rugged bushwear: gumboots, plaid Swanndri coats, knives belted around the waist. Their horses were fitted with rifle scabbards; sheepskins padded the hunters' ride. Two ill-tempered dogs trotted at the horses' flanks.

"What are you after?" I asked. "Deer? Pigs?"

"Both, anything," they grunted back and kept moving. The hunters passed and we gave them a wide berth.

● ● ●

We walked separately for a time on the way out from Tawhiwhi Hut. I waited at a fork in the track and started back when Kate didn't show. As I rounded a corner, there was a movement and I froze. Thirty meters ahead stood a red deer stag. Velvet hung from the stag's newly forming antlers. Another thirty meters behind the stag I saw Kate's purple pullover, half-concealed in some tall grass. The three of us formed a perfect line. We all remained quiet for several minutes. Then the stag shied and ambled off down the river bank.

Red deer, an Old World cousin of the American elk, were introduced to New Zealand by Europeans. In the past, red deer multiplied so fast that they were thought of as pests. Now, spotting one in the bush is a rare enough occurrence to be a special moment. There are still plenty of red deer to see, though, on New Zealand's four thousand game farms. Aside from meat sales, the deer are farmed for their antlers. The antlers are a staple in the pharmacopoeia of the Far East, for everything from arthritis medication to aphrodisiacs.

● ● ●

Andy picked us up at the trailhead. Back in Ruatahuna, we washed our clothes and our bodies, then settled into the Forest Service hut. Later, we walked over to visit Russell. We found Russ inside, barefoot and in shorts. He grabbed a terry cloth hat, red instead of blue this time, and joined us at the picnic table. Russ listened intently while we told the big fish story. His face grew animated, his eyes happy. Our enthusiasm seemed to take him back to other times, private memories.

"I've got this whenever I want," he said with a smile. "But it does my heart good to see you visitors have some fun, too."

I recounted the pig hunting stories we'd heard, and mentioned the hunters on horseback. "Those guys were carrying rifles," Kate said. "Are there many accidents? Should we be wearing orange in the bush?"

"Course accidents happen," Russ replied, "though I don't reckon anything like youse folks are used to. Just part of the game." Russell pulled off his hat and ran a hand through his short-cropped hair. "Last year a bloke I knew quite well, Forest Service man, got shot and killed durin' the roar. Roar's the worst time. Everybody goes out then–big advantage bein' able to know where the deer are. Trouble is you got other hunters out there roaring, attracting deer. People don't always know what they're shooting at."

. Russell pulled out his pack of cigarette papers, picked one off the top, and stuck it to his lip. "This forestry bloke and his mate were in the bush, roaring. His mate bends down to pick something up when BOOM!–a shot rings out. Bloke says he could feel the wind right across the hairs on his neck. He hits the ground and by the time he gets his wits and sits up, he finds his mate dead, bullet right through the head."

By now, Russ had rolled some tobacco in his palms and pulled the paper off his lip. "This friend of mine," he continued, "'bout fifty-nine he was, been hunting all of his life. Not doing anything wrong that day. At the inquest the bloke that shot him swore he was following a deer, heard the roar, saw a movement in the bush, and fired. Strange set of cards that can be dealt sometimes."

Russell licked the paper, gave it a roll, then settled the stubby cigarette into the corner of his mouth and lit it. "Some of us fellows sat around for hours trying to sort it out. Everybody knows you shouldn't shoot at something 'fore you know what it is. But the bloke was sincere. Strange cards...."

Talk soon returned to fishing. "Don't go far much anymore, now." Russ said. "Hell, if I wanted to catch a bunch of fish, I'd go up to Minginui. Got more fish in one hole on the Whirinaki than the Whakatane's got in a half mile. Lotta people, though." Russ paused to relight his cigarette, which had gone out. "Got four pound rainbows down the road five minutes from here. No reason to drive to Minginui."

With that Russ invited us to go fishing later in the evening at his favorite spot, a beautiful hole far up a bush-lined gorge. I felt like a kid stepping into fly fishing manhood. Dinner went untouched. Two hours before departure time, I was ready.

Russell sent me up into the gorge alone while he and Kate waited at the car. Two big trout worked the surface as I approached. Darkness started to fill the gorge; the moon was on the rise. Earlier, I errantly tied on a nymph when "Dry fly!" was being shouted from the heavens. Without a flashlight, I couldn't see to thread the hook. I sweated profusely, hands quivering, quietly swearing up a storm. While I struggled to change flies, the two monsters continued to peacefully slurp the top, eight feet away from me. I tried to catch the moonlight reflection off the pool, but couldn't focus because of the ripples caused by the feeding trout. After fifteen minutes, I finally shook my way into the eye of the hook.

The fish ignored a dozen casts. I pulled up my line to find a huge rat's nest—fifteen more minutes to untangle. By the time I was finished, I was finished. The fish were down and inky blackness overwhelmed the gorge.

I had "fished" three quarters of an hour, only fifteen minutes of which my fly was on the water. I returned to the car, limp like a wet rag, but with a certain air of philosophical dignity. After all, I had to return with something. Kate laughed; Russell smiled knowingly.

● ● ●

The next day was the day that Russell ran us out to the start of our second tramp, the tramp where the possum kept us awake at Parahaki Hut. The possum wasn't the only thing that hindered our sleep during those first trips into the bush. Sandfly bites kept us scratching long into the night. Sandflies are small, but their bite packs a wallop and itches like the blazes. Our skin quickly grew splotched with red welts. I scratched my shins so hard that I drew blood. Nightly, Kate rolled around in her sleeping bag, desperately trying not to touch her bites. Eventually she'd cry out in anguish, rip the bag open, and start itching fervently.

We spent much of the walk out from Parahaki Hut talking about getting back on the bikes. Kate retained a lingering phobia from our three summit ride into Ruatahuna. "I hated that!" she lamented.

"But look how it paid off," I returned. "Meeting Russell and the great fishing and tramping."

"I don't care what you say," she shot back as we waded the stream. "I'll never have anything good to say about that miserable ride."

"If we can make it through that day we can handle anything," I argued.

Kate, however, couldn't forget the pain so quickly and worried about our next ride: fourteen kilometers of metal road up a pass higher than any on the way to Ruatahuna.

"That's gonna kill us," she said.

We walked on in silence. The days, we both knew, would not all be perfect. We needed open minds and positive outlooks to prosper through the day-to-day trials of a transient lifestyle. We each had a strong desire to learn about New Zealand and its people. But there was more. We were also traveling to stretch ourselves and learn more about each other. After almost five years together, we both understood that our Kiwi travels would likely decide the future, if any, of our relationship.

● ● ●

Russell met us back at trailhead, two cold brews in hand. He laughed with us about the possum story as we rattled back to Ruatahuna. We planned to stay the night at the Forest Service hut, then return to the bikes in the morning. When Russ pulled up to the hut, however, we found a monstrous Chevy Suburban, complete with American side drive, parked in front. "Damn them," Russell muttered. "I told them the bunkhouse, not the hut."

"Who?" Kate asked.

"Just some floozy Cabinet Minister. You'll see her, silver-haired lady."

"Cabinet Minister, as in Wellington, as in the national government?" I asked.

"Sure," Russ said. Without getting out of the truck, he leaned on the horn and yelled, "You're in the wrong place."

A silver-haired head woman stepped out the door, followed shortly by an older man and a young couple. "I said the bunkhouse over there," Russ barked. "You'll find it a bit nicer. We save this place for itinerants like these Yanks here. They'll be over in a while to use the shower, so you'll have to share." The last comment was a statement, not a question.

With a collective sigh of relief, the four in the hut started carrying boxes of food and wine back to the Suburban. Kate and I climbed out of the truck, grabbed our packs, and then helped them vacate the dilapidated hut. The Minister, a stately-looking woman, said hello and then, as if in explanation, "Strange trip we're on, jumping from first class hotels to places like...er...this...."

Kate and I had stopped in the bunkhouse for a shower previously and knew the Minister was still in for a surprise. Unlike the hut, the bunkhouse had a kitchen and even some padded furniture. No one, however, had stayed in the bunkhouse for some time. Thousands of dead flies graced the floors and window sills. When I walked over for my shower later, the sound of furious sweeping echoed out the door.

Russell was disappointed that we'd done poorly fishing on our second tramp and invited us on a private tour of his special river.

We parked at the "swimming hole," a deep pool surrounded by rocks. Maori kids dove from the rocks, screaming and hooting in the cold water. The Minister and her entourage sat on the bank enjoying the sun.

Russell sent me out on an old wood bridge over the gorge, right above where I'd performed so dismally a few nights earlier. The bridge was thirty or forty feet up, three feet wide, and had no railing. No trout moved in the pool below; the observer above found only vertigo.

The guide, who had referred to himself as "ol' Russ," quickly dispelled any worries we had about him getting around in the bush. He plummeted into the gorge, hopped fences, slid on his bum, and walked waist deep in the stream. Kate and I had our hands full keeping up with him.

The sides of the gorge rose straight up away from the stream. Boulders and fallen trees littered the edge of the water. Bush encroached wherever it could get a foothold. The stream was narrow, often only fifteen feet wide. Casts, by necessity, were short.

Russ pointed out likely pools with his walking stick.
"Try next to that rock, they usually sit along there...Never taken a trout in that pool, some pools just don't hold trout...Saw a monster in that pool last year, no strike. Never seen him since...."

While I fished, Russ charmed Kate with his endless stories. Russ, a pakeha, was enamored with Maoris. His daughter had married a Maori. Russ understood Maori traditions, their lore, their tongue. He explained that Maori society is arranged in maraes–tribes of sorts. Each marae has its own building, usually decorated in traditional wood carvings, which serves as a gathering place in times of celebrations or sorrow. Russ taught us some Maori phrases: "kia ora" for good luck or good health, "haere-mai" for welcome, and "tapu" for forbidden.

All too soon the gorge and my fishing ended. We hadn't seen a fish. For the second time with Russ, I had snatched defeat from the gaping jaws of certain success.

● ● ●

We walked back on the bluffs above the gorge, crossed a fence, then followed the edge of a potato field. Russell pointed out a ridge he used to hunt deer on. "Steep enough to slide 'em down to the road," he said.

Like all great storytellers, Russell loved an audience. In us he had an eager one. Russ had guided sportsman for a while, hoping to make big money off rich Americans, but soon gave it up for lumber and Forest Service work.

"Had one old boy, bout seventy-two, up for a fish one time," Russ began. He stopped to look into the gorge, as if remembering.

"This bloke's old tart drank like a fish–for breakfast, lunch, and tea she did. Set this bloke up in the gorge and told him I'd pick him up on the other end in a few hours. His tart had a beer or two, that being a great lunch for her. Came to pick him up and he was all smiles, had three beautiful trout. Couldn't stop talking about it, he was so excited."

We started walking again. "I took him down to the swimmin' hole for a bit of dry fly work, and damn me hide if he doesn't hit into a big one. Well that thing is across the pool, up and down, out of the water–a real monster. It starts running on him and I'm standing on shore yelling 'Let 'em go, let 'em go!'"

Russ hopped a small ditch without a pause, lost in the story. "The old boy's got these big hip waders on, standing on slippery rocks, so I grab him around the waist to help him down. The fish is way into his backing by now. We chase it three pools down and finally slow it on an open stretch. The fish is getting tired and this old bloke works him up onto a sandbar in the middle of the pool."

Russ stopped and faced us to give the story added emphasis. "We're almost ready to go after the fish when all of the sudden, sensing one last chance at life, it makes a final effort. Boom–then nothing. Dead silence. Damn me hide if the monster wasn't gone. Well that old bloke just stood there and slapped his line on the water over and over, moaning all the while. I says to him, 'That's your luck, mate.' 'Bout broke his heart."

We walked on quietly for a bit, enjoying the sun, looking into the gorge, and then Russell started anew.

"'Nother time we had one of your sports heros, bloke named Ted Williams, over here for a Tourist Council promotion of hunting and fishing. 'Bout nineteen fifty-eight, it was. Baseball's not big here. What was Williams famous for?"

I told him that Williams is considered one of the greatest hitters of all times.

"Tourist Council had this idea," Russell continued, "The Big Three. Wanted to see the shortest time to take a big game fish, a trout, and a deer. Film crew, press, the whole deal. With a bit of wit, they thought they'd take the big game fish in the Bay of Plenty, float plane Williams into Rotorua for a trout, then fly him in here for a deer. Me mate was in on organizing all this, so he calls to tell me to get ready for a deer."

Russ slowed up to prod a clump of dirt with his walking stick. "I waited three days. For some reason we didn't know exactly when it would be. So for three days I didn't move out of sight of the phone. Finally I says, 'This is hopeless,' and head for the river and a bit of fishing. Damn me if Williams doesn't take his big fish and head for Rotorua. Me mate gets excited when he hears the word 'cuz now the clock is started. He rings me in a big hurry, but Mother tells him I'm down at the river. So he jumps in the truck and hurries down from Rotorua."

"Well damn it if it doesn't take 'em two and a half hours to take a trout!" The disgust in Russell's voice was apparent. "I'm down there on the river with three beautiful trout when here comes me mate flying by on the road. I scramble up the bank and flag down a lady I've never seen. Finally catch me mate and we head over to the airstrip. We wait for the racket of the plane–it's getting dark by now– then turn on our lights. They never see us and end up landing in Minginui, twenty-five miles away. Some Forest Service chaps hurry them down here to where we're waiting."

"I'd seen deer coming out of the gorge here," Russ stopped and indicated, "so I figure we'll get out the spotlight and pick one up right quick." Russ leaned on his walking stick, pulled off his hat, and wiped the sweat from his forehead. "Spot-lighting wasn't real popular in the States, so they didn't want to do that for releasing the film back there. Well, the clocks a running and they had a war council, and damn me hide if they didn't decide, 'Let's get one anyway.'"

"So we jump in the farmer's Land Rover and come around the corner over there." Russell pointed across the field to the scenes of action. "My mate was on the spotlight, I think. He turns it on and the paddock lights up like a Christmas tree–bright, shiny eyes everywhere. Then the deer scatter. Williams finally drops a hind and we wave the light. That was the signal that the kill was made and to stop the clock. All the sudden there's cars all over the field, blokes shaking hands and congratulating each other, some bloke from *Field and Stream* running around trying to record it all."

We started walking again and soon jumped a fence near where we'd dropped into the gorge. "We had dinner later," Russ continued. "Mother had steak and kidney, but when I pulled out those three trout, Williams got excited. Wanted to stay right then and fish, but they had him traipsing off for publicity stunts and there was no time. Got a few cards from him over the years, but he never made it back."

As we started down the hill to the car, Russell waved us on. "You two go ahead," he said. "I'll be there in a second. Gotta see a man about a dog."

● ● ●

Kate and I joined Russell's group for a farewell beer that night. The Cabinet Minister and her underlings were also there. Only in New Zealand, we were learning, could you sit in a tiny bush town sipping beer with the most powerful woman in the country.

The Minister was pleasant but, like most politicians, liked to hear herself talk. I gave her an enormous amount of credit for being in Ruatahuna at all, not to mention that she seemed genuinely concerned about public land management. She and Russell were a well-matched pair. They discussed the possibility of him working for the Park Service board. As we departed, the Minister gave us her card in case "any of those floozies in immigration" gave us any problems with visa extensions.

Russell accompanied us outside. For a moment we stood under the stars, listening to the sounds of the night; then he wished us success with the rest of our travels. We thanked Russell for his help and friendship. He asked us to close the gate on our way out.

THE "EASY" EAST COAST

Chapter 4

Leaving Ruatahuna was not easy. Kate and I had found much of the New Zealand we'd come searching for in this tiny bush town. Also, the question of returning to the bikes lingered. Our last day pedaling, we couldn't forget, was the fiasco of December 24. Now three-thousand-foot Taupeupe Saddle stood between us and Lake Waikaremoana, our goal for the day.

The seats felt hard and uninviting as we pedaled out of town and started to climb. Strangely, however, the monster saddle had no teeth. Even though the vertical change was great, the incline was gentle. Two and a half hours of mild pedaling carried us to the top. Crossing Taupeupe Saddle with such ease helped us over a big mental hurdle. It was the first of the many lessons of bike travel that we would learn: in hill-climbing, grade, not elevation change, determines difficulty. We pushed on happily, buoyed with new confidence.

Our first view of Lake Waikaremoana was mesmerizing. We rode up onto a bluff, pedaling hard. As we crested the top, the bush gave way to nothingness. Kate and I walked carefully to the edge and peered over. Hundreds of feet below lay the lake, deep blue and unrippled. Dark mountains, draped in uninterrupted sky, lined the water's edge.

Caravans and tents jammed the motor camp at Waikaremoana Point. Contrary to our earlier thoughts, holiday season does come to New Zealand. We climbed the next bluff and searched for a spot to pitch the tent.

On top of the bluff stood the former site of the old Lake House Hotel. Established in the early nineteen hundreds, the hotel became popular after trout were introduced to the lake. The first recorded catch was fourteen pounds! The historic hotel expanded through prosperous times, but was deemed uneconomical and torn down in the early seventies.

The hotel had been perfectly situated high above the lake. Kate and I set up the tent on the south side of the site and started cooking dinner. The sun slid towards Panekiri Bluff, a yellow block that dominates the southern end of Lake Waikaremoana. Blue yielded magically to pink, then orange, as the sun sent low-angled beams of light into the lake. We sat close on our pads and watched, our boiling rice neglected.

We planned to continue south in the morning but dawn brought heaping buckets of Urewara rain. After ten days of sunshine, the time for rain was definitely upon us.

Summertime weather in New Zealand runs in reasonably consistent patterns. We soon learned that if it rained for a couple of days, a few days of sunshine would follow. Self-forecasting, which we did daily, proved every bit as scientific as the voodoo meteorology practiced by Kiwi weathermen. New Zealand weather, according to them, is always "fine." This term applies to rainstorms as well as sunshine, gale force winds and peaceful calm. Forecasters declare, "Cloudy and fine today" or "Expect rain with periods of fine extending through the weekend." Newspapers run weather briefs for ten towns. The listing under every town will read "Fine" even though two snowstorms and a hurricane are in progress.

"Fine," in Kiwi weather forecasting, means "we have no earthly idea."

● ● ●

After a day huddled inside, Kate and I itched to move on even though the rain continued. The sky cleared soon after we dropped off the lake plateau. Our goal became reaching the end of the Urewara gravel.

"Only half an hour more pedaling will get you off the metal and onto the tar seal," a shopkeeper in Tuai told us. Her estimate, like most given by automobile drivers, was off by a factor of three. It took us an hour and a half.

The road onward to Wairoa wound through rolling hills. We rounded a corner and came upon a young boy riding a pony bareback. Suddenly the pony veered ninety degrees; the boy continued in the previous direction. He landed belly first in the mud as the pony bolted for the farmhouse, almost a kilometer distant. By the time we reached the next corner, the pony waited in the farmyard. The boy was only halfway home.

Kate and I set up camp in Wairoa, then talked with a German biker who pedaled in at dusk. The German claimed to frequently ride over two hundred kilometers a day. On this day he had put in a hundred eighty-five kilometers. The German's bike and physique substantiated the stories; both were lean and built for speed.

"I am by myself, you see," the German told us. "You are two, together. You can talk, do things, share things. For me, there is nothing to do, so I bike many kilometer. I am lonely...I fill my time with biking. To be with someone is better, I think."

The German wore a Hawaiian marathon shirt and claimed to have run the marathon in 2:30. We believed him, but stared wide-eyed as he rolled and smoked a cigarette. When he noticed our looks, he explained, "A cigarette after a long bike ride helps me relax."

The German departed at seven the next morning. Kate and I piddled around until ten, then started south. Frequently, we had heard that riding along the East Coast meant easy flats and coastal plains. In fact, the "easy" East Coast turned ugly. The road shot straight up a hundred ridges then plunged into a hundred gorges. Every corner revealed another monstrous challenge. Kate began to fall far behind; her high gear ratio was really beginning to tell.

"I'm ready to die," Kate declared as we climbed out of a deep gorge. I felt much the same. At the top of the gorge we pulled into Putorino for a cold beer.

Seventeen kilometers still separated us from our desired stop at Lake Tutira. We continued to climb past Putorino, then dropped into another deep gorge. Halfway out of this one, Kate stopped to walk. I churned on, yelling, "Smile, we're almost to the top."

A few minutes later Kate pedaled up to where I waited, her eyes full of tears. "Don't tell me to smile when my legs are numb!" she anguished. "I can't feel my legs! They're mush! My knees are killing me! How can you be so damn cheerful?"

The hills had taken their toll. But even with our dues paid, Lake Tutira was still fifteen kilometers away. Kate cried the entire way. My feeble attempts to comfort her accomplished little more than aggravation. When a truck approached and I cautioned Kate to move over, the flame reignited. "Don't tell me what to do!" she yelled. "Just get away from me. "

"But I...,"

"No, don't say anything–I don't want to hear it. "

"But I. . .,"

"GET AWAY!"

Sore knees and mushy legs do not answer to reason. A lower gearing ratio was imperative for Kate, otherwise the hills would kill her.

We pulled into a roadside picnic ground at Lake Tutira. I helped Kate into her sleeping bag and took care of the tent and dinner. She mumbled incoherently until mollified by hot tea. Kate's humor and color slowly returned. We listened to the birds in the Lake Tutira sanctuary, then passed into a hard sleep.

In the morning we switched bikes in hopes of giving Kate's knees a rest with the Rockhopper's granny gear. The day's ride, however, took us out of only one deep gorge. I stood up the entire three-kilometer length of the rise while Kate pedaled effortlessly. I felt empathy for Kate--seeing a giant hill and realizing the agony required to get up it must have been disheartening.

From the top of that final gorge, we plummeted to the sea through five or six glorious kilometers. Tired bodies translated to a couple of rest days in Napier. Kate and I made use of the time by sampling the local brewmaster's fare, but not without the help of some of the locals. We arrived at the tour of the Leopard Brewing Company on time only because the city bus driver broke his route and delivered us to the front door. Later, a helpful Kiwi driver stopped three times to guide us on our way to the Hawke Bay vineyards. Try as we might, we never did convince the man we weren't lost.

• • •

Kate and I biked south from Napier to Waipukurau along flat, coastal plains and peaceful backroads. Pedaling side by side, we rejoiced at finally reaching the "easy" East Coast we kept hearing about. The land was dry with no bush. Surrounding hills blazed with scorched yellows and golds.

At the Waipukurau motor camp we met Ursella, a Canadian biker. Ursella stood almost six foot, an attractive northwoods woman who cooked for the forestry service in British Columbia. In the middle of custard, Ursella blurted out, "What do you think of your president? Personally I can't see one good thing about him." US-bashing was very popular with the budget travel set, with Canadians often being the most vocal.

The nuclear issue was the hottest topic of conversation in New Zealand. In 1984, David Lange's Labour Party came to power under a pledge of ridding New Zealand of nuclear weapons. Part of the policy includes a ban of American nuclear-armed and nuclear-powered ships from Kiwi harbors. The ban did not come without threats of reprisal from the U.S. government, including economic sanctions, withdrawal of defense obligations and shared military intelligence, and the freezing of New Zealand from the ANZUS (Australia, New Zealand, US) alliance.

Even under the threats, Kiwis show a remarkable grass roots resilience. A poll revealed that seventy-four percent of Kiwis applauded the refusal of port entry to the first US ship to test the nuclear-free policy. Young and old Kiwis alike defended the virtue of the ban to Kate and me. The only Kiwis we met that did not support the ban were Vietnam vets who had fought alongside Americans.

• • •

The ride southwest to Dannevirke continued through flat, dry countryside. A farmer leaned on his fence as we ground to the top of the only hill along the way. "You shouldn't put such big hills in front of your place," I hollered to him.

He laughed and replied, "I reckon that'll slow you speedsters down a might."

From Dannevirke, a welcome wind pushed us down Highway 2 to Palmerston North. The road follows the Manawatu River out of the flats and through the Manawatu Gorge, a gap between the southern end of the Ruahine Range and the northern end of the Tararuas. The feel is all wrong; a river passing from flat land, through mountains, back into flat land.

In Palmerston North, we explored gearing options for Kate's bike at the Pedal Pusher bike shop. Installing a triple crank required a complete overhaul: a new bottom bracket, new derailleurs, and heaps of money. An easier, and less costly, solution to Kate's high gear ratios was to replace her chainrings with smaller ones and spread the rear cluster. The man at the bike shop assured us that the ride to Wellington was flat, so we decided to mull it over until then.

South of Palmerston North, the pull of Wellington drew cars from everywhere. Backroads dwindled; we stayed to the main road for lack of other choices and battled head winds and heavy traffic to Levin. Shoulders appeared intermittently but mostly we squeezed onto the foot of crumbled pavement on the road edge. Semi-trucks and buses never considered slowing from a hundred kilometers per hour as they passed. Initially, the blast in front of the big vehicles forced us sideways off the road. Just as we turned inward to compensate, the push disappeared and a draft sucked us in. Another frantic yank on the handlebars frequently left us in the ditch. One bus passed so near I had to pull my elbow in to keep from being hit. Later, the same bus passed going the opposite direction; a sign on the side declared, "RENT ME." Great, I thought, death at the hands of a nonprofessional.

In the morning we continued to battle traffic until Paraparaumu, then threw in the towel and took the suburban train into Wellington. Wellington, New Zealand's beautiful capital, spills off the hills and into the harbor. We spent a few days touring the city, ever aware of the South Island, our next destination, looming majestically across rugged Cook Strait.

Village Bikes helped us work out Kate's gearing problems before we crossed over to the South Island. We picked up a thirty-six-tooth chainring, popped her forty up a level, and spread the rear cluster to include a thirty-two-tooth sprocket. Kate tossed her old fifty-two-tooth chainring, which had been unused freight since Auckland. Her new 36/32 combination resulted in a smallest wheel of thirty inches, as compared to the previous low of thirty-nine inches. We both looked for improvement in Kate's sore knees and hill climbing disposition.

● ● ●

Wellington's celebrated winds blasted out of the hills as we rode along Waterloo Quay to the ferry terminal. The ferocious winds accompanied us on the ferry ride across Cook Strait, but died out as we approached the tip of the South Island.

I left Kate below, went topside, and began talking with a "granola girl" from the States. She and her boyfriend were traveling the South Seas and, in particular, had dreamed of New Zealand. Of late, however, they'd become disenchanted.

"I don't know how we're going to find enough stuff to do for the six-month time slot we've allotted here," the granola girl carped. "Nothing in New Zealand is new, everything is the same as at home: mountains and outdoors. The food is terrible here; we can't find anything healthy. They treat the environment so badly. And if I see another sheep, I think I'll die."

I didn't reply, just leaned on the railing and watched as the ferry passed into the labyrinth of Marlborough Sounds. Tall ridges, blanketed in deep bush, dropped to sheltered inlets. Secret waterways led to hidden bays. The sun descended slowly, leaving the calm waters of the sounds glimmering. The wind stood still; the air had just the right sweatshirt chill to it.

The entirety of the South Island stretched beyond this overwhelming introduction. I watched in silent awe. How could anyone be disappointed in New Zealand in the face of such beauty?

As I fell deeper and deeper into my philosophical musings, the granola girl's boyfriend approached her and said, "God, I'm so happy not to see any bare hills. At least if there's sheep, we won't be able to see them."

South Island

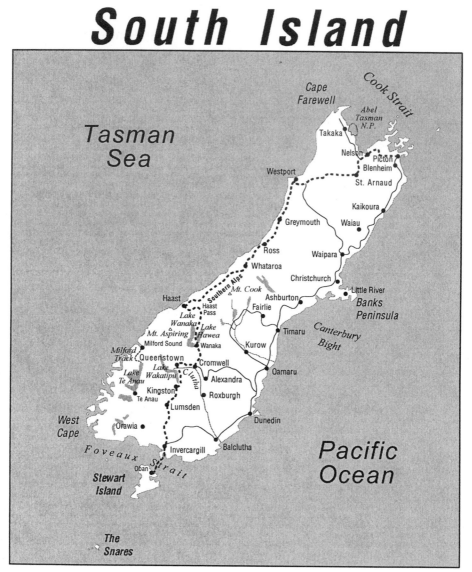

Tasman Sea

Cape Farewell

Cook Strait

Abel Tasman N.P.

Takaka

Nelson

Picton
Blenheim

Westport

St. Arnaud

Kaikoura

Greymouth

Waiau

Ross

Waipara

Whataroa

Christchurch

Little River

Mt. Cook

Ashburton

Banks Peninsula

Southern Alps

Fairlie

Haast

Haast Pass

Lake Wanaka

Lake Hawea

Timaru

Canterbury Bight

Mt. Aspiring

Milford Sound

Wanaka

Kurow

Milford Track

Queenstown

Cromwell

Lake Wakatipu

Clutha

Oamaru

Lake Te Anau

Alexandra

Kingston

Roxburgh

Te Anau

Lumsden

West Cape

Orawia

Dunedin

Foveaux Strait

Invercargill

Balclutha

Pacific Ocean

Oban

Stewart Island

The Snares

SOUTH ISLAND HELLO

Chapter 5

An irate biker burst into the motor camp kitchen at Momorangi Bay. "This trip sucks!" she groused. "I'm flying home." It was the day following our ferry crossing to the South Island, but we'd only made it a scant fifteen kilometers from the ferry terminus in Picton. Queen Charlotte Drive, which winds in and out of secluded bays and waterways, so enchanted us that all Kate and I cared to do was stop and enjoy the beauty of the Marlborough Sounds.

"God damn three solid weeks of rain coming up the West Coast," the incensed biker muttered to herself. "I should have stayed home where it was sunny." Outside stood an expensive new mountain bike. The girl wore lavish bike togs, color-coordinated right down to the stripes on her helmet and the tassels on her socks.

A big space quickly cleared around the sourpuss, but amiable Pat, a biking friend we'd made in camp, decided to try and break her shell. Pat was from East Glacier, Montana, slightly round, baby-faced, and, like me, tooled around on a Rockhopper. Kate and I quickly found him to be easygoing and unpretentious. When

Pat started to ask the sourpuss about the South Island's West Coast, she cut him off. "Listen, buddy, it's wet, miserable, cold, lonely. There's no place to eat or buy anything. In fact, there's nothing there but stinking rain!"

Pat let the sourpuss's brashness run off him and continued his attempt to engage her. "How do you like your bike?"

"Give me some space, OK?" she bristled. And then, as she turned her back on him, she said, "I just want to eat and get out of this God-forsaken place."

Pat stood up from the table and spoke to the cold shoulder. "You know, where I come from rudeness is considered bad manners. You definitely qualify." With that he walked out the door.

Later Kate, Pat, and I sat around the tents talking. The night air was warm; stars twinkled in a cloudless sky. Quiet settled over the camp, except for a the hum of radios reporting the status of the America's Cup yachting duel between the US and New Zealand. Kiwis buzzed with dreams of bringing the Cup home. The Bank of New Zealand offered bonds that increased in value every time the Kiwi boat, *KZ7*, won. Dairies offered *KZ7* ice cream–"the only *KZ7* Dennis Conner will ever lick." Buttons and t-shirts proclaimed "KIWI MAGIC!" and "THE PLASTIC FANTASTIC!" the latter referring to *KZ7*'s fiberglass hull . When at length that night Chris Dixon and *KZ7* crossed the finish line ahead of Dennis Conner and *Stars and Stripes*, a collective cheer rang out through the camp. Sadly, for the Kiwis, the Yanks atoned for the loss in the coming days and won the race series four to one.

We bid Pat farewell in the morning and biked forty kilometers to Pelorus Bridge. The ride engulfed us. Dark waterways, a salty odor, still air, bird calls, and sunshine combined in sensual orgy. As the days passed, we were becoming more and more at home on the bikes. Car travel now held no appeal. Biking allowed us to pass through a scene as vibrant participants rather than as passive observers.

Kate and I camped on a grassy knoll above the Pelorus River. The river cuts deep into rock and runs through emerald pools that cry out for swimmers. Many on this hot day answered the call. We moved upriver, found a secluded pool, and soaked away the heat of the ride.

In the morning, we swam with two Kiwi girls who were touring the South Island. They wore jandals (that's Kiwi for sandals) and rode rickety bikes–life can be very simple when you're not an equipment junky. The girls introduced us to a biker we noticed the previous night. He was remarkable first because he carried a big red backpack instead of panniers, and second because he camped under the toilet overhang. Gary, in fact, was from the University of Colorado and we quickly discovered a couple of mutual friends.

Gary and I talked as we pedaled for Nelson. Gary's sense of equipment priorities was unique. "My bike was the main toy I got to bring along," he explained. "Weight-wise, I couldn't bring much more. I've got panniers and a front bag at home, of course." Gary wore racing cleats and rode a mountain bike. When we talked about fly fishing, the quagmire deepened. "Yeah, I really wanted to fish over here," he told me, "but didn't figure I could bring too many toys, like I said, 'cuz of the weight. I've got my reel and some flies, but I left my rod at home."

I laughed heartily with Gary; he was so darn good-natured and easygoing I couldn't help it. On the run to the ocean, Gary pounded off. Even carrying a big pack he easily outdistanced me on the flats.

I continued on to find Kate in Nelson, where we planned to spend a rest day. She had biked far ahead for most of the morning and chugged easily over the three major climbs along the way. We both felt thankful for the successful first tests of her new gearing.

● ● ●

Departing Nelson, Kate and I pedaled hard to reach the morning tour of McCashin Brewery. There we talked at length with Stuart, a bearded biochemist, after the tour. Stuart had traveled around the world and thus was interested in our journeys. We, on the other hand, were interested in tasting his beer, so the conversation proved mutually satisfying.

An hour after the tour group departed, Stuart stuffed our front bags full of beer and poured us out the door. As we struggled to mount the bikes, he offered a suggestion, "Stop in at Mapua tonight. It's not far and I think you'll find it an interesting place to stay."

Kate and I wobbled off, trying hard to find our lost equilibrium. Thirty kilometers down the road signs appeared touting the Mapua Leisure Park. Why "leisure park," I asked a man at the gas station, instead of the normal title "motor camp"?

He smiled and laughed, "That's the nudey place. Only clothing optional camp in New Zealand."

We biked into the camp with slight trepidation. Immediately, a naked toddler scurried across the road. Kate, who wasn't nearly as excited about the opportunity for titillation as I, announced, "There you go, big guy, your first nudist." The camp looked like any other we'd been in: caravans, ablution blocks, clothes lines. Somehow, though, nudes playing tennis and bouncing on trampolines gave the camp a slightly different flavor.

California Bob arrived near dusk. Bob sported a dark beard and wore turquoise pants. Even in the fading light, he continually popped his Vuarnets on and off. Bob questioned us incessantly about the camp—how many folks went nude, where nudity was allowed and so on—then set to work putting up his tent. Moments later a pungent odor wafted over and we knew Bob was bolstering his nerve. Shortly he emerged, nude, and strode to the beach. Bob must have been in search of a twilight tan. Kate and I chuckled; we were both well into our bunting jackets.

Actually, the "leisure park" surprised us. We left believing that our preconceptions of a nudist camp were way off base. Nude or clothed meant nothing; there were no hangups. Kate summed it up best in one of her letters: "It's not as weird as it sounds, just a bunch of old men running around naked."

● ● ●

Kate and I biked from Mapua, along the Tasman Bay, to Motueka, where we landed in a health food restaurant called The

Place. I started talking with a girl in line who was from Holland, but had lived in New Zealand for three years. "They call me Dutchy," she said. "I won't tell you what else they call me!"

Dutchy wore skin-tight black pants, a loose tank top, a woven ankle bracelet, and assorted jewelry. The exposed portions of her legs were unshaven. She brushed her short blonde hair straight back; silver John Denver glasses tilted on her nose as she smiled at me. "I wanted to get away from the stink and flatness of Holland," Dutchy continued, "so I came here."

Dutchy joined us at our table after lunch. She asked about our trip, then clued us in on some nice areas of the South Island. When she found out we planned to walk the Abel Tasman Coastal Track, Dutchy asked where we were going to store our gear. We didn't know.

"You could leave your stuff with me," she said, "but I just got evicted from my place. Right now I'm just jumping from bach to bach around the bay." We thought Dutchy meant "from bachelor to bachelor." Months later, while reading, I learned that a Kiwi "bach" is a small home or vacation cottage. Upon the discovery, I sat bolt upright in the tent and exclaimed, "Bach! That's what she meant!" Kate looked at me as if I'd lost my marbles.

Dutchy championed New Zealand's opportunities. "You can do anything here," she said. "You gotta be willing to work, but shit, sky's the limit." She sat forward in her chair, excited. "Anything you damn well please. I started a clothing shop in Wellington. I'd just come over from Europe so I knew what the styles would be in advance. Everything is so piss-ass backwards here. So I rented a shop and started. Did real well but I left after a few months. Had crime problems. Turned out–I found out later–that some gang had been in the spot I rented before me. Rival gang kept breaking my windows. Twice I got up in the middle of the night and found 'em inside. 'Shit on this,' I says. 'I sure as hell don't need this.' So I just up and left. Left all my stuff behind."

Dutchy worked out a way for us to leave our bikes and gear at her place of work, a home for mentally handicapped adults, while we tramped through Abel Tasman National Park. The home was empty when we met her there later. The students were on summer holiday. As a counselor, Dutchy taught crafts, checkbook balancing, counting, shoe tying. Whatever their level, students were encouraged to improve. Mostly, Dutchy taught self-confidence and self-worth.

Dutchy pointed out a patchwork pillow made by the students. "Wonderful," she beamed. "Even the most severely handicapped can have a part in cutting Styrofoam pieces to stuff the pillow with. It gives us a real sense of accomplishment when we all take part and see some goal reached. They can be real monsters sometimes, but they can also be wonderful."

After storing the bikes and our extra gear in the garage, we thanked Dutchy vigorously. She stood in the drive and grew reflective. "I've traveled enough," she said. "I know it's the people who help you that you remember. I've had help and I like to help others now whenever I can."

● ● ●

Suddenly Kate and I found ourselves ready to walk the Abel Tasman, something we hadn't planned on doing until a few days later. At the edge of Motueka we stepped onto the road, transformed. Our backpacks bulged with food and gear; nothing hinted that we were bikers. We stuck out our thumbs for the first time in New Zealand. We hoped to hitch to the northern end of Abel Tasman National Park, walk the coastal track south, then catch a short bus ride back to Motueka and the bikes.

Soon an ancient man in an ancient car opened a creaky door and motioned us in. The ancient man drove half in, half out of the ditch for the next five kilometers. Guardrails cringed as he approached. At his turnoff we thanked him for the ride, then more thankfully stepped out of the car.

Twenty minutes later a young computer operator from Wellington picked us up and took us over the Takaka Hill. At least we think that's where Mario Andretti took us. Kate and I both closed our eyes for most of the trip. Mario was the antithesis to the ancient man. Hard rock shook the car. We raced along at a hundred kilometers per hour, even when signs said that prudent folks would be doing half that speed.

At Takaka, we spilled out of the car and assured Mario that he didn't have to take us farther. As he squealed off, we staggered into a pub for a nerve-settling beer. Later, we tempted fate again by hitching a ride to Pohara, where we planned to camp. Thirty seconds after we stepped out of the pub, we sat in another car. This time the driver was sane.

Kate and I walked along Golden Bay after dinner and discussed how we'd get to the start of the coastal track at Totaranui, some twenty or thirty kilometers distant. We considered breaking down and buying a bus ticket in hopes of avoiding another harrowing hitchhiking experience. But later a couple stopped, from out of nowhere, said they'd seen us come in with backpacks, and asked if we wanted a ride to the start of the track the following morning. The power of good clean living never ceases to amaze me.

Our benefactors dropped us at the national park building in Totaranui. Abel Tasman National Park is named for the Dutch explorer Abel Tasman who, in 1642, became the first European to sight New Zealand. He called his discovery Staten Landt. The name was later changed to Nieuw Zeeland, after a Dutch province.

The Abel Tasman Coastal Track crosses several large tidal flats. The flats are only passable within about a two-hour window on either side of low tide. Missing the window means hours of waiting for the next low tide, a long detour, or a cold swim. Kate and I departed Totaranui posthaste in hopes of crossing Awaroa Flats, the first and largest of the flats, before the tide rose too high. We arrived at Awaroa Flats at eleven-thirty; low tide was at nine. Still we crossed the kilometer-wide flat without topping our waists.

After a lunch break at Awaroa Hut, we continued on for another couple hours to Onetahuti Beach, a mile of stunning yellow sand sloping gently into a magnificent blue bay. At the end of the beach we found a small campsite with running water, brought down via hose from a cold pool in the bush. "We're home," I announced.

Coastal view from Abel Tasman National Park.

Kate and I walked along the beach later in the evening. Stars dazzled the clear sky; the ocean stood still. We discovered a shallow cave at the beach end and crawled inside. Thousands of glowworms sparkled in the blackness of the cave, perfectly mimicking the sky outside. Glowworms emit a light that attracts bugs to their sticky excretion. Our flashlight revealed another inhabitant of the cave, the giant weta, a grasshopper-looking insect about three inches long.

The following morning's walk wound through bush to Bark Bay, and later crossed a long swing bridge over the Falls River. The span and the height of the bridge demanded pause. Yet the bridge held sturdy enough that I jogged across. The couple who crossed before me did not fare as well. The woman was ashen. As they stepped onto the bridge, she jumped back and decided she couldn't carry her pack across. The man took the pack. Then they discussed who should lead. The woman eventually started first but, ten steps onto the bridge, she balked.

"No...no...go back...GO BACK!"

Reorganized, he led. She wrapped her arms around him and closed her eyes. Every step he took was immediately filled by one of her feet. They moved slowly across, as if glued.

After a night at Torrent Bay, we set off for Watershed Cove, a water resupply point of the French explorer Dumont D'Urville in the early eighteen hundreds. The clear stream was important to us as well, not only for drinking but also for reconstituting rice, soup, noodles, and powdered milk.

The day's walk couldn't have been more than a kilometer or two as the bellbird flies, but that fit with our relaxed attack on the Abel Tasman. One woman we met walked the length of the track in a single day. Most folks do the walk in three days. We, however, chose to squeeze three days into five.

As we set up camp, Kate and I greeted the Greens–Brian, Eleanor, Steve, and Bronwyn–a family we'd crossed paths with several times on the track and now shared the small camp with. The six of us sat on the beach, got acquainted, and enjoyed the peace of the day's final hour. The sun slowly dropped towards the horizon. Surf lapped quietly. The Bryant Range loomed dark far across Tasman Bay, while nearer at hand a rainbow formed, one end disappearing behind Adele Island.

As the sky streaked pink and shadows crept across the beach, we moved to start a campfire and prepare dinner. The Greens, Kate and I learned, lived near Christchurch. Brian, the father, was an electrical contractor who'd worked for farmers for twenty-five years. Steve had received the highest scores on his university entrance exams. Embarrassed by the praise his mother lavished upon him, Steve exclaimed, "I reckon they must of gotten my scores mixed up with someone else's!" Bronwyn was mature and polished for thirteen. She loved to tramp, though lamented that only one of her friends shared her interest. Eleanor, the matriarch, was the glue that held the group together.

The Greens worked and played in tandem. Everyone seemed comfortable in their role. Sports played a big part in their cohesiveness and the conversation slipped easily from squash to skiing, tennis to rugby, lawn bowling to field hockey. Eleanor talked about two other sons; the affection in her voice assured us that they also melded easily into the group.

We fed the fire and talked late into the night. Anything much past dark rated as "late" for the two Americans. Later, lying in the tent, Kate and I for the first time heard the haunting cry of the morepork–a small, nocturnal owl whose call mirrors its name.

Kate and I caught a small fish before our departure in the morning. The Greens, en masse, gave us a sitting ovation from their position (Brian called it a "pozzi") on the beach. That afternoon Kate and I moved on to Apple Tree Cove. Twilight descended quiet and cool. We camped alone, the peace of our evening broken only by a small mouse who rifled through our packs.

Super Monday (Super Bowl Sunday on the other side of the International Date Line) found us in a heated argument as we worked our way to the southern end of the Abel Tasman Track. Questions about the future reared their ugly heads and Kate and I tussled bitterly. Marriage? Religious affiliation? Jobs? Home town? Tough questions followed by emotional answers. Part of the joy of our trip resulted from the deferral of those questions. Exactly five years had passed since we'd met, yet sometimes we felt like strangers. We talked uneasily and the only solution seemed to be to change the subject, to ignore the questions a while longer.

● ● ●

Kate and I departed Motueka early the next morning, pedaling south, but uncertain of our destination. The ride along the Motueka River crossed through lush farmland consisting principally of tobacco and hops. The sun beat down and no traffic bothered us. Better still, mountains poked skyward far to the south. We felt their magnetism and pushed hard all morning.

We stopped in Tapawera to ask directions to St. Arnaud and Nelson Lakes National Park. A back road through Golden Downs looked promising and uncrowded. The locals were evenly split about the distance, if the road was sealed, and how many ranges the roads crossed. Our queries left us more confused than informed, though that wasn't all that unusual. Locals, it seems, always give the worst directions.

In Golden Downs State Forest we pedaled towards the head of the Motueka River, then climbed an enormous hill to cross the watershed. Fifteen kilometers of chunky, miserable gravel wound through the bottom of the next valley. Wavering bike tracks marked the road in front of us. We soon spotted two bikers making their way up a hill a half a kilometer away.

Curt and Cynthia greeted us cheerfully. They hailed from Rapid City, South Dakota, were on a honeymoon of sorts, and, unlike most bike travelers we met, were middle-aged and well established. We pedaled into St. Arnaud together and stopped at the hotel for celebration. For Kate and me anyway, one hundred ten kilometers was a long day of riding and reason to celebrate.

The refreshments set us all to giggling, especially Cynthia, who needed no outside anesthetic to loosen up. The bar served only chicken nuggets and chips. Kate wrung the grease out of her chips and eventually surrendered them to me in disgust. The rest of us, meanwhile, alternated inhaling the gut bombs and telling each other how we never ate greasy food at home.

● ● ●

Kate and I set out to walk around Lake Rotoiti, in Nelson Lakes National Park, the following day. Lake Rotoiti is enormous, bush-lined, and surrounded by rugged mountains. We made the far end of the lake in three hours. Rain and a lone fisherman arrived as we sat on the veranda of Coldwater Hut. The fisherman greeted us, then climbed into his small boat and backed out. A moment later he returned to the dock. By now the rain raged. "Gonna rain all afternoon," he yelled, "Do you ...." He didn't have time to finish, we were already sprinting towards the boat.

Kate and I biked back to our West Bay camp in darkness and rain. Our first sight of the tent since the early morning showed it to be surrounded by two inches of standing water. The inside of the tent, however, was relatively dry. We secured the bikes under some heavy bush and climbed into our home, zipping away the wet.

Heavy rain pounded the tent all night. We were still almost two hundred kilometers inland, yet the presence of the West Coast was upon us.

THE WET (AND WILD) WEST COAST

Chapter 6

The rains passed sometime in the night. Kate and I rose early and walked to the edge of Lake Rotoiti. Dawn revealed a glorious blue sky; wispy clouds clung to the side of Mount Robert. At the outlet of Rotoiti, the powerful Buller River began its race to the West Coast and the Tasman Sea.

The Buller, our companion for the next three days, started big–far too swift to wade. Twenty kilometers downriver the Buller was too wide to throw a stone across and still growing. We biked to Owen River, stopped for lunch, then pedaled on to Murchison and set up camp.

Later I biked to the local pub, stepped inside, and asked for, "One Double Brown to take away please." Moments later the bartender returned with one–one case of quart bottles! "Wait a minute mate," I laughed, raising my hands in surrender. "I'd love to take those beers from you, but I don't know how I'm going to strap them on my bike."

The pub crowd all hooted. A bloke across the bar yelled out, "Drink eleven of 'em here, mate, and that'll leave youse one for the road."

"After eleven," another quipped, "he wouldn't be able to find the road."

● ● ●

Below Murchison the Buller flows through a rugged gorge. The road parallels the river, but often climbs bluffs or dives in and out of steep side valleys. Near Inangahua Junction, the gorge ends and the river spills into an open valley. The day Kate and I pedaled through the gorge was cloudless, our second cloudless day in a row. Little did we comprehend our luck.

Other bikers had told us to call the Roessinck family in Inangahua Junction. The Roessincks put travelers up for a nominal charge. Mrs. Roessinck started the service after wayward travelers began to break into the old church to seek shelter from the rains. Inangahua Junction had no hotels, motor camps, or camp areas. Travelers learned about the Roessincks by word of mouth, like Kate and I, or from the gas station in town.

We pedaled up Brown Road, turned right at the plow, and found a pleasant farmhouse sitting just above the Inangahua River. In the paddock, a muscular bloke wearing only shorts and gumboots tended cattle with his dog. We exchanged waves. At the house, barefooted Natasha Roessinck, who wore a drab singlet and flowery skirt, and her boyfriend Scotty, who sported a broken ankle, greeted us. Mom and Dad Roessinck, Natasha explained, were in Wellington working on a house that Mr. Roessinck was building.

I fished for an hour while Kate talked with Natasha and Scotty. Otto, from back in the paddock, and I joined the group simultaneously. A twenty-four year old dairy farmer, Otto possessed the most amazing physique I've ever seen, particularly for someone who'd never touched a barbell. Blood-gorged veins protruded from every well-defined muscle, even down the washboard of his stomach.

A group of friends congregated and a big barbecue ensued. The occasion was twofold: the departure of one of the friends for trade school "over the hill" in Christchurch, and the homemade raft race down the Buller River the following day. The barbecue consisted of mutton sausages and chops, heaps of salads, and lots of DB (Dominion Breweries)beer.

With the arrival of darkness, eating slowed and DB consumption accelerated. We soon learned that while Inangahua Junction sits some fifty kilometers inland, the locals consider themselves West Coasters. "Nobody on earth drinks like Kiwis," Scotty told me. "And nobody in New Zealand drinks like West Coasters." In Inangahua Junction, apparently, we stood on a pinnacle of sorts.

We walked over to the shelter concealing the group's battleships for the race down the Buller. Otto and crew had constructed a log craft of gigantic proportions. The monstrosity was shaped roughly like a F-14 bomber; it looked likely to float as well as an F-14.

"Sinking's not a problem," Otto claimed with a toothy smile. "Our only worry is the damn thing keeps trying to get airborne!"

Discussion had it that the raft would be dragged to the Inangahua River with a tractor, then floated down to the confluence with the Buller and the start of the race. After the race the raft was firewood...that is unless somebody came up with a crane and a flatbed truck to get it back to the farm. Natasha and friends planned to man a small raft and run interference for the big craft. The $100 prize necessitated warfare. Cheating was not only required, but encouraged.

Back at the fire, beers in hand, the crew settled into a comfortable conversation centered around Otto, the undisputed leader. Otto's amiable character lent itself well to such a role. "Mom and Dad came over on the boat from Holland," he told us. "Reckon you could say I was brought up on the boat. Dad wasn't much for farmin', that was always Mom's love. Dad took to construction after a bit and Mom kept things goin' on the farm. I had gone back to Holland. Dad helped out with fence mendin' and the like, but didn't have his heart into it. Guess they were sort of thinkin' I might be back."

We stopped to reload our DB's. Kiwis have a great knack for popping the cap off one bottled beer with the cap of another bottled beer. I never did get the hang of it.

Otto continued, "I did some farmin' down in Southland, but the way that bloke treated his animals put me right off dairying. Didn't really know what to do, but then I got some good advice from a friend. 'Write down what's good and what's bad about dairy farmin',' he says to me, 'and by the time you're done, you'll know what to do.' Mostly I decided I liked workin' by meself and doing physical work. So I'm back here. Don't like having somebody tell me what to do and I could never work inside. Haven't read a book in three years. That's nothin' to be proud of, I s'pose. Scotty here reads one every month. Can you imagine that?"

Otto paused to roll a cigarette, something he did almost constantly when he wasn't smoking one.

"Anyway, I've got seven more years. Gave meself ten years, three's already done, to make dairy farmin' work. If I'm no good at it by then, I reckon I should be doin' somethin' else."

The talk became more lively as the evening pressed on: pig hunts, goat snatching, possum trapping.... A wind came up and the temperature dropped. As we talked, I rested my foot heavily on the fire grate and suddenly the whole thing–grate, coals, and fire–flipped skyward in a brilliant display. The group scattered. I stood stunned, luckily wearing only a few of the embers. Everyone reconvened around the fallen fire, laughing wildly.

Otto spoke first, "So much for subtlety, Scott. Do you mean to be wanting to go inside?"

Kate joined in, "Well, you left them something to remember you by anyway. Good one mate."

● ● ●

Rain pelted the roof in the early morning hours. "That's West Coast rain," Otto explained as we sat at the breakfast table. "She'll likely be here all day."

The rain didn't dampen the enthusiasm of Otto's clan in their race preparations. Rain is a way of life on the West Coast and certainly not about to spoil a day dedicated to fun. Friends and a case of beer arrived from Nelson as Natasha fed me a big breakfast of mutton sausage and eggs. Kate ate porridge.

Kate and I set out for Westport in the rain and were quickly soaked. The rain decreased to a fine mist as we started into the lower Buller Gorge. The mist continued until an hour outside Westport. Then the heavens released. We plowed through the deluge, through puddles and mud and sheets of rain that hurt. Finally we splashed out of the bottom of the gorge, but still the rain pelted down. Ahead lie the Tasman Sea and our official welcome to the West coast. We couldn't see the Tasman through the downpour.

We pulled into a motor camp in Westport, water squishing from our socks, and ran smack into an unfriendly hostess who had her ire up against bikers. "No bikes under the walkways!" she growled. "No, there's no other spot for them. And don't let me catch you leaning them up against any buildings. We consider people more important than bikes."

"Funny," I told her, "we treat our bikes better than you treat people." Just one more log on her fire.

● ● ●

Finally, officially, the West Coast. The biker's grapevine reported rain, endless stretches without food or break, rain, grueling rides along rugged coastline, more rain.... We stopped for church in the morning before tackling the coast. A nun allowed us to park the bikes at the convent. The friendly priest spotted us before Mass and asked about our trip. He had long hair and smelled of cigarette smoke.

Kate and I pedaled south in divinely-inspired sunshine and landed at Punakaiki for the night. After setting up the tent, we biked to Dolomite Point to see the Pancake Rocks. The odd formations look like tall stacks of thin pancakes, a result of wind and water erosion on the limestone headland.

A second nice day accompanied us along the coast to Greymouth. The sunshine, we knew, couldn't last, and as we left Greymouth the rains returned. Kate and I took shelter for a time at Shantytown, a New Zealand historical society remake of a mid-1800's mining town. Gold, coal, and greenstone (jade) are the heritage of the West Coast. Greenstone, in particular, was prized by the Maoris of old for jewelry and weapons.

The downpour continued through the afternoon and evening.

Low, dark clouds blanketed the sky far out to sea. We biked hard for Hokitika and arrived soaked. A stand of trees provided a measure of shelter for the tent and bikes through the evening. About five a.m. the next morning, however, the rain turned ugly. The previous twenty-four hours had been a pitiful prelude. Rain sheets buckled trees and set old cans afloat. Cats hid under dumpsters; cars stayed off the roads; mothers worried for their children. Five seconds outside drenched the body and spirit.

Kate and I found shelter and waited...and waited.

Eight hours later the deluge ended and we assessed damages. Everything we owned dripped. We found some dryers; four cycles later the only thing dry was our supply of coins. We pedaled out of Hokitika late, and headed for Ross under still threatening skies.

● ● ●

Month three was beginning. Kate and I had almost two thousand kilometers of touring under our belts and no longer felt any trepidation towards bicycle travel. We had developed techniques to deal with rain (principally garbage bag pannier covers and positive attitudes) and other adversity. We considered ourselves seasoned bike travelers now–happy with, if not downright defensive of, our mode of travel.

The West Coast provides a great forum for bikers to shape and hone their road wits, biking style, and opinions. Biking partners ride side-by-side and frequently more bikers pass than cars. Towns are few and far between. What towns there are cling lovingly to points of interest. Motor camps huddle alongside the small towns and in the evenings the cyclists gather to swap stories and trade information.

We met in numerous bikers along the West Coast, from folks that knew Kate's brother to the well-manicured Canadian girl who wore a silk scarf while she rode. And there was Nigel from Perth. Following New Zealand, Nigel told us, he planned to fly to Vancouver. "Then I'll carry on down the West coast and pop inland a few times, maybe to Colorado for a day or two." Nigel coached us on biking in Australia; we gave him some help with

American geography.

But the best story of West Coast bikers came to us second hand, from another Aussie pedaler. Over tea, he told of an enterprising American biking couple he'd met earlier along the West Coast. "These two were on a self-proclaimed 'World Bike Trip for Peace,' or something equally obnoxious, "our Aussie friend snorted. "This bloke sells bloody memberships to his ride for $25US each! Subscribers get a monthly newsletter telling of their latest adventures. Here, look at this. The joker gave me one. Did he think I was going to subscribe or something?!"

I read the newsletter the Aussie offered. It related an entertaining story about the couple being kicked off a farm in New Caledonia. A footnote on the last page urged people to renew their subscriptions, lest their vicarious forays into the "World Bike Trip for Peace" should end. How biking and world peace fit together, I couldn't figure out. I must confess to not being highly idealistic. Our trip, given a title, would surely have been bannered "The Kiwi Bike Trip for Fun."

● ● ●

"The computer is down," Kate announced. Kate's bike computer kept daily and trip mileage, and told speed and time of day. It proved particularly handy for predicting the remaining distance on a long, deserted highway. Over the months the computer gave us intermittent problems, but we did our best to always keep it operating.

Only a herd of sheep in the road interrupted the flat ride south to Ross. In town, we learned that there was no Bank of New Zealand, where we got cash advances, until Wanaka. At over four hundred kilometers, Wanaka looked to be a week away. We carried only $100NZ($60US). "No worries," a postal clerk assured us. "There's almost nowhere between here and there to spend money anyway."

Kate and I picked up groceries and pedaled off to the local rugby paddock. A thick canopy of trees along the sideline sheltered a perfect tent site. We paused long enough for three adolescents to finish sneaking their cigarettes, then set up the tent on soft pine needles. Rains came in the night but did not penetrate our shelter.

In the morning we loaded up before the first rain of the day hit. We departed an hour later, after the squall passed. Much of our ride through Westland went like that, an hour of rain followed by an hour of sun in which the clouds gathered for their next release.

With about half of the West Coast behind us, Kate and I felt extremely lucky. No day had been wiped out by rain. We'd even been blessed with a couple of days completely void of wetness. Still we met bedraggled, disheartened bikers who inevitably were on short, tightly-scheduled rides. We had the luxury to sit out an hour, or even a day, and to select the best window of weather for cycling.

After pushing through thirty kilometers of hills, we flushed out onto the flats north of Harihari. Intermittent cold drizzles caught our attention, but not so much as the magnificent glimpses of the coming mountains. The ocean and the Southern Alps trapped the road for the first time. Peaks leaped skyward, so near the sea that every inch of a fifteen hundred meter mountain was vertical. The sun and clouds played games with our visual perceptions: one mountain face stood brilliantly illuminated while the next was shrouded in haze and mist. Water drops sparkled in mid-air and rainbows hopscotched from valley to valley.

Part way to Harihari a number of bikers, sans panniers, trickled by us. The support van showed that the group belonged with "Backroads," a touring company from the States. Most of the riders greeted us cordially. They were remarkable for two reasons. First, of the dozen bikers, none rode a mountain bike. Second, each biker wore impeccable biking togs: black stretch tights, colorful riding jerseys, and high-tech cleats. Their carefully orchestrated color combinations presented a vivid contrast to the budget-minded, gear-laden bike travelers we usually met.

Kate and I sought out another rugby paddock in Harihari, hoping to again find a place to pitch the tent. The grass was saturated, however, and we sank in up to our ankles. A band of rain clouds rapidly approached. Necessity directed our attention to the Harihari Rugby Clubhouse. Moments later, tea boiled in the billy and our sleeping bags covered the concrete under the veranda. We prayed that no functions were scheduled for the club that night. Darkness arrived. I peered through the clubhouse window and my flashlight illuminated a sign over the sink: Love starts when you sink in his arms and ends with your arms in his sink.

We departed for Franz Josef early, not wanting to push our luck with any indignant rugby players. South from Harihari the road crosses some hills, then the Whataroa River. We stopped at the river for an energy boost. Because we'd missed purchasing morning groceries, however, our food supplies held only a single muesli bar. No worries, we thought, Whataroa is just ahead.

The day was February 6th, yet a sign on the only store in Whataroa read, "Closed for the Holiday." February 6th, the gas station attendant explained, is Waitangi Day, a celebration of the 1840 treaty signing which brought the Maori people under British protectorate. The gas station sold only candy bars, a revelation that set Kate to shaking. I decried the inequity of it all while happily cramming the bars in my mouth. Kate choked down just enough chocolate to sustain her for the rest of the day's ride.

We hit Franz Josef just before the rains. Franz Josef Glacier, and nearby Fox Glacier, are unique in all the world. Nowhere at this latitude–about equivalent to southern Oregon–do glaciers so nearly approach of the ocean. Kate and I couldn't see Franz Josef Glacier, much less the fifteen or twenty kilometers to the sea, as we hurried to make camp. Dark clouds blanketed the treetops. We considered pedaling to the glacier anyway, but then the rain began, so we moved into the motor camp kitchen for an evening of reading and traveler's talk.

● ● ●

I awoke at five the next morning to the sound of banging garbage cans. The ruckus continued and at five fifteen, sleep impossible, I peered outside. Ten feet away hopped the noise generator, a kea, the mischievous Kiwi mountain parrot. I stepped outside, shivering, and shined my flashlight on the imp.

River gorge crossing near Franz Josef Glacier.

Undaunted, the kea hopped to the next tent, carried on through the vestibule, and stuck its head inside. "Get out of here you crazy bloke!" came a yell from the tent, followed rapidly by a bare foot kicking wildly out the door.

I slipped on my shoes and walked quietly around the camp. Keas wreaked havoc on all fronts, turning the early morning calm into pandemonium. The cheeky parrots rolled rocks off garbage can lids and soon the lids clattered to the cement. Every calculated act resulted in another crash. The grand master, without a doubt, was the big kea who repeatedly picked up stones, flew to the roof, and dropped them dead center on a garbage can lid below.

Around the camp, cabin lights began to flick on. I stopped into the kitchen to heat up some coffee. A fat kea unabashedly hopped in the door, then surveyed me curiously. Kate approached and the chubby bird hopped back outside. Kate stepped back, but the kea didn't fly to safety. Instead, the brazen bird took two giant hops towards my innocent partner, sending her scurrying.

Later we packed, ate, and biked up to Franz Josef Glacier. The road was quiet because of the early hour. We dumped the bikes at the car park and walked to the glacier terminus. Sunshine and lifting mist accentuated rushing waterfalls and glistening slabs of schist. Ice chunks tumbled into the till-laden torrent at the base of the glacier. As we headed back to the bikes, a guided group of glacier walkers passed, studded boots clicking on the rock.

● ● ●

The ride from Franz Josef to Fox Glacier is a mere twenty-three kilometers, yet squeezed into that short distance is one of the most tortuous stretches of highway in New Zealand. The road digs a precarious foothold into steep, bush-filled walls and repeatedly reverses itself as it crosses three major ridges.

Kate and I crawled over the first ridge and enjoyed a windy descent into the valley. Pedaling hard, we crossed a bridge and mounted the second hill. We cranked up and up, every corner revealing another incline, and finally topped number two. Two down, one to go. Piece of cake. Plummeting off the second ridge, we rounded a corner, popped out of the bush, and spotted the bridge that marked the bottom of the valley. As our gaze continued, the road disappeared. Vanished. Gone. Finito.

I lifted my eyes two notches higher and saw a line in the bush that marked the road. The line climbed straight up to heaven and didn't dally getting there. We both stopped, mouths agape. It couldn't be, we assured each other....

It was—a bona fide two-picture-taker.

We stood in a vast potential well with no place to go but up. So up we started, pedaling, laughing, joking at the idiocy of a road that defied gravity. Up, up, up. Half way through the ascent

Kate became delirious. As always, she released her delirium through illusions of foods long left behind. "Could I get some nachos and salsa over here, please?" Kate joked as she weaved to overcome the pull of the hill. "While you're at it, get me a big pizza with lots of sauce on it. And don't forget to bring me a Dos Equis."

I stood up on the pedals for power. "Could I finish you up with a big chocolate chip cookie, ma'am?"

"Why most assuredly."

The top mercifully arrived before we began to believe our delusions. We flew down into Fox Glacier and at the motor camp discovered Curt and Cynthia, the Rapid City couple we'd met near St. Arnaud. As they were on a tighter schedule, Curt and Cynthia had done some bussing and ended up ahead of us. They reported that East Glacier Pat, our camping partner in Nelson, had been in Fox the previous night. The bikers' grapevine on the West Coast is like that. With only a single road and two choices of direction, bikers cross paths frequently and almost everyone knows someone you've camped with on another night.

Cynthia charged through the evening in rare form. She possesses the singular ability to laugh at her own jokes, yet still carry everyone else along on the enjoyable ride. As we talked, a German fellow sat in one corner of the kitchen beating whipped cream–"tink, tink, tink." He beat that cream silly for over an hour. Every time our conversation lulled–"tink, tink, tink"–reverberated through the room and we broke up.

"Why's he doing that?" I whispered.

"He's trying to beat air into the cream to make it fluffy," Kate answered quietly.

"In that case he must be trying to get the whole roomful in there," Cynthia giggled. Then she swooned, "See, it's working. I'm getting light-headed already."

"Quick somebody open a window...."

● ● ●

Kate and I took a brisk sunrise ride to Lake Matheson in search of New Zealand's most famous reflection. A wooden walkway surrounds the lake, giving easy access to the mirrored images of Mounts Tasman and Cook. Clouds covered the peaks, but gradually Tasman and then the top triangle of Cook poked into the sunshine. The emergence of the peaks came twofold, thanks to the placid lake waters.

Later we packed, then pedaled up the grueling road south of the Fox River. A rushing stream crossed the road near its end. Kate and I dismounted and walked through. A couple from Idaho, excited to try out their mountain bikes, plowed into the water and promptly dumped. A handlebar pack bounced down the stream.

We started up the track to the Chalet Lookout for a closer view of Fox Glacier. A stream beside the track has sculpted smooth waves in solid rock. Deep in the valley the Fox River, grey-white with rock flour, roared seaward. At the lookout the bush split to reveal Fox Glacier, a blue zigzag of ice and rock spilling out of the Alps. The scene oozed surrealism: we stood in shorts and t-shirts, surrounded by subtropical forest, yet in front of us was a valley of ice thought to be over a thousand feet thick.

Kate and I left Fox Glacier at two and put in sixty kilometers by dusk. The final hour of the ride hurt me. I was weary and drained. No wind, no hills, no rain, no stress—still I needed an act of mind over body to finish the day. I just didn't have it.

"When are we going to get there?" I yelled at Kate, who was pedaling ahead. "My legs ache, my bum feels like it met up with the wrong end of a jack hammer, my water bottle's empty, and to top it all off, I'm starving."

My diatribe ran right off Kate. She slowed to let me pull up even and gave me a sideways smile that seemed to say,"You're pitiful." Then she coolly remarked, "Quit whining. Would you rather be at work?" Kate said no more, just pedaled off.

We eventually found a pullout along the Mahitahi River, then fought through curtains of blood-thirsty sandflies to set up camp. Dinner ceremonies were held in the refuge of the tent. Every bathroom call necessitated a renewed attack to rid our home of unwelcome intruders.

● ● ●

The final seventy kilometers to the town of Haast held a single tea room at Lake Paringa. The woman inside seemed unhappy to be alive. Until the West Coast, we'd barely run into a frown in New Zealand. But on the West Coast, we were treated poorly several times by irate motor camp managers and sour restaurant operators. All seemed to spite the bikers who made up a big part of their clientele.

Riding on through scattered showers, we crossed the boulder battle zones of flooded out creeks. The West Coast's big rains produce gully washers that tear down mountainsides and leave giant scars. The last of the big rains had come while we took shelter in Hokitika. Tall rubble piles recalled washouts that had closed the road in numerous places. Near the worst spots, bulldozers awaited their next cleanup duties.

The road south of Lake Paringa returns directly to the sea, then climbs over a couple of dizzying bluffs before crossing coastal plains to Haast. In the flatlands, I picked up my first puncture of the trip, the result of a quarter inch split in my rear tire. A sharp rock slipped inside the split and ripped the tube to shreds.

Sandflies sucked us into a frenzy of action. Each tube-changing movement was punctuated with a swat, a slap, and a scratch. As Kate and I worked on replacing my tube, a Backroads biker, from the touring company, passed. Not forty meters away he pulled up, also with a flat. Within five minutes the support van arrived and loaded on the biker and the bike.

New tube in place, we pedaled for Haast, trying desperately to outrun the sandflies. A biker streaked up and hailed us just as we crossed the Haast River. The girl rode a white Healing, looked tall and fit, and wore a silly Kiwi riding helmet. "Where are you camping tonight?" she asked. We told her we planned to camp wherever we could find a nice patch of grass. "Mind if I join you?"

Janet, we soon learned, was a nurse from Vancouver. She came to New Zealand with a girl friend. They decided to bicycle tour after arrival, bought gear, then later split up because of incompatible biking paces and goals.

The three of us pedaled into Haast, what little of it there was.

Where "town" should be is a gas station and, looking entirely out of place, an enormous modern motel. A single group of shops stands several kilometers away. We purchased groceries at one of the shops, then pedaled back to the motel pub for a beer and, more importantly, luxurious shelter from the now pouring rain.

Backroads bicyclers began to file into the pub, fresh after a shower and change of clothes. "I have to warn you," I told Janet, "we have a habit of taking friends to strange places that frequently don't work out, trips they wish they'd never been a part of. You may want to reconsider staying with us tonight."

Janet looked between the rain outside and the comforts of the motel, considered, then said, "No, I really should get out and camp. I haven't used my tent that much. I don't like to free camp by myself 'cuz I don't feel real comfortable about it."

Janet soon found herself camped under the veranda at the Ministry of Works. The spot was truly idyllic, providing everything a happy camper might need: a water spigot, an overhang for shelter from the rain, and a cement sidewalk for lumpless sleeping. With darkness, even the sandflies quieted. Perfect.

Then a bright light clicked on directly overhead. The light was great for cooking and reading, but terrible for sleeping. Even worse, the light attracted every mosquito on the South Island. The wall under the light grew so thick with mosquitoes we could scribe our names on it. Kate pulled a mesh sack over her head and crawled into her sleeping bag. The constant buzzing of hungry mosquitos waiting inches from her face, however, soon drove us out to the wet lawn to setup the tent.

Meanwhile Janet, who kept muttering, "I don't believe I'm doing this," decided to set up her tent under the veranda. When I suggested the grass might be more comfortable, Janet came out with an interesting revelation. Here, just hours before we'd be moving inland over Haast Pass and thus finally escape the sodden grasp of the West coast, Janet admitted, "I don't really like getting my tent wet."

The Matukituki Valley and Mount Aspiring.

INSPIRING ASPIRING

Chapter 7

I jumped out of my sleeping bag at six a.m., hoping to get us all moving before the first Ministry of Works people arrived. Janet waited inside her crumpled tent. "I heard some plastic rattle in the middle of the night," she said, "and haven't been able to sleep since."

We ate, scrubbed our faces under the faucet, and hurried to pack. I was zipping the last pannier shut when two carloads of highway workmen drove in. Seven men stepped out of the cars, all dressed in orange coveralls. We saddled up with an attempted air of dignity, said "Gidday!" to all, then pedaled off as the workers scratched their heads and mumbled.

Janet, Kate, and I started up the Haast River, riding three-across, just as the sun began to fight its way into the valley. Clouds and mist hung low and tight against the mountainsides. Gradually the sun gained the upper hand and clothes were joyfully sloughed off.

Kate and I were happy to have a new and interesting companion. The three of us laughed as we rode and talked of Haast Pass.

Haast Pass, the only southern road over the Southern Alps, was completed in 1965. Horror stories about the pass filter through the bikers' grapevine, with adjectives like steep, agonizing, rugged, frustrating. From the grapevine, we knew that the pass contained long sections of chunky gravel which made for tough riding. The gravel proved doubly worrisome for us as I continued to pedal with a quarter inch split in my rear tire. The next bike shop was in Wanaka, two days away, so we couldn't afford to have the tire disintegrate.

Surprisingly, the road stayed sealed and horizontal all the way up the Haast River valley. We pulled into aptly- named Pleasant Flats for lunch at ten thirty. Actually, ten thirty was way past lunchtime as we'd pedaled continuously since seven fifteen.

The first incline began shortly after Pleasant Flats. Janet, who was a powerful biker, often pedaled ahead, then waited. Soon we hit the sharp rise up to the Gates of Haast, where the river battles enormous boulders for a path through the mountains. The roar of the tumult was awesome.

Ten turns of the cranks later we ran into a wall. I stood up in my Granny gear but still struggled up the pitch. Once on top, I went back to help Kate who, even with her new gearing, stood no chance against a grade like this. Kate struggled alongside the bike, arms extended far out as she pushed. She wouldn't surrender her bike when I offered to help.

"This is a matter of pride," Kate puffed. "I'll get myself over Haast Pass."

As quickly as that it was over. The rest of the short climb passed imperceptibly, even when we finally hit the gravel. Haast Pass, a single difficult pitch, did not live up to its accursed reputation.

On the last rise before crossing the watershed we caught a couple on a tandem. Wayne and Carol, from Nevada, rode bare; earlier in the day a couple in a car had offered to carry their gear. We had a small celebration at the sign marking the pass, then started down. The down side of the pass proved tougher than the up as bone-jarring washboard and rock chunks hammered us. Wayne and Carol, who rode on skinny tires, particularly struggled.

The five of us called it a day in Makarora, a combination store, motor camp, petrol shop, tea room, and park office. We lounged around the pool in glorious sunshine, discussing the multitude of changes since Haast Pass. On the east side of the Southern Alps many of the hillsides stood bare. Mosquitos and sand flies were less prevalent. Gone, at least for this day, was the rain. We had survived the West Coast.

A Contiki bus and its many occupants commandeered much of the camp. Contiki tours are famous for carrying young adults who like to socialize. Their evening gala–loud music, tight jeans, comments like, "What are you two doing in there alone?"–sent our group scurrying for the sanctity of the kitchen, the one not labeled "For Contiki Group Use Only." Our conversation flowed smoothly until a bottle of detergent decided to blow up.

I was squeezing our new bottle of Lux to see if the spout leaked. The spout did not leak. The pressure buildup, however, blew the entire cap right off the bottle. A two foot long, two inch wide steam of detergent shot out in a brilliant arc through the air. For one terrible, wonderful moment time stopped.... I alone saw the stream of heavy liquid arching towards Janet's bowed and unsuspecting head. An instant later, Lux covered her from head to toe. The maps Janet had been diligently studying dripped. She said nothing. I apologized profusely while the others roared in laughter.

When I tried to help Janet wash her hair out under the faucet, she waved me away, mumbling, "I don't think I need anymore of your help." Janet ended the scene by retiring to bed rather than blowing up. Mostly, I think, Janet wanted to get away from me. Sleeping on cement the previous night, the long ride over Haast Pass, and the ordeal by Lux probably were enough togetherness.

● ● ●

Janet slipped out early the following morning; Wayne and Carol left soon afterwards. Kate and I lounged through the morning, and got a late start for Wanaka.

The road from Makarora to Hawea was chunky and washboarded in places, deep and soft in others. Biking turned sour just past the Neck, a small strip of land separating Lakes Wanaka and Hawea. A heavy wind blasted across Lake Hawea and the road deteriorated. We zigzagged but the washboarding proved pervasive. A small pickup jolted past; the driver waved wildly. We know, we know–get out of the middle of the road.

The driver continued to wave, then stopped and hopped out. "Well, do you want to throw 'em in the back of the ute?" he yelled. "Saw you struggling through that miserable muck." "Ute" is a Kiwi abbreviation for "utility vehicle."

Kate and I considered the idea. We had never taken a ride but this offer was enticing. After a quick exchange of "Will you feel guilty?" looks, we threw the bikes aboard. The bloke deposited us twenty or thirty kilometers later, just outside of Wanaka. Back on the bikes we snickered like two kids who had just gotten away with something.

● ● ●

Following a day of relaxation, Kate and I deposited our bikes with the Wanaka camp manager, who was kind enough to store them, then pulled on our tramping hats. We bought food, packed, and caught the shuttle for Cameron Flats, the drop for trampers bound for Aspiring Hut. Along with Sue, the driver, we were joined by Andrew, a tall, slim bloke from Melbourne.

"Like Prince Andrew," I said, "that's easy to remember."

"I assure you," he replied dryly, "the name is all we have in common." At the time Prince Andrew was frequently in the Kiwi news, though mostly in a subjugate role to the overpowering presence of his new wife, Fergie.

Sue filled us in on local history, the ski areas, the problem of breaking into the circle of Wanaka locals. She noted that the school system was extremely keen on outdoor education. This manifested itself in a curriculum which included skiing, rock climbing, and canoeing.

A heavy rain fell at Cameron Flats as the three of us started up the West Branch of the Matukituki River. Andrew supported two weak ankles and spindly legs with a pair of broken down running shoes. He carried an overstuffed backpack with an ice ax mounted precariously on the side. We enjoyed Andrew's company, but worried at every muddy turn that he'd slide over a cliff or slip and impale himself on the ax.

The Matukituki valley is open, bordered by bush-clad mountains, and, on this day at least, wet. The rain slowed as we approached Aspiring Hut, which sits on the valley's edge. Aspiring Hut serves as the base for mountaineers, trampers, and day hikers. The hut includes a thousand feet of floor space, bunk room for a small army, and a kitchen full of pots and pans. A rain catch outside supplies water; the toilets sit in the woods fifty meters away. Like many of the busier huts, Aspiring has a warden whose job is to collect fees, maintain the hut, and dole out information.

In the morning the clouds dissipated, revealing the rugged mountains that line the valley. Dark bush climbed two-thirds the way up the mountainsides only to be replaced by golden tussock, which in turn gave way to shimmering glaciers. Mount Aspiring poked its head high into the sunshine. Aspiring towers 3027 meters and is New Zealand's highest peak outside of Mount Cook National Park. The peaks of Mount Aspiring National Park are rugged and untamed; witness the names given by early explorers and surveyors: Mount Defiant, Mount Doleful, Mount Dreadful, Mount Awful, The Blister....

In the morning Kate and I decided to walk up to Liverpool Bivouac, a base hut for ascents on Mount Liverpool and directly across the valley from Mount Aspiring. The track took us two hours along the flat west branch of the Matukituki River, then veered ninety degrees away from the river, straight up into the bush. We climbed five hundred meters, frequently scrambling over sliderock or pulling ourselves up by exposed roots. Once I scratched my ear and found a pea-sized pebble in it.

Eventually we emerged from the bush and spotted Liverpool Bivy, a pink pimple of a shack on Mount Liverpool's chin. A drizzle hurried us inside. The musty shack contained a couple of dirty mattresses and a dusty table. We couldn't see Mount Aspiring through the bivy's window; a cloudbank covered the valley and obliterated the view. After lunch we decided to move off the bare mountainside before the drizzle turned to rain.

That night I didn't move from the fire at Aspiring Hut. My body drifted in and out of a catatonic state, the result of the day's exercise and a stomach bug that would follow me for a week. Valentine's Day was upon us and Kate, bless her heart, pampered me.

• • •

We departed Aspiring Hut for Cameron Flat in the company of three new Montana friends. Jack, Rachel, and Kathy worked in Glacier National Park. We'd spent a couple of enjoyable nights talking with them by firelight about grizzlies, wolves, and the lack of large, indigenous mammals in New Zealand. They agreed to squeeze us in to their rented car for the drive to Wanaka.

An old Swiss gentleman approached me just before we departed Aspiring Hut. "I am seventy-two yar alt," he said. "Yesterday I come from Dart. Today must go Wanaka to eat, I am out of eat. Aspiring–look, look–sie ist sehr beautiful." The old man wore shorts, a singlet, wool socks, and boots. He sported a majestic white beard, flecked with silver. His face was deeply tanned and wrinkled; white hair flowed back from a receded hairline.

As we walked, I mentioned the old Swiss gentleman to Jack. "He's incredible," Jack exclaimed. "We saw him up on Cascade Saddle yesterday and he just flew past us down the hill–no sign of a stiff joint in his body."

The old Swiss gentleman started after we did, passed us, took a detour to Cascade Hut, passed us again, took a detour around a rough spot in the river, and passed us again. The last time he cut straight down through a series of switchbacks without breaking stride. From behind, his sinewy legs churned like a racehorse; his arms pounded away like well-lubed pistons. The pack hid his white head and most, judging the passing blur, would mistake him for someone a third his age.

In the coming weeks the old man became a folk legend. Every tramp we took someone told another story about him. One person had it that he lived in a hut high in the Swiss Alps. Another told that he had crossed Cascade Saddle in just over six hours, a trip that takes most trampers closer to nine hours.

I believed every story. By the time we loaded the car and passed him, the old Swiss gentleman was already a couple kilometers down the road towards Wanaka, some thirty kilometers away. We wanted to offer him a ride, but the small car already bulged at the seams. Later, when we arrived in Wanaka, we spotted the old Swiss gentleman sitting outside the ice cream parlor, soaking in the sun.

"Apparently," Jack deadpanned, "he just likes to walk."

• • •

That evening a big contingency of folks from Aspiring Hut met for dinner in Wanaka. The group included several Aussie climbers, and Fran and Kevin, a couple we'd run into at Liverpool Bivy. Fran is a vibrant Kiwi with dark hair and a great smile; Kevin is a brick-solid Aussie from Melbourne, Victoria.

It wasn't long into the meal that Bruce, a Tasmanian climber, took over. Bruce loved to talk. He was quick-witted and sharp-tongued and particularly liked to take shots at Victorians. "It's always easy to tell Victorians in the bush," he reported with a wink to Fran, "because you can hear them coming. The pots and pans they strap to their packs are banging and clattering away."

Not to be outdone, Kevin countered with, "Don't take much stock in what a Tazzie tells you. They're all inbred down there and a little crazy anyway."

Soon Bruce turned his wit on one of the Americans present. The Yank was helplessly overmanned until Bruce said, "We Aussies often think you Yanks are slow and dimwitted because you don't understand our sophisticated humor."

That gave the Yank an opening and he replied, "The reason Americans don't laugh at Aussie humor is because it's usually hard to pick up the words. Aussies talk fast and jumbled. With you though, Bruce, I don't worry. If I don't pick up the first thing you say, it really doesn't matter. I know there'll always be something more coming."

That broke the group up. Bruce, who'd been talking for three hours straight, turned red but also whooped in laughter. "I'm happy to finally meet an American chap with a sense of humor," he chortled.

• • •

I retired for the second night in a row with shivers and a fever. In the morning the fever departed but my stomach convulsed and I threw up several times. Kate and I packed and started pedaling for Cromwell anyway. Twenty minutes out of town I bent over the bike in agony. We returned to Wanaka and I collapsed into thirteen hours of uninterrupted sleep.

We resaddled for another try the next day and raced to Cromwell on the wings of a friendly wind. The wind did not treat us so kindly as we pedaled for Queenstown. It hit us head on the minute we took to the road and never slackened. My stomach cramps returned, worse than before, and threw spasms through my body. I had no energy. Kate took the lead to battle the wind, but I couldn't keep close enough to draft her. She waited constantly. The same distance we traveled in three hours going to Cromwell took us six hours going to Queenstown. At one point we pedaled only three kilometers in thirty minutes. A cold rain and some sandflies would have pegged the misery index at ten.

Mercifully, we finally reached The Remarkables, newly covered in a dusting of snow. Queenstown and shimmering Lake Wakatipu soon appeared and helped quell the day's frustrations. We found a pleasant campsite at the "Bottleshop"–a motel/campground where the buildings are constructed partially of bottles–set up the tent, and collapsed.

Kate and I spent a couple of days in Queenstown relaxing, reading our mail, and getting ready for tramping. We planned to spend two weeks exploring the Southern Alp valleys emanating from Glenorchy, a small town on the opposite end of Lake Wakatipu from Queenstown. The night clerk at the Bottleshop kindly offered to store our bikes while we tramped.

Before departing Queenstown, however, Kate and I stopped for our first Mexican food in three months. Stomach cramps continued to plague me. Mexican food probably wasn't the best selection for my queasy stomach, but by this time we'd convinced ourselves that burritos and nachos held medicinal value. And indeed it wasn't too long afterwards that my stomach finally came right.

WELCOME TO PARADISE

Chapter 8

We met the Magic Bus, a silver soup can on wheels, for the ride from Queenstown to Glenorchy. Twenty-four people crowded aboard for the Routeburn Track, five more for the Caples, Kate and I for the Rees-Dart. The Magic Bus, marketed specifically to trampers, substantially undercuts the state owned New Zealand Road Services (NZRS) buses. Rarely are its hard wooden seats empty.

The Magic Bus dropped us at Glenorchy, the small town which serves as the base for tramping in the area. Kate and I planned to do a loop up the Rees River and back down the Dart River, then to walk the Routeburn and the Milford Tracks, and finally to return to Glenorchy via the Caples Valley.

The Glenorchy motor camp shuttled us the final fifteen kilometers to the beginning of the Rees Track. We shouldered our packs and started up the open valley floor of the Rees River. The river ran in a great torrent through the alluvial braids of the flood plain. High mountains rose straight up out of the flat valley with no pause for transition.

We opted to camp at Clark Slip, two hours below Shelter Rock Hut. In the morning the track continued on through a moss-covered forest, then out onto an open, grassy hillside. The mountains ahead quickly closed ranks. We crossed the Rees, a small stream by this point, on a swing bridge near Shelter Rock Hut. The hut was new and posh: an indoor sink supplied water from the rain catch, there was a shiny "Fatso" stove, and the mattresses were clean. After lunch we yawned, looked up the valley and considered the walk to Dart Hut, then took a nap.

Malcolm, from England, and Tim, a Wisconsinite, arrived at the hut on the wings of big storm. Malcolm is short, trim, and fit, with a handsome face and blonde hair that parts high above one ear. Tim is tall, also fit, with dark, curly hair and a deep laugh.

The four of us talked from light through dusk into darkness to the accompaniment of heavy wind gusts and pounding rain. Tim told of the year he'd lived in Beijing, China, teaching English at a research institute. He talked of the cultural revolution, of the oppression of the Chinese people, and of how every one of his two hundred students dreamed of escaping to live in the US.

The conversation often turned to climbing. Malcolm, a hardcore climber, complained of needing a "fix" every week or so back in his younger days. He had recently been on a twenty-four day trek in Pakistan to the base of K2. It was a fantastic, horrific story about sherpas and tea rooms, falling boulders and a crazy German swimming an uncrossable river.

All was quiet as we crawled into our sleeping bags for the night. Then Malcolm's voice came out of the dark. "I once had a friend who claimed that climbing was better than sex. I've been trying to prove him wrong for years."

• • •

Kate and I got an early start for the Rees Saddle. Sunshine and showers battled as we chugged up the sloping valley of golden tussock. The Rees River shriveled to a trickle, then disappeared. On the final, steep climb, the sun broke through. A wet, sparkling rainbow rose from the base of the saddle–it was thick and close enough to throw rocks through.

We bucked a strong wind to climb a knob above the saddle. In one direction, the tiny Rees River started its rocky drop to Lake Wakatipu. A slight turn revealed a huge waterfall racing off the face of Headlong Peak, and farther up the valley, Mount Tyndall, covered in white by the Tyndall and Isobel Glaciers. Continuing the circle gave life to Snowy Creek and its hurried drop to the Dart River.

Tim and Malcolm caught us on the saddle. The four of us set off for Dart Hut together and soon descended in a cold drizzle. Wet snowgrass and schist made the going slow. We slipped along from point A to B, marked by rock cairns and orange stakes.

Scott, the Dart Hut warden, looked up from a voluminous book on women's rights and greeted each of us as we entered. He had thin blonde hair, a scraggly beard, and a demented smile. Over afternoon tea, Scott told us that he spent seven months of the year based at the hut, looking after the Rees and Dart Valleys. In quiet moments, Scott often burst into song or carried on public conversations with himself. "I guess maybe I'm a little stir crazy," he admitted. His only repetitive contact with the outside was the myriad of trampers who passed through the hut. Scott made new friends nightly, only to see them disappear by morning light. He coped through a deranged personality, psychosis being the best way to handle loneliness.

Two bunkrooms sandwich the hut's main room, which in turn houses a cast iron stove, a couple of tables, and some gas burners. Malcolm joined me at one of the tables and we talked through much of the early evening. "My wife died after a long illness," Malcolm said quietly. He supported his chin on folded hands. "I guess I'm still trying to cope with it. Part of the reason I'm traveling, I suppose, is for an escape, maybe a transition."

Malcolm lowered his folded hands to the table and tapped his thumbs together. "I quit my job, so there's really nothing for me to go home to. I'm just hoping I can find a new direction for my life."

Darkness settled into the valley. Scott lit a couple of gas lanterns and hung them from the rafters. Malcolm stepped over to the stove to get some hot water for tea. Kate who had been talking with Tim, rose and said she was making it an early night. I excused myself to step outside. Stars filled the sky; the air stood still. Far above the glaciers glowed white.

Malcolm's mood was brighter when I rejoined him. The conversation turned to rock climbing and he related the story of a thirty foot fall. "My handhold gave way and I fell free from the rock. I kept trying to turn and finally got flipped around and ended up face-down, spread-eagled." Malcolm spread his arms and made a horrified look, as if falling. "It was incredible, like slow-motion. The trees and ground were coming up and all I could think of was 'This is it!' After that I had another single, all encompassing thought–'WHEN IS THAT BLOODY ROPE GOING TO CATCH?' Folks around us looked over to see what the commotion was about. "Well, the rope finally caught, gave me a tremendous pop, and wrenched me back to the rock. I ended up with a broken hip but didn't know it at the time. After my belay lowered me down and I stopped shaking, I climbed back up and cleaned the route."

Tim and Scott joined us. Soon rib-splitting laughter rocked the hut as Scott and Malcolm played out their favorite Monty Python skits. No one in the hut could sleep due to four crazy new friends, joined for one special moment in the New Zealand bush.

● ● ●

Kate and I made for Daleys Flat Hut in the morning. Scott, the hut warden, sat on the porch delivering a demented goodbye as each tramper moved away. Tim was off to Aspiring Hut. Malcolm would join him to Cascade Saddle, then return for another night with the crazy man.

We crossed through thick bush, stepping over roots and splashing across small streams, then hit Cattle Flats, a magnificent expanse of golden grass paralleled by the milky Dart River and glacier-covered peaks. The track eventually passed into the forest and then back into more endless flats. The flats gradually ceased to be so engaging. Kate plodded easily on but I dragged us down. My legs ached.

The walk was advertised to be six hours. Eight and a half hours after departing Dart Hut, Kate and I arrived at Daleys Hut. We ate a weary dinner with ten thousand sandflies and read the intentions book. Most trampers mentioned four to six hours as their walk time from Dart Hut. One tramper, however, admitted to thirteen hours, and that without lunch!

A note on the hut wall claimed that the walk out to the road took seven to nine hours. Based on this day's performance, that meant eleven or twelve hours for me. The van pickup for Glenorchy departed at three thirty. Some high math revealed that I'd have to depart at four a.m. to arrive on time. In this depressed state, I grabbed a pen and made my own entry in the intentions book:

Left Dart Hut at 10:06 and arrived here at 6:30. Beautiful weather continues to follow us. What is it with all these four to six hour hikes from Dart? Do you people eat lunch? Do you sing songs when you tramp? Do you LOOK at the mountains.... Better question–do your watches work?

> Happy Trails!
> Scott and Katie
> Boulder, Colorado/USA

Following dinner, we grudgingly pulled on the packs, put in a final hour, then set up the tent in dying light.

We hit the trail at seven fifteen the next morning, moving fast. Mist covered the river, dew soaked the grass. Sandy Bluff rose out of the river valley and we climbed its rock face slowly through a maze of dangling cables and rickety ladders. Kate raced off the bluff. I plodded, consistent if nothing else, but she still waited five minutes of every thirty.

We took a lunch break at Chinaman's Bluff and surveyed the map. The pick up point, conspicuously named Paradise, looked easily in reach. We pushed on across Mill Flats and eventually came out onto an enormous green paddock. The track to Paradise ended at a gate; on the other side of that was a dirt road and more green paddocks. Diamond Lake glimmered ahead, and across the Dart River the Southern Alps jumped skyward.

An older English couple stood by the gate watching our approach. A small rental car sat behind them. When we were within earshot, the man waved and yelled, "Cheerio and welcome to Paradise." The man and woman chuckled at his cleverness, then climbed into their car to leave. We waved back, doffed our shoes, and collapsed in the cool grass.

• • •

Kate and I spent a night in Glenorchy before departing for the Routeburn Track on a NZRS bus. The giant bus carried five people, including the driver. "Need twelve to break even," the driver grumbled. "Bloody Magic Bus is driving us into the ground. We should have never been here anyway. I told 'em. Not enough business and the bloomin' road is tough as hell on the bus. Some college boy brain in Wellington decided we should be here. Knows lots about figures, nothing 'bout drivin' a bus."

We walked through pouring rain to the Routeburn Flats Hut. Hordes of folks wedged into the hut. The Routeburn Track, like the Milford Track, is an extremely popular tramp. Unlike the Milford, however, no quota system has been instituted to decrease the traffic. Kate and I put the tent up in the pouring rain, much to everyone's surprise. It was a loud, stormy night but we stayed dry and were happy not to stay in the crowded hut.

The storm passed in the early morning hours and the following day began beautifully. Clouds and wind, however, greeted us atop Harris Saddle. We blew down through the tussock, then descended through mist and beech forest to Lake Mackenzie and Mackenzie Hut.

The hut holds bunks for forty, though this night closer to sixty people sought refuge from the rain. Kate and I cooked with Pete and Rita, a couple from Wellington. The conversation flowed easily and evolved into a shared walk out to the Divide and the end of the track the following day. Pete and Rita drove us to Te Anau, the start of our Milford Track trip, then departed to visit relations farther south. Before they left, we all shared a beer and a promise to meet later for a bike ride in Wellington.

Kate and I spent a rest day in Te Anau preparing for the Milford Track. We packed the tent and food in a box and left it with the motor camp. The Magic Bus would pick the box up several days later, meet us at the end of the Milford, and shuttle us to the Divide. From there we'd start the walk through the mountains to Glenorchy, via the Caples Valley.

● ● ●

The Milford Track is the best known walk in New Zealand, perhaps one of the best known walks in the world. The beauty of Mackinnon Pass and the relative ease of the track attracts masses. The walk is so popular that a quota system goes into effect for the busy summer and reservations must be made months in advance.

There are two ways to walk the Milford. THCers (Tourist Hotel Corporation) pay around $500NZ($300US), drink catered tea along the track, have their gear shuttled from hut to hut by helicopter, and sleep in sheets at day's end. "Freedom walkers" pay around $50NZ($30NZ), carry their own gear, cook for themselves, and sleep on dusty mattresses. Still, the freedom walkers have it pretty cushy: roofs, toilets, drying rooms, gas burners....

The Milford is a social walk. Forty freedom walkers and forty THCers start daily throughout the summer. Waiting out bad weather is not an option as trampers coming up the track have their names on every bunk. The track has three overnight stops; hence, over three hundred trampers are on the trail daily. Travel, however, is unidirectional and huts for the freedom walkers and THCers are spaced an hour or two apart. Thus, perceived traffic can be remarkably low.

Here, then, is one of the most popular tramps in the world--the only track that many will ever walk, or the launching pad from which novices can start their backcountry experiences. Here, more than anywhere, New Zealand should put her best environmental foot forward to make a lasting impression about proper backcountry etiquette. Here New Zealand could shine.

Instead, she falls on her face.

● ● ●

Kate and I caught the NZRS bus to Te Anau Downs, then the ferry up Lake Te Anau to the start of the track. The ferry provided our first chance to meet with the freedom walkers we'd be tramping with for four days. Also on board were the THC group. Thirty-seven of the forty THCers were from a running club in Auckland. Chief among them was a witty bloke named Trevor whom we'd met on the Routeburn Track. The runners were mostly older, Trevor being something over sixty. Trevor stood tall and solid; age lines crossed his face but his legs looked young and strong. A crushed orange hat, complete with a nametag, topped his head. Trevor traded jibes with his group as he introduced us around.

We de-boated at the head of Lake Te Anau with another of the freedom walkers, Doug, from Oregon. Doug carried an enormous blue pack and sported a Baltimore Orioles cap. We quickly passed Glade House, the first stop for the THCers, then made our way along the heavily bushed Clinton River.

Doug talked about his father, a preacher. "He's a Baptist, but they're in no way related to the Southern Baptists." Doug hopped over a puddle in the trail, then continued, "At one time they were fooling around with the trinity. I even asked my Dad if he believed in God, because I wasn't sure."

Kate and I met more of the freedom walkers that night at the Clinton Forks Hut. Tom and Stacey were a friendly husband and wife team from Oregon. Tom may be the only person ever to walk the Milford Track in a button-down oxford shirt. Eberhardt and Alfred were two older Germans who claimed to speak no English. Kate and I served as their unofficial translators for a few days until Eberhardt started laughing when an older woman, thinking she was safe, described how she'd like to take a roll in the hay with him.

Kate and I set off in the morning thinking trout. We stopped at Dead Lake, which is neither dead nor a lake. Dead Lake is a widening of the Clinton River which resulted when a slip partially crossed the valley. Rotting trees and stumps line the shore.

A lure fisherman stood at the only opening. He was a stoney-eyed, blonde Kiwi with big muscles. The lure fisherman's boots were so broken down that he walked on the sides rather than the heels.

We bypassed the fisherman and stopped at the head of the lake. Here the river ran slow, flat, and clear. Big fish meandered through the water. Bush engulfed the shoreline. Kate played

A fine rainbow from the Clinton River on the Milford Track.

guide, leading me up and down the river as she spotted fish, but our efforts proved fruitless. The bush displayed a voracious appetite for my flies.

We eventually departed for Hidden Lake, where we found the lure fisherman, now accompanied by six Dead Lake trout dripping blood from a heavy stick. Five of the six weighed over five pounds. When the muscle man asked us to take one of the fish, we declined.

I caught and returned two nice rainbows at Hidden Lake, but the spectacle of those big fish nibbled at me. After promising subservience for life, I convinced Kate to make the half hour walk back to Dead Lake. We moved to the vacated opening and I cast a streamer far out into the channel. A moment later the streamer headed for the other side of the valley, line still attached. I struck hard, the line hesitated then continued on its original path across the channel. I slowed the fish's horizontal progress ten meters short of the other side, so it decided to try the vertical direction. Three heavy jumps revealed a beautiful rainbow, stunning in size and strength. We played a game of retrieve and run for fifteen minutes, until the big fish finally wearied and came to my hand.

Kate, who'd been watching and coaching, cheered. I popped the hook free, then lowered the six pound rainbow back to the water, holding its tail. The big fish sat for a moment, catching its breath, then broke free and swam strongly away.

We pushed up the valley for Lake Mintaro Hut and found everyone there marveling over the fish dinner they'd just eaten. Mr. Macho, as we'd started calling the muscle-bound lure fisherman, was a hero. Several people couldn't comprehend that we'd let our three fish go.

The hut warden appeared later in the evening and delivered a frolicking speech about the next day's hike to Mackinnon Pass. He broke everyone up with stories about how keas, the mischievous parrots, strip toilet paper out of the bathrooms, bang on the roof, and steal gear. Then he made some disturbing comments.

"The keas hang around all morning out on the porch, entertaining. Go ahead and feed them, but if you're going to give them chocolate...DON'T! Toss it down to my hut instead." He motioned towards his hut to the accompaniment of uproarious laughter. "The keas eat here, then fly up to Mackinnon Pass where they'll meet you again. They know a good thing when they see one. Go ahead and feed them while you're taking your break. By this time they're so bloated they can't fly, so they roll down the hill (more laughter) and arrive back in time for breakfast the next day."

I couldn't believe what I was hearing. This talk set low impact camping principles back thirty years. I could see a new breed of Milford keas being genetically selected. Those that put on the best show for the tourists would get fed and survive; the others would starve.

● ● ●

Day three is the big day of the Milford Track, the day of the climb over Mackinnon Pass, the day that good weather is a must for the views. The promised keas never showed, much to almost everyone's dismay. The disappointment, however, was tempered by a brilliant sun that shone brightly for the first time in four days.

Gentle, groomed switchbacks carried us up the mountainside. A gas-powered grass cutter sat abandoned on one corner. Above bushline, we began to see back down the Clinton River. Billowy clouds clung to the peaks bordering both sides of the valley. Wind bounced and prodded the clouds, but couldn't free them from the mountaintops.

We overtook John, an older Kiwi, near the top of the pass and walked on with him. John said that he had recently retired and was fulfilling a lifelong dream of walking the Milford. Elderly Kiwis can be a resilient lot. Another freedom walking couple, again Kiwis, were both over seventy. The woman wore a skirt throughout the tramp, but carried a pack just like everyone else.

John, Kate, and I arrived at Mackinnon Pass together, dropped our packs, and sidled over to look out into the Arthur River Valley. Before us were high mountains and deep valleys and glaciers and sky and clouds and wind and sun and tussock and bush and rock and two thousand foot dropoffs. We stood silently, stunned, for several minutes. Then John voiced all of our thoughts, "Kind of makes you feel a bit silly and insignificant, doesn't it?"

Kate and John took off over the small hump to the pass hut. I stayed, hoping to cement the images in my mind. The sun, having just slipped over the peaks, accentuated the greens and golds of the valleys with soft, angled light and deep shadows. Electric blue sky offset the peaks. I sat and tried to drink it all in, feeling the wind and the sun, straining to open my senses to the full scene but having no chance. There was too much beauty, too much country.

No keas appeared at the pass hut. Even those masters of beggary had to think twice about braving the wind gusts coming over the ridge. I leaned hard just to stay upright. Kate and John waited in the hut, drinking tea before starting down into the Arthur River valley.

Kate and I were resting in the sun at Quintin Hut when Trevor and the first of the THCers arrived. The THCers stay at Quintin on night three while the freedom walkers continue on another hour to Dumpling Hut. Trevor waved and moved inside to drop

Sutherland Falls on the Milford Track.

his gear. A moment later he reappeared and discreetly produced two oranges for Kate and I from his pocket. "They've got a bowl full in there," he whispered. "There was some sponge cake, too, but I couldn't figure out how to get it in my pocket."

A short detour to Sutherland Falls yielded an awesome display. Sutherland, the seventh tallest falls in the world, is five hundred eighty meters and three tiers of water plunging from sky to earth. Cold mist, which hung heavy for sixty meters around the base of the falls, checked our approach.

Dumpling Hut proved to be another drop into the bottomless abyss of screwy Kiwi backcountry logic. While we prepared our meal, I noticed a sign posted on the wall. "Kate, come here," I said. She looked up, surprised at the tone of my voice. "Read this to me. That can't say what I think it does."

Kate stepped over and read the sign, "Please use the river for washing clothes. It has endless water, we don't."

This was too much. I stomped over to the hut warden's house and knocked. The door opened. A short, solid young woman with kinky auburn hair smiled and said, "Gidday." She was dressed in typical bush clothes: wool jersey, sweat pants, and jandals. Through the door I could see another girl sitting at a table eating dinner.

"Looks like you're eating," I said. "I'll come back after you're done."

"No, that's OK. What is it?" she asked, still standing in the doorway.

"I'm a little upset about a sign I saw in the hut," I replied.

"What sign?" She looked puzzled.

"There's a sign up encouraging people to do their wash in the river. That's certainly not national park policy, is it?" The astonishment in my voice must have been evident.

"No that's not park policy, that's my policy." Her eyes hardened and the smile on her face disappeared.

"What?" Now I was puzzled.

"The problem is that I have to pump water up from the river to the tanks. Lately I've been going up and finding people washing their clothes in the sink and simply running the tanks dry." Her voice softened as the explanation ran on. "I just get tired of pumping water up there all the time."

"You know soap suds are tough on plants, insects, and fish," I offered. "Also, the suds are a visual pollutant. They collect in backwashes and on lake shores and look terrible. Don't you think a better sign might read, 'Rinse, DON'T Wash your clothes at the river?' Or better yet, 'It's only one more day...save your wash 'til you get out.'"

"Oh I don't think many people do their wash down there anyway," came the reply. "Plus, you're not allowed to wash in Lake Mintaro or anywhere the soap might collect."

"But the suds here go somewhere–to big pools in the river or to Lake Ada." I was getting nowhere fast.

"Sure, but there's endless water." Jan's reach for the door signaled that her patience was wearing thin. "It's just washed right out so it's no problem."

"But it goes somewhere!" I can be a persistent little cuss.

She finally gave in a little. "Well, I suppose it goes into Milford Sound eventually."

"And that's all right?"

"Listen," Jan said, her voice strained, her face turning red, "not that many people go down there, so it really doesn't matter." Back to that.

I decided on a final tact. "This walk is done by thousands of first time trampers, and not all Kiwis. Can't you just imagine them saying, 'Well if it's all right to wash clothes in rivers on the Milford Track, it's certainly OK anywhere else'?"

This time she only grunted and closed the door.

On the last day of the Milford, Kate took off without me as I was getting my characteristic slow start. I had spent the night dreaming about the backwards bush ethics of a country that prides itself on being a world leader in environmental policy. I remembered watching the hut warden take a soap bath in the river at Routeburn Flats, and of being encouraged to bathe in rivers in the Urewaras. In New Zealand, the common tramper thinks nothing of killing a multitude of trout, feeding wildlife, burying garbage, or dropping orange peels along the track. "But orange peels are biodegradable," a number of Kiwis argued. So are old car bodies, given sufficient time.

Similarly, the Kiwi hut system is a paradox. Huts localize environmental damage to small areas, helping maintain the surrounding wilderness. Yet at the same time, huts concentrate people and destroy a sense of self or aloneness.

With these laudable thoughts rifling through my mind, I decided a photo of the offensive sign would be a treasure. A Canadian bloke, equally as incensed as I, had made an addition to the sign. It now read:

PLEASE USE THE RIVER FOR WASHING CLOTHES
it has endless water, we don't
But Don't Use Soap.

I added my own "PLEASE!!" in front of his message, then tried to take a picture of the sign but found it too dark. After a moment of pondering, I carefully untaped the sign and moved it three feet to the left, onto the window. The morning sun showed strongly through the translucent paper. The message was written on the backside of Fiordland National Park letterhead.

Suddenly the hut door burst open and in raced Jan, the hut warden. She was mad. Jan stomped to the window. "Do you get some kind of pleasure moving other people's signs?" she fumed. Then, searching for something really important to get mad about, she growled, "I can't believe you put this on the glass." With that, Jan ripped down the sign, gave me a disgusted sneer, and marched out the door.

I charged down the track, full of overblown self-righteousness and piety. Luckily, Lake Ada interrupted my indignation. We had to be at Sandfly Point at two p.m. to catch the ferry across Milford Sound, but I thought that gave me ample time to cool down with some fishing.

I took eight or ten unsuccessful casts from a narrow log that stuck out into the lake. My watch signaled departure time for Sandfly Point. As I turned to survey the tenuous walk back to dry land, line started ripping off the reel. That got my attention quick. Thirty feet out I turned the fish, then slowly worked it in. The sight of me sent the fish off on another run.

Kate climbed down through the bush to the lake's edge. "Let's go, we have to catch the ferry."

I shrugged, pointed to the doubled-over pole, then let the line go in desperation, hoping that with slack the fish might shake itself free. Peach line disappeared into the deep, but the fish stayed hooked.

Meanwhile, Trevor and the first of the THCers stood in the bush above, watching the comedy unfold. They weren't due at Sandfly Point until an hour after us. Trevor was hidden from our view but his voice boomed over the lake. "Get it in and let's see it."

"It's got lots of strength left," I hollered back at the bush.

"I don't want excuses," came the hidden reply. "I want results!"

The fish eventually tired. The THCers gave mock applause when I held the four pound brown high and then quickly released it. Kate and I jogged the remaining distance to Sandfly Point and caught the ferry just as the skipper cast off. After a sparkling ride through Milford Sound, we headed for a cold beer and a close to our Milford trip.

• • •

The Magic Bus, with our food and extra gear on board, met the ferry in Milford. This bus, as luck would have it, was on its final journey. A recent engine test, the driver reported, had failed to locate any compression. We crawled slowly away from the ocean, up into rugged country.

Passing through Homer Tunnel was like crossing into another dimension. Our dim headlights barely cut the inky blackness. Water dripped from the rugged, unfinished walls. A small stream flowed down the road, which was chunked and broken. The grade was decidedly up and we crept along like a slug in wet soil. Supertramp pounded through the bus's speakers, adding to the unreal imagery.

The Magic Bus dropped Kate and I at the Divide and we struggled into Howden Hut. A corner under a table served as our camp; no beds were available. We stayed two nights, resting, rejuvenating, and talking with the myriad of trampers. Our only physical endeavor was a slow, joyful climb up Key Summit.

The hike from Howden Hut over the saddle into the Caples Valley shot straight up through beech forest. We scrambled over roots and rocks and, after an hour, emerged from the bush into a rain cloud. An old fellow approached who, aside from the normal backpack, carried two small suitcases, porter style. "I always carry eight days of food," he offered as explanation.

The track dropped off the saddle into cool, mossy forest. The Caples River, initially a trickle, grew to a stream and then a river over the next couple of days. We spent a night at the Upper Caples Hut, and another night camped near the Lower Caples Hut.

The morning we were to walk out of the bush, Kate and I woke to the sound of drizzle on the tent. Low clouds covered the Caples Valley. The debate in the Lower Caples Hut was whether to get an early start and arrive at the road first, thus assuring a ride on the shuttle to Glenorchy, or to wait and stay warm and dry until the last possible moment. We opted for the latter plan.

Rugged Southern Alps views from Milford Sound.

Once we left the hut, the drizzle didn't waste any time turning into rain. From there it rapidly progressed through the downpour stage and became a full-fledged tempest. Gore-Tex stood no chance; we were soaked in an instant.

I was splashing through a puddle when a voice behind startled me. "Playing through!" It was Michael, a free-spirited fisherman we'd met on the trail. My backpack, including the elongated fly pole case, was covered in a black plastic bag. As Michael charged by, he turned and yelled, "Your pack looks like it has an erection." I chuckled heartily, raindrops shaking off my nose.

While Kate and I walked, our bodies generated enough heat to offset the icy rain. When we reached the car park at the end of the track, however, the story changed. A brisk wind blew off Lake Wakatipu and sent us into a fit of shivering. Within ten minutes, both of us were frozen to the core.

The other fifteen people who'd walked out crowded into the one shelter available, the longdrop. It was the only place in sight to escape the rain. Kate and I jumped around for twenty minutes before deciding they'd have to make room for us. Dave and

Susie, other acquaintances from the past couple of days, moved everyone aside, coaxed us into dry clothes, and found us a hot cup of tea. The longdrop's smell was arguably tolerable, though no one gave it a mention. With seventeen folks jammed in, we were lucky it was a two-seater.

The van showed up right on time. Seventeen frozen bodies swarmed out of the loo, much to the driver's amusement. Rather than catching another shuttle back to Queenstown and the bikes, we took the path of least resistance to a hot shower and stopped in the Glenorchy motor camp. Dave, Susie, Michael, Kate, and I decided to share a room and within moments transformed it into a dripping mess.

The five of us planned to catch the bus back to Queenstown in the morning. The rain, however, had other thoughts. It pounded down without reservation throughout the afternoon and night and into the next morning. Michael, who went to breakfast before the rest of us, stuck a soaking head into our room. "Dragoon, folks. Road's out, big slips in two places. At least that's the rumor in the kitchen. I'll go verify." After talking with the camp manager, Michael returned. "False alarm. I was wrong...road's out in three places."

Nobody was going anywhere, not even tramping. The day was a wash across the boards. Stranded trampers drank heaps of tea, fought for the washer, and watched the rain. There was plenty of rain to watch.

Kate and I spent the day getting to know our roommates. Michael, a lanky bloke, had stringy hair which was supposed to reside in a pony tail; actually it spent most of the time in his eyes. Michael and I discussed fly fishing from every angle. His knowledge dwarfed mine. He was shocked that I didn't know the scientific names of trout. "Rainbow trout? C'mon, that's an easy one: Salmo gairdneri."

Susie and Dave lived in Calgary, Canada. Susie has an interesting accent; she originally came from Gibraltar, one of only thirty-seven thousand people. Dave is an emergency room doctor. Dave and Susie arrived in New Zealand after an African safari. Lions milled around their camp and a five minute walk required an act of courage. The idea of escape to the Land Rover provided little comfort–the doors were kept locked to prevent baboons from looting the truck.

The rain stopped somewhere into its third day. Glenorchy generally soaks up forty inches of rain a year. Ten percent of that total had fallen in a twenty-four hour period. Trampers stepped outside and looked skyward. A few hopped across the sodden grass and headed for the store. Trips to the Routeburn and Rees-Dart got going, but the Queenstown road remained closed. The five of us drank tea and waited, played hackey-sack and waited, drank more tea and waited....

A few cars trickled into Glenorchy around noon. A couple hours later, twelve cabin-fevered souls loaded into the motor camp van and started for Queenstown. The remnants of several washouts slowed our progress. In one spot a creek had stormed out of its culvert and eaten a twenty meter gash across the road. A front-end loader struggled to open a second lane as we sloshed past.

● ● ●

Kate and I crawled into the tent, back at the Bottle Shop in Queenstown, with mixed emotions about returning to the bikes. In the past month we'd barely pedaled a hundred fifty kilometers. Climbing back in the saddle meant reacclimating the muscles and hardening the bums up again. We planned to head south to Invercargill, and from there to Stewart Island, the end of our southward travels. Our enthusiasm for being on the road again, however, far outweighed any hesitancy. Three and a half months into our journey, we found ourselves more eager to continue than ever.

Happily, we also found ourselves liquid. Kate, the budgeting task master, had early on laid out a daily budget of $40NZ (initially about $20US) for the two of us, all inclusive. There weren't any new clothes or fancy gifts in our portfolio, to be sure, but we were toeing the line. Still, we considered ourselves destitute, aware that the budget was designed to take us through the year on our savings.

While mulling over our finances, I smiled inwardly,

remembering an incident at Quintin Hut on the Milford Track. We sat in soft grass, soaking up the dazzling sunshine and reliving the beauty of Mackinnon Pass. A fellow next to us stretched his legs, lay back, and popped a section of orange into his mouth. Then, to no one in particular, he said, "I wonder what all the poor people are doing today?"

Kate leaned over and whispered in my ear, "We're here."

THE ANCHOR STONE
OF NEW ZEALAND

Chapter 9

Climbing back on the bikes after three weeks of tramping proved to be an awkward adventure. I almost fell off twice in the first kilometer. Still, the legs worked amazingly well. Considering all the tramping we'd done, I guess that wasn't so surprising.

We pedaled south from Queenstown, destination Southland and Stewart Island. A few kilometers out of Frankton, Kate's bottom bracket started to click miserably. She laid the bike on its side and tried her best to work some chain oil into the crank. It wasn't the prescribed fix, but shortly the click disappeared.

Much of the reason we'd been trapped in Glenorchy was the preeminent demand on work crews to open the road south from Queenstown, the road we now traveled. The big rain was four days past, but small streams dropping from The Remarkables still roiled. Piles of shoveled muck recalled great gully-washes which had blanketed the road.

The Remarkables climb straight out of Lake Wakatipu's eastern shore, so rugged and dry as to hold little vegetation. As we worked our way around a big bluff near the south end of the lake, Kate spotted something ahead and said, "What is that, a marching band?"

"A marching band! Those are cows, you dingbat."

A mob of Herefords, a hundred of them, were being driven down the road by a bloke in a Toyota pickup. They continued to pound the highway as we approached. To the left was a steep embankment, to the right a sheer dropoff to the lake. We pedaled cautiously forward. The cows, bewildered by the odd spectacle of two bikers, froze. Then they spooked and stampeded back towards the Toyota.

The bloke in the Toyota would have none of it. He started beeping and swerving and eventually got the cattle turned. The cows came straight at us. We pressed together, figuring that if it was time to die we might as well be trampled together. Just as the lead bull was upon us, however, he swerved. The others split, thundering by like a stream racing around a boulder.

When the last cow passed and the ground stopped rumbling, the farmer drove slowly forward, leaned out the window, and with a sideways nod said, "Gidday. You be 'right there?"

"Sure, no worries. Guess they don't like bikes."

With a wry smile, he replied, "Either that or bikers," and drove off.

● ● ●

Following a night in Kingston, we continued south along the Mataura River, which ran high and muddy. Reverberations of the big rain would put famous Southland fishing on hold for weeks. The countryside began to open and fill with green paddocks. Mountains, still near at hand, rose in dark contrast.

Southland, like so much of New Zealand, is sheep country. One paddock held a thousand sheep. They had grazed the grass to golf green nubbins. I stopped for a drink near a gate in the paddock's corner. A lone sheep spotted me and decided I was about to open the gate and allow him into an ungrazed field. The sheep started trotting towards me. Others joined him. The cascade picked up numbers and soon a thousand sheep were trotting my way.

Sheep entertained us daily. When twenty ton trucks flew by, they wouldn't flinch. Yet our two-wheeled, two hundred pound approach sent them scurrying in fright. Numerous times sheep raced head-on into solid wood posts while trying to escape us. Kate came up with a simple explanation. "I think they breed sheep so they don't have horns. Somebody must have got mixed up and removed the brains, too."

We pedaled past Five Rivers, pumped over some low hills, and coasted into Lumsden. A big match was in progress at the cricket park near where we set up camp. Cars lined one edge of the field. Folks sat on the grass enjoying picnics and the sunshine. Shadows engulfed the players–their white togs provided a striking contrast to the dark green of the surrounding trees.

Kate and I exited Lumsden for Invercargill on the wings of a tail wind, made tremendous time for a couple of hours, and crossed the Oreti River to pedal down a quiet side road. The mountains now fell distant. As the day wore on, the wind shifted one hundred eighty degrees. By early afternoon, a heavy southerly whipped across the flat Southland plains. We pedaled hard, but progressed slowly and pulled into Invercargill beat.

Invercargill marked the end of our southward biking, so we hired a caravan at the A&P campground to celebrate. Our plan was to hop over to Stewart Island before starting north. Youth Hostel members, we soon learned, could fly to Stewart Island for half the normal $50NZ($30US) fare. We weren't hostel members, but justified joining because of the fare savings and the potential need for winter shelter. Also, flying eliminated a rough ferry ride across Foveaux Strait.

The same rain that trapped us in Glenorchy also flooded the Invercargill airport; thus the Southern Air van dumped us at their temporary office, a gas station storage shed. Kate and I found a couple of old tires off to the side, and sat. An official looking man–he wore a Southern Air shirt–jammed gear, groceries, and a flight box into the back of the van. Then a woman stepped out of the shed to say they had a standby opening on the next flight. Kate sent me ahead.

With the airport closed, Southern Air was flying from the local motor raceway. That's right, the oval kind. Following a short, crowded drive to the raceway, pilot and passengers spilled out of the van. The pavement of the race track oval was cracked and pitted. A large sign on one end championed Dunlop tires.

Once the goods were transferred to the rear of a ten-seater plane, the passengers began to pile in. Then the pilot climbed on board and started flicking buttons. The first engine flipped on but the second wouldn't turn over. The pilot beat on the instrument board as if fully expecting to remedy the problem. When the engine still didn't start, he flipped the first engine off and said, "No worries, we've got another one."

"Another engine?" the nine of us asked in unison. I was happy to see I wasn't the only one closely following the proceedings.

"No, no," the pilot laughed, "another plane." Quick as that he jumped out of his seat, ran down the infield, and hopped into a waiting plane. Moments later, the new plane and nine jittery passengers sat at the corner of the race track oval. After a cursory look at the gauges, the pilot hit the throttle. The plane rocketed through the turn, shot onto the straightaway, then lifted off without a hitch.

The small plane crossed low over Foveaux Strait. I closed my eyes and thanked the heavens that our craft was amphibious. Just as my ears became accustomed to the drone of the engines, Stewart Island appeared. It was far bushier than I expected. In fact, the entire island looked blocked in.

A short, dented runway rose up out of the bush–no tower, no hanger, no welcoming banners. The race track oval, with its Dunlop tire sign, looked official in comparison. We landed without incident. A van pulled up to swap departees for arrivees and haul us to Oban.

Stewart Island measures sixty-four by forty kilometers. It is not urban. Oban, population three hundred, is the only town. Tourism, fishing, and salmon farming keep most of the residents busy. The island has a manual telephone switchboard, thirty kilometers of roads–many gravel–and no community electricity. Every night the evening calm is broken by the sound of a hundred diesel motors.

According to ancient Polynesian mythology, the demi-god Maui created New Zealand. One day he set sail with his brothers on a fishing expedition. Legend says that the North Island was the fish they caught, the South Island was their canoe, and Stewart Island was Te Punga o te Waka a Maui–"The Anchor of Maui's Canoe." The Maoris gave the island another name, Rakiura–"The Glowing Sky." The colorless pakeha name, Stewart Island, comes from the First Officer of the ship PEGASUS, which made the first survey in 1809.

Kate arrived on the next flight, somewhat less upset about the flying conditions than I, but disgusted that the pilot picked his nose throughout the flight. We spent some time at the Forest Service asking about tramping, and eventually decided on a three day, two night loop to the Port William and North Arm huts, then back to Oban. We walked five kilometers north, around Horseshoe Bay, and came to the end of the road and the start of the track.

The sound of a quiet ocean lapping against the shore accompanied us most of the way to Port William. Lush bush pushed right up to the water's edge. Much of the track was boardwalked, making mud, the scourge of Stewart Island trampers, virtually nonexistent.

As we dropped into Port William, two Forest Service workers passed in the opposite direction, carrying traps baited with meat and fruit. They told us they were after possums and domestic cats gone wild. Both animals are considered vermin on Stewart Island because they destroy native bird life, including kiwi birds.

The kiwi, and other flightless birds such as the takahe and kakapo, were once prevalent in New Zealand. Europeans, however, brought cats, weasels, and ferrets. These exotic predators have rushed many species of flightless native birds toward extinction.

The Port William Hut is old and worn, with soiled walls and torn mattresses. The kitchen holds a couple of wooden tables and a big stove. While we ate dinner, one of the Forest Service trappers, a shaggy, baby-faced blonde, trotted away from the hut with rifle in hand. The other, a slim joker with a curly brown beard, joined us at the table.

"What do you do with the cats and possums you catch?" I asked naively.

"We take 'em out to the ocean for their baptism." The forestry man grinned on the word "baptism."

"What do you mean?"

"We just drop the cage a foot under the water and hold our foot on it until they drown," he answered without hesitation. "Cats are weenies. They kick a bit and die in thirty seconds or so. But possums are great." The dying daylight couldn't hide the excitement in his eyes. "They're bloody rats, you know. Possums thrash around for three or four minutes, sometimes up to fifteen." The forestry man spoke with great relish about this part of his job. Perhaps it was better than digging a new loo, his job for most of the day.

In a quiet moment, a single shot rang out. Our man said, "Great, deer. God, I'm so sick of rice and noodles. I want some meat."

Shortly, the baby-faced trapper returned, empty-handed. "Couldn't find a bloomin' deer," he moaned as he set the rifle down. "Got frustrated, so I shot a possum in the stomach."

In the morning, the forestry boys left two newly trapped possums sitting beside the hut while they went off to dig their loo. The two nocturnal creatures sat in utter confusion. Several of us discussed how ghoulish it was. A quick twenty-two shot to the head or fast acting poison had to be more humane than drowning. At lunch, the forestry boys slid broomsticks through the cage handles and took the enemy off for baptism. They apparently left the gruesome task until midday as a reward for their first half day's work. I suppose it made the morning go faster.

• • •

The first portion of the Link Track, which runs between the huts at Port William and the North Arm, was newly boardwalked. The planks provided striped contrast to the dark swirls of green bush. After the boardwalking ended, the track rolled across hills, over logs, through mud, and under dangling ferns. Bush overwhelmed the track, sucked at us, clawed at us, pulled us in. Often the sun couldn't fight its way through the canopy. Only once in five hours did we see over the top of the bush, and for that we climbed a rock in a man-cleared opening.

Darkness comes early to the bush. Kate and I hurried through the last couple of kilometers, unsure how far our destination lie ahead. Just at dusk, the North Arm Hut appeared. It was a dilapidated old place with tiny, clear bugs swimming in the water supply. Rakiura lived up to its name with a sunset sky glowing in pinks and purples. The quiet waters of the North Arm repeated the display. As twilight settled in, we retired to the hut and spent the night reading by candlelight.

In the morning Kate and I climbed away from the North Arm and back into the bush. Mud soon covered us to the knees. Sandflies, as always, heralded our passing. Nothing, however, could dull the excitement we felt for our impending return to the bikes. After six weeks in the bush, our tramping season was ending.

Interspersed with the talk of our turn north, was jovial banter about what a misguided soul I'd been before we met. Bell-bottoms, cowboy shirts, and long hair, as far as Kate was concerned, didn't cut it. "It was the eighties, for goodness sake!" she cried in mock horror. Then, after pausing to climb over a log, Kate assured me, "You were lucky beyond belief that I happened along and straightened you out."

I thanked her with a gracious bow, and we walked into Oban.

● ● ●

In town, I cranked up the operator from a pay phone and asked for Ann at one-nine. The operator didn't sound upset that I had no change for the pay phone. Also, she was certain I'd find Ann home, and I did. Ann runs a small business accommodating trampers and hikers. I asked if she might have a place for us. "I'm not sure what the ones from last night are doing with coming and going," Ann answered. "But once it gets sorted out, I'm sure we can squeeze you in."

I rang off to let the operator know we were done, and then Kate

Trekking in the mud of Stewart Island.

and I walked across the street to Stewart Island Travel (also home
to Southern Air, a tea room, a souvenir shop, video rentals, and
a guiding service). The bloke behind the counter was tall, with a
long bushy beard and flowing hair reminiscent of Medusa. He
laughed when I asked how to find Ann's, waved his cigarette, then
did a jig to accompany his answer. "Go up the hill, down the
other side, cross two bridges and take the first left. We got only
two bridges on Stewart Island, so if you don't see 'em, mate,
youse really lost."

We walked over the hill, found the bridges, and turned in at a
hand-scrawled sign which invited trampers up to the house.

Ann's house, green and weather beaten, sat plunk in the bush. A vegetable garden filled much of the yard. We found Ann elbow-deep in a patch of potatoes. She was a solid woman with a warm, worn face and gray hair. Ann wore gumboots, athletic shorts, and a soiled sweatshirt.

Ann showed us the small annex to her house which serves as a trampers' rest stop. The annex had two small rooms, three beds, a table, a tattered easy chair, a shelf full of dusty books, and two stoves (one gas, one wood). "Usually turn the generator on about half six for lights," Ann said as she pointed out the bathroom. "Shut her down about half eleven, depending on how tired I am. There's candles about in case you want to stay up later than that. Just be careful of fire. Also, I get the stove in the house going at night and heat up some water, so if you want a shower, it'll have to wait til then."

Ann's place is not conducive to loners. The small, two room attachment to her home has bed space for about eight, if you count the floor. Any overflow moves into the main house. The crew this night included a Scot, a park naturalist from Canada, a student from Idaho, and a sheep farmer from New York.

With acquaintances made and stories told, everyone drifted off to their own spaces. The drift was necessarily short. Kate and I shared one of the rooms with the Scot. We showered off the grime of three days in the bush, then read for an hour until the roar of the generator died and the lights blinked off.

We spent much of the following morning beating our laundry mercilessly in Ann's concrete wash basin, and then running it through the hand-ringer. That evening we walked to Harold Bay in search of the Little Blue Penguins who nest there. We didn't see a splash for an hour and a half, but we did sit through another special sunset. Pink sky haloed Oban. As night slipped into the harbor, we listened to the sounds of the shore, felt the cool sea breeze, and rested back-to-back.

● ● ●

At four forty-five the following morning, a possum knocked over a barbecue outside Ann's annex. Three warm pairs of feet, all male, reluctantly hit the cold floor. Moments later, we departed for town through thin fog and heavy darkness. The stimulus for our early walk was the dedication of a Maori carving at the Forest Service building. The carving was a gift from some Maori carvers to the people of Stewart Island.

The Maoris believed that the carving could not be exposed to light in its new home until it had been properly blessed. The blessing closes the eyes of the spirits who dwell in the carving and renders it safe for all to see and enjoy. If the spirits see light, they are released to come and go as they please, and the carving becomes dangerous.

Solemn ritual accompanied the dedication of the carving. Still the dedication lasted only a half an hour. Sunup fast approached.

The dedication was conducted by a Maori priest. Fifteen men stood in a dark circle around the carving. The priest alternately said the blessing in Maori and relayed what he was doing in English. He had dark hair and skin and wore glasses, purple pants, and a bone carving around his neck. His sweater bore a star and a crescent moon.

The carvers took on a sober attitude as the priest chanted. Following his prayers, the priest asked the local Presbyterian minister to add his blessing. The minister called on God to use the carving to promote understanding between the Maoris and the people of Stewart Island.

The carving was large, perhaps six feet by four feet, and stained blue-green to represent the sea and bush of Stewart Island. The six apprentice carvers struggled to mount it on the wall, then sang several songs. Dawn hinted from the east. The head forestry man, who was dressed officially for the ceremony, invited everyone to stay for breakfast. Ann and another woman were out back in the garage preparing a full bore Kiwi feed: eggs, toast, jam, mutton sausages, and tea.

In the preceding days, signs posted around Oban invited men to the early morning dedication, but forbade women. Oti, the head carver, explained that in the month they had been preparing the carving, neither he nor his six apprentices had associated with women. The reason was tied up in a woman's power to give life.

The carvers also were trying to give life: to their work and the spirits that dwell in it. When my confusion at the explanation showed, Oti smiled and tried to make it clearer. "Some women have big walla wallas and make us lose our concentration."

Following breakfast, dignitaries on both sides expressed a desire for understanding and harmony between the Maoris and the people of Stewart Island. Then, as everyone began to get up to leave, one of the apprentice carvers let out a grunt. He was a stout, Sumo wrestler-looking bloke, fully tattooed down the arm, with long black hair. The Sumo grunted again, this time louder, and the rest of the carvers and the Maori priest broke down, hands on knees, knees wide apart, all answering the grunt with one of their own. Seven of them stood in a line, just inside the garage door; the leader stood apart. Then a chant began–great reverberations of grunting and yelling and guttural sounds accompanied by stomping feet, fists pounded into hands, and arms thrust downward in powerful motions. All this came in a rhythmic, stunning fashion, often punctuated by a cry and a return between the Sumo and the group. The chant was loud, erotic, and it transfixed everyone in the room. The chant ended slowly, dying a quiet death, and the audience clapped.

I watched, dumfounded, and when the chant was over, I questioned Ann. She explained that the Maoris had performed a "haka," a ceremonial dance, but she couldn't provide an interpretation. I queried the Maori priest, who was sitting off by himself. He leaned back in his chair, pondered for a minute, then said, "Well, I can tell you what it means if you want to know. A haka can be made up to do with any situation: birth, death, marriage. If I wanted, I could make one up about coming to Stewart Island to dedicate this carving."

"Right, I understand that," I said. "What about this one?"

The priest smiled before continuing. "Back about 1937, the Maoris had a great chief. He was newly married and had sexual intercourse with his wife for the first time. He decided he wanted to write a haka about it. I suppose he just lay back, lit a cigarette, and figured it out. The part at the beginning where we were kind of quiet was when his penis is limp and waiting. Later, he becomes much more excited and the sound and tempo grow.

Finally it's over and we become quieter again, thoughtful."

I couldn't help but chuckle, remembering the Presbyterian minister tapping his finger to the rhythm of the haka.

Later, I joined the Maori priest in an office of the main Forest Service building. He sat in a chair; I stood. The priest expressed great concern over the problems facing young Maoris, particularly the growth of gangs like Black Power and the Mongrel Mob. "These groups are tearing the young Maori people apart," he said. "They rape women, defenseless women, some in their seventies and eighties, and think what big men they are. Then they get their ten mates to take a turn. It's a crime, a pity." His voice and eyes echoed great sadness. "Alone they are often OK, but the power of the mob will start them doing crazy things."

The priest took off his glasses, leaned back in the chair, and paused, reflective. After a moment he looked up, eyes hard, and continued. "Knifing and shooting and beating people up. I think the best thing they could do is line 'em up and send them off to war. Let them fight someone who's trained to fight back. I know–I was in Vietnam."

The priest sat forward, chin in his hands. His eyes no longer focused on me. "We followed a bunch of your boys in on a jungle raid. We were backups, about a half mile behind. The Cong were waiting in ambush. They're a terrible people...wiped out the lot of your boys..."

The priest sat silent for a moment, then rubbed his eyes and put his glasses back on. He looked at me again. "We try to get between the gangs, to bridge the gap. It's not working, though, and I wonder if we're at the end. It all starts with the family. Mom and dad don't care and pretty soon the kid's on the streets, then into a gang. White man, Maori walk together in New Zealand. We do things like the carving to help build understanding. We do protest dances at the government so they know what people think. But we're losing our young ones too fast and I'm not sure what else we can try."

● ● ●

Later I walked to Ackers Point, alone, and spotted ten Little Blue penguins. The sun was low, the ocean calm, and light penetrated deeply. From my vantage high on the point, I could follow the penguins' undersea antics. They dipped and darted effortlessly through the water. For a moment blue glowed off their backs, then white from the belly as they banked through a turn. After a quick breath at the surface, the penguins dove again, took wing, and soared away.

I started back for Ann's in fading light. Darkness overtook me, but the hum of Ann's generator signaled the way. A new crew was assembled in the annex, including a girl who stared unabashedly at Kate. When she caught our questioning glances, Trish apologized for staring. "Kate just looks so much like my sister it's unreal."

Trish was a pretty twenty-three year old blonde, with apple cheeks, gorgeous eyes, and a robust laugh. She was appalled that we thought of New Zealand as a rural wonderland and insisted that we come to visit her in Auckland so that she could show us the city life. "You'll have to hurry, though," Trish warned. "I'm in training for a five year travel stint. Going to Canada first." Like so many young Kiwis, Trish wanted to get out and see the world.

Ann's annex had picked up a few more bodies that night, largely of the North American variety. We sat in a group in the annex, some eating, some weaving wrist bands, all talking. As the lone defender of the Motherland, Trish took the brunt of the Kiwi jokes. Semantics played a large role in the light-hearted conversation. "It's so confusing," someone said. "You say biscuits instead of cookies, open the boot and the bonnet instead of the trunk and the hood, drive on metal roads that don't have anything on them but dirt and gravel, and have nanas instead of grandmas. Don't you get confused?"

Trish laughed incredulously with each comparison. "Of course not. It's you people that don't know how to speak English. For example, what do you call the serviettes?" Blank stares. "You know, the paper towel you wipe your face with at a meal."

"Napkins, of course."

Trish broke into hysterics. "Nappies are what you put on a

baby!"

"How 'bout this?" I asked. "You say tea when you mean dinner. Tea is something you drink but people see me fishing and say, 'Fishing for your tea, mate?'"

That brought Trish out of her chair in search of a dictionary. The English Oxford, of course, backed up her argument, saying that "tea" can be an evening meal.

"I win that one," Trish beamed. "OK, what do you say when you're going to buy someone a beer? You say, 'I'll shout you a beer,' right?"

"No," someone replied. "I think we just say, 'I'll buy you a beer."

It took us thirty minutes to get over the pronunciation hump of scons versus scones.

Trish tried one on us. "What do you people mean when you say 'Mickey Mouse?' That always confuses me."

Kate explained that Mickey Mouse meant cheap or low in quality. Trish still looked puzzled, so Kate made a wavering motion with her hand and said, "You know, so-so."

Suddenly it dawned on Trish; her face lit up and she exclaimed, "Oh! You mean higgilty-piggilty!"

● ● ●

A cold drizzle fell as we walked to town early the next morning. For seven days we'd enjoyed perfect sunshine and not a drop of Stewart Island rain. Still, the first day of fall was upon us and we knew it was time to move north. The warm days of summer were numbered and the numbers were small.

Kate and I filled two standby openings on the first plane out. Our feet rested on boxes of frozen salmon. The pilot lifted off, waggled his wings over Oban, and pointed the small plane towards the South Island. We did not land at the race track oval. The floodwaters had subsided enough to partially reopen the Invercargill airport.

I made a fateful decision on our hike back to the A&P motor camp. For several weeks I'd been walking the fence about running

New Zealand's premier marathon, the Fletcher Challenge. A Kiwi runner had lobbied hard that I give it a try. "C'mon mate," he argued, "you'll be plenty fit. You've been biking all over the bloody country!"

We were fit, all right, yet my journal showed only five runs in the past year. Six weeks and a thousand kilometers of biking separated us from the Rotorua marathon. The prospects for adding to my year's running total looked slim. Can I survive a marathon, I wondered, on the strength of my biking and tramping alone? In the war between reality and romance, Steinbeck once wrote, "Reality is not the stronger...." I sent the entry form in, and then forgot the marathon in an act of ignorant bliss.

For the moment, the east coast of the South Island loomed ahead, an area we knew little about. We did know that winter fast approached, and that we wanted to beat the cold weather north.

South Island

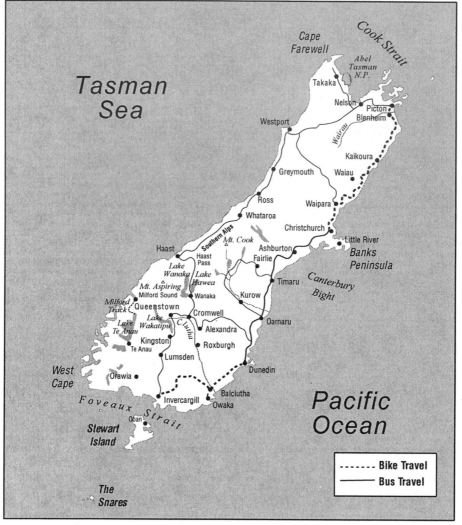

Tasman
Sea

Cape
Farewell

Cook Strait

Abel
Tasman
N.P.

Takaka

Nelson

Picton
Blenheim

Westport

Wairau

Kaikoura

Greymouth

Waiau

Ross

Waipara

Whataroa

Christchurch

Little River

Haast

Southern Alps

Mt. Cook

Ashburton
Fairlie

Banks
Peninsula

Haast
Pass

Lake
Wanaka

Lake
Hawea

Timaru

Canterbury
Bight

Mt. Aspiring
Milford Sound

Milford
Track

Queenstown

Wanaka

Kurow

Cromwell

Lake
Wakatipu

Clutha

Alexandra

Oamaru

Lake
Te Anau

Kingston

Roxburgh

Te Anau

Lumsden

West
Cape

Orawia

Dunedin

Foveaux Strait

Balclutha

Invercargill
Owaka

Oban

Pacific
Ocean

Stewart
Island

The
Snares

------ Bike Travel
——— Bus Travel

THE RIDE NORTH

Chapter 10

We pedaled out of Invercargill on March 24th. Rain pounded Southland for the second day in a row. With the rain came a new element, cold. This day began the test of our long-held theory that by biking north at the proper time, we could stay one step ahead of the coming winter.

Amidst the weeks of tramping, Kate and I had biked hard only three days. A cold rainstorm was not what we needed to herald our return to the road. By mid-morning, however, a delightful sou'wester drove the dark blanket of clouds away and pushed us all the way to Gore. Even with the tailwind, sixty-five kilometers of pedaling provided an ample reintroduction to biking for our leg muscles and bums.

More rain and another blessed tailwind chased us east to Balclutha. The final thirty kilometers pitched and rolled through rounded hills and green valleys. It was like biking through the folds of a loosely dropped blanket. Enormous thunderheads hung heavy in the sky, trailing a wet veil that stretched to the ground. Sparkling water drops and bright patches on distant hillsides showed the presence of a hidden sun.

Balclutha sits astride a mighty river of the same name. The salmon were making their yearly spawning run and a group at the motor camp hoped to catch a few. Stan, Jerry, Mavis, and Kath came over every year from Dunedin. Kath was the best fisher, but Stan was definitely the ringleader.

After dinner, we all sat around the kitchen table listening to Stan. Stan was short and wiry, with weathered skin and eyes that twinkled. When talk turned to salmon fishing, he looked to Kate

and I and said, "Yessiree mates, we got a mess of 'em last year."
The others hung on his words, expectant of the story they all
knew.

"Had one special lure that was a bloody good one," Stan
continued. "Caught a mess a salmon on that lure. I got the
biggest on that lure, too, a seventy-five k-g'er. What a beauty she
was, mate!" The others giggled and chimed in that indeed that
had been a beauty. Kate and I knew Stan was having us on.

"Seventy-five kilograms? Isn't that a pretty big salmon, Stan?"
I had to ask.

"Who said anything about salmon, mate?" Stan chortled with
a big grin. "I was talking about Mavis, I was. Put that great lure
right through her! What a fighter, let me tell youse! Funny thing,
the doctor couldn't understand why I wanted the lure back so bad
when he got it out of the ol' girl. Mavis was a might hacked off
about it, too."

● ● ●

The Catlins Forest Park is one of New Zealand's secret
treasures. Even Kiwis stay away in droves. We pedaled south
from Balclutha to Owaka, the northern end of the Catlins and,
unbelievably, had our third tailwind in as many days.

Owaka felt deserted: no cars, no people, no animals, just cold
wind. But the wind brought a clue, the sound and smell of cattle.
Auction Day!

We pedaled through town to the stockyard and suddenly were
surrounded by cars and people, cattle and commotion. Farmers
walked the tops of the pens, sizing up stock and making notes.
Others sat in the stands, listening to the auctioneer and watching
intently as cattle were bought and sold. Our biking togs looked
out of place among the plaid Swanni pullovers, terry cloth hats,
and gumboots, but few noticed in the excitement of the auction.

Kate and I found a superb campsite at Pounawea, four
kilometers away near the mouth of the Catlins River. The camp
whispered; the only guests besides us were an old man and a
couple, and they both had cabins.

We stayed at Pounawea for a rest day, which also happened to be my twenty-eighth birthday. An instant chocolate pudding pie served as the birthday cake. It wasn't, however, the same old instant pudding we ate every third night. Kate whipped up a graham cracker crust and topped the pie with one of our tramping candles.

That afternoon we took a short ride to the mouth of the Catlins River, then climbed off the bikes for a hike to the False Islets. A driving rainstorm hit as we walked along the beach. The tide ran high but was just turning. A fishing boat fought to enter the inlet, but a powerful westerly wind and strong outflow held it in place. After five futile minutes, the skipper sought easier passage near the shore.

The scene grew even more violent when we rounded the point to Surat Bay and got our first look out to sea. Giant waves crashed in a line across the river terminus. Wind and water met in an awesome battle. Powerful gusts blew the top foot of water off cresting waves, but the water pounded relentlessly forward. Farther on, huge waves ravaged the False Islets. White froth enveloped the enormous rocks for seconds at a time, yet the Islets always reappeared–the sea all powerful, the rocks defiant.

Nothing in Kaka Point, a village up the coast from Pounawea, seemed open but the pub. The motor camp was closed for the year, but the stout caretaker climbed down from repairing his roof and agreed to let us stay. He even turned on the water heater and electricity, then charged a grand total of $2NZ($1.20US).

After setting up camp, we pedaled ten kilometers back down the coast to Nugget Point. A grass-carpeted walkway leads to the solitary lighthouse on the headland. Fences on each side of the walkway guard against two hundred foot dropoffs. Far below, giant chunks of rocks, the "Nuggets," rise unnaturally from the sea. The motor camp caretaker had told us to be sure and look for seals. "Look close, they look like little turds down there." It was a crude but apt description of the view from the lighthouse. Hundreds, maybe thousands, of droppings lined the water's edge and littered the Nuggets. As we climbed down to the sea, the inanimate wasteland came alive with seals. They fought and played, yawned and slept. The seals were ungainly on land, but graceful in the sea even as they pin-balled through the rock reefs.

Riding North to escape the cold grip of winter.

The Nuggets provide the seals with safe haven from pounding waves and the worries of land. Two of the Nuggets were particular favorites. The first, a massive triangular slab, emerges vertically from the sea. Seals blanketed the rock even a hundred steep feet above the water. The other favorite held a protected pool that deepened with each surge of the ocean. A continuous stream of seals plunged into the pool, swamping their neighbors like kids in a swimming hole.

Kate and I pedaled out of Kaka Point the following morning under dreary skies. It was as if the weather decided to take the day off: low clouds but no threat of rain, no sun, no wind, not hot, not cold. We worked our way back to Balclutha, then pushed north through the hills to Milton. A carload of joyriding teenagers, music blaring, beers sloshing on the dashboard, swerved out of their lane as if to hit me. They laughed and ricocheted back across the road as I extracted myself from the ditch.

The ride from Milton to Dunedin was not greatly inspiring.

Wind blasted us, stinky swamps lined the road, and shoulders disappeared as the traffic grew heavy. At Mosgiel, the road shot straight up and we were soon pedaling through the suburbs and giant hills of Dunedin.

Dunedin's roads, a local biker explained, were laid out in Scotland with no regard to local topography. Someone dropped a grid over the map and where it fell is where the streets went. The result is a series of straight, steep roads.

As we attacked one of the precipitous climbs, an angry rain started. Two inches of water rushed through the gutters by the time we reached the Octagon at the center of town. A statue of Robbie Burns, the great Scottish poet, presides over the Octagon. Scottish Free Church immigrants founded Dunedin in 1848 and the Scottish heritage has never been forgotten.

Elegant Victorian architecture dots Dunedin, particularly at the University of Otago, where we stopped to look at the museum. One of the museum's displays showed the gargantuan moa, a ten foot flightless (surprise) relative of the kiwi bird. The moa, a sort of original Big Bird ala Sesame Street, is now extinct, though rumors persist of sightings in the rough bush of Fiordland National Park.

Dunedin provided our first mail stop in over a month. We spent two hours in the center of the Octagon reading and rereading our mail. Passersby wondered at our silly laughter and backslapping. Life continued at home as we knew it would: cars and washers and houses had been purchased, promotions received, new jobs taken, children conceived, marriages made and broken. Letters, unlike phone calls, did not reestablish a direct umbilical cord to home. Rather they gave us time to reflect on the importance of our journey, and on how we missed our family and friends, not jobs and purchases.

● ● ●

Dunedin became a transition point of sorts. First, our fourth month on the road was ending. Second, Kate's sister, Kim, was about to arrive for a week's visit.

Over three hundred sixty kilometers separated us from

Christchurch, where Kim landed. So at four a.m. we found ourselves pedaling through the deserted streets of Dunedin, toward our first bus ride since departing Auckland some thirty-two hundred kilometers previous. We were the only passengers.

On our way up the coast, the bus driver pointed out the bright lights of squid fishing boats far out to sea. "Japanese, the lot of 'em," he claimed. "By crackee, they catch our fish then sell them back to us for a tidy profit."

The terrain for biking looked tough until Palmerston, then mostly flat to Christchurch. At least that's how it seemed. Riding in the bus removed us from sore muscles, sun on our faces, the famous Canterbury winds, the smell of sheep-ripened paddocks. Six days of biking flashed by in six hours with no sensation of passage. Bus travel was inert: no agony, no fun, no sheep antics or farmer's "Giddays," no hill struggles...no memories.

● ● ●

Kim, a flight attendant with United, arrived looking impeccable, as always, even after twenty-seven hours of flying. Her visit reconnected Kate and I with home. We resumed forgotten identities; we laughed and joked about stories of friends and family. Kim's visit brought a welcome rest for us—no biking or long tramps for a week, just relaxation and happy thoughts of home.

Kim's week took us over most of the north half of the South Island in a small rental car. As with the bus, I was struck by the fact that although we were traveling so much farther by car, we were seeing so much less. After being happily bike-bound for four months, car travel felt like making the jump to light speed.

At the end of the week, we found ourselves on the West Coast. Westland welcomed us back with rain, heaps of it. In Hokitika, Kate and Kim called their parents and found out that their grandmother was near death. Both wanted to go home. It was a sad, dreary afternoon.

● ● ●

Following Kim's departure, Kate and I descended on our Christchurch liaisons, Jim and Judy, with flowers and Steinlager beers in hand. Jim and Judy were Americans working in New Zealand. Jim had worked with my Dad at one point in the States. He and Judy agreed to be our mail stop and forwarding agent.

Kate and I stayed with them several different times when we passed through Christchurch. We quickly grew to think Jim and Judy, and their kids, Jarred and Jenny, as our adopted family. Our enjoyable evening conversations often centered around the differences in Kiwi and American society. One thing was the same, according to Judy—Jim worked too hard in New Zealand, just like at home.

During one of our stops, Jarred, Kate, and I biked to the Canterbury versus New South Wales (Australia) rugby match. Jarred hopped on my mountain bike and wound us along the Avon River to Leicester Park. At the match, Canterbury jumped out front 24-7 early in the second half, then coasted to a 25-24 loss. The crowd cheered and screamed fanatically, the weather was superb. I was reminded of a fine fall afternoon at a football game, except for eating meat pies instead of hot dogs.

● ● ●

Returning to the bikes after a period of no pedaling, as always, felt strange. But when we passed the first green paddock, and the pungent smell of sheep dung wafted over the road, we started to feel at home. And when the first sheep truck rocketed past and a mist of sheep urine enveloped us, we knew we were back in business. A mental check of legs, lungs, and bums reported all a little sore, all happy to be back at work. Kate and I sidled around Christchurch, then started north to Picton, the ferry, and the North Island.

T-shirts sufficed for the next day's warm afternoon ride. Winter, for the moment, trailed in the race north. We sang loud and obnoxiously out of tune until the shadows began to lengthen and the road turned steep. Just as the sun dropped behind the Kaikoura Range, we rolled into Hawkswood, which consists of a stop on the train line, a ranch, and a motor camp. Shafts of light hung over the valley and dew sparkled in the close-cropped grass. Silhouettes of sheep and horses moved through the paddocks. Before we were off the road, a sense of calm surrounded us.

A big man stepped out of the ranch house to greet us. JD carried a pronounced belly, had white hair, a grey and white peppered beard, and bright blue eyes. He walked with a limp and sometimes used a cane. JD's belly, as well as his pants, were held in place by a leather belt. The belt didn't pass through the prescribed loops, nor were his soiled pants buttoned.

"Why don't you two just bunk in that cabin back there?" JD said. "Gonna be a cold one tonight. Be better than your tent. After you get settled in, come on over to the house for a cup of tea." Afternoon tea turned into "tea," the dinner variety, which turned into conversation in front of the television.

The motor camp, JD informed us, served only as a sidelight to the eighty-eight hundred acre sheep ranch. "Don't make any money off any of this," JD explained. "Don't care if I do. Mostly, just like to meet people." JD sat in a soft chair and sometimes suspended our conversation for short snoozes. He kept an open door to all and frequently travelers stopped to stay a week or longer. Two young women presently worked for JD, one from England, the other from the North Island.

JD showed us around in the morning. The setup was extensive: a shop with power tools, a run down tennis court, horses for riding, a big barn, rustic cabins, caravan sites, fruit orchards, a swimming pool, domestic deer. A wooden stage hosted dance and theater in the open air of the bush; a string of lights illuminated the narrow path to the clearing. Posters showed that *Cabaret* had once been performed there.

But JD's pride and joy was the Hawkswood Flyer, an excellent reproduction of an old Cobb and Company stagecoach. "American chap stopped for a night once–stayed four and a half months to help me build the Flyer," JD explained. He paused to run his hand lovingly along the hitch. "There's a few others around, but ours looks the best, works the best, is the best." JD and his team of horses take the Flyer to parades and outings for a fee.

JD's next plans included building a clapboard wagon, making some furniture, and constructing a mud house to enclose the antique printing press he owned. He lobbied hard for us to stay and work on his myriad of projects in exchange for room, board, and companionship. "Something you'll remember all your life," he said convincingly. "Just like the chap who put together the Flyer." We gave JD's proposition some serious thought, but the lure of the road, the oncoming winter, and the marathon all compelled us north.

● ● ●

From Hawkswood, Kate and I crossed the Conway River and then some rugged hills. Atop the final crest, a bloke on a mountain bike caught us. Peter, a dairy farmer from Victoria, Australia, wore a funny orange kayaker's helmet, but biked like the dickens. We glided down to the coast together, and then shared lunch.

Peter had been to the States and done some farming through connections in the Baptist Church. His biggest gripe about the US was the frequent American attitude that nothing outside the States is worth worrying about. Several folks even had the audacity to ask him how it felt to be in a democracy for once! Yet he did like some aspects of US life in comparison with his homeland.

"I reckon Aussies don't realize their potential," Peter lamented. "So many blokes there are just happy to live on the dole." Peter alternated his talk with hungry licks of an ice cream cone. "For some reason Aussies just expect to be taken care of. I could even be on the dole as an out-of-work Aussie in New Zealand, getting money for just pedaling around enjoying meself."

Gigantic hills and gentle surf sandwiched the remainder of the road to Kaikoura. Up the coast, snow-covered mountains rose directly from the sea. The rugged landscape and eight thousand foot peaks rivaled the beauty of the West Coast.

In Kaikoura, Kate called Glennis and Richard, a couple we met on the Milford Track. The phone went unanswered, so we headed into the grocery store, almost knocking Glennis over in the process. Without so much as a pause, she said, "I was starting to wonder when you two would show up."

A six pack of beer and some gooseberry wine later, we were well beyond reliving stories of the Milford and instead concentrating on homeopathic medicine and walking the Appalachian Trail. Glen is a pretty woman, a nurse, and much intrigued by Shirley MacClaine and her claims of channeling.

Richard, an electrician, had recently been in a bad electrical accident. "Got tangled up in a three-phase circuit. Didn't want to shut the power down because there was a meeting going on." Richard paused to show me the scars running up and down his arms. "I'm 'bout ready to go back to work, but still a bit worried. I guess having a close brush with death really makes you stop and think."

Glen and Richard insisted on giving us a head start on our ride the next day. We hoped to pedal one hundred thirty kilometers to Blenheim so we could catch Peter and Rita, our friends from the Routeburn Track, before Easter. Glen and Richard zipped us twenty kilometers up the road, then decided another twenty kilometers wouldn't hurt us and drove on.

Even with the forty kilometer head start, the day became a monster. We turned inland a couple hours up the coast, and ran directly into a powerful headwind and a big range of barren hills. One giant hill after another fell, only to be replaced by more imposing climbs. The wind fought us every pedal of the way for seventy kilometers, no matter which way we turned. The wind even robbed the downhill respites; we had to pedal on the descents to avoid being stopped in our tracks.

Past Seddon, we struggled on through rolling country. Wind gusting through cuts in the hills batted us around like ping pong balls. We reached Blenheim just before dark, in remarkably good spirits despite the trials of the day. "Hey Scott," Kate yelled as we pedaled through town.

"Yeah?"

"You know how the winds have been against us today, no matter which way we've been going?"

"Yeah."

"Those winds have a name."

"What's that, Kate?" I knew from experience that something very profound was coming.

"They're called 'againsterlies.'"

"Right."

Our camp selection that night left a lot to be desired. The tent sat at the base of a railroad track which carried trains hourly. The ground shook like an earthquake every time a train passed, causing the tent to roll and tug at its stakes. We bounced around inside like marbles in a tin can.

● ● ●

The cold April ride to the North Island contrasted greatly with our warm southward crossing in mid-January. Hundreds of gulls, some flying, some riding, also made the passage to Wellington. At the head of the Marlborough Sounds, a seal hopscotched along a rocky point and later, in the middle of Cook Strait, fifteen dolphins raced along with the ferry.

Wellington, as usual, was windy. We pedaled to the train station and met Peter, our friend from the Routeburn Track. Pete's a handsome fellow, with reddish hair, a trim mustache, and a mischievous smile. He wore a dress sweater and tie, leather shoes, and a new Gore-Tex coat. On the train ride to Plimmerton, a small suburb north of Wellington, we caught up on our travels since the time we shared on the Routeburn, and heard about Pete's job as a computer programmer.

Pete and Rita's flat faced directly to the ocean and Mana Island. Rita pulled up on her motor scooter shortly after we arrived. Rita, who works with handicapped kids, is a porcelain doll–petite, with olive skin, wire glasses, dark hair, and a wonderful Portuguese accent. She and Pete met while he was in Portugal on holiday.

Pete and Rita shared the flat with Nigel and Cheryl, another couple with an international history. They met while Nige studied in the States. Cheryl, a displaced Californian with long, dark hair, was always upbeat and loved to egg Nige on about returning to America. "God it's great to talk with Americans," she exclaimed when we met. "Pancakes, Steamboat, Easter egg hunts! Hooray!

Real life lives on!"

Nige, a wiry sort with a wry sense of humor and an extra dose of Kiwi accent, quickly gave us the word, "You two won't be staying on long. Otherwise it'll take me months to get this nonsense out of her system."

This group were among the few young professionals we encountered in New Zealand. Male and female held jobs, all drove or commuted to work, clothing went beyond wool jerseys and Swannis, wind surfing and cappuccino were the passion. Urban life exists in New Zealand, mainly in Auckland, Wellington, and Christchurch, but by choice we mostly avoided it. Still, if I must ever commute, let it be in Wellington, where the suburban train passes along rugged coast and bush-covered hills.

We spent several days in Plimmerton. One afternoon, Nige climbed into his dilapidated Citroen and managed, after thirty minutes of effort, to start it. He sat in the drive for another ten minutes with a big grin on his face because of his accomplishment. I sauntered over and leaned in the window. "Hey Nige," I said, "I'm not sure if you know this, but starting these things is only half the battle. Back where I come from cars actually move. We don't just sit in them and smile."

Cheryl chuckled from the passenger side while an incredulous look came over Nigel's face. "You know, dearie," he said to me with a sneer, "I'm going off you quite rapidly." With that Nige drove off, black smoke trailing the Citroen.

That evening I sat on the front lawn and watched the sun set along the north side of Mana Island. Pinks and golds streaked the sky. The sun was an orange ball, so far away and cold that you could look straight at it. The ball moved towards the horizon, contacted it, then slowly disappeared.

Pete stepped out of the house to call me for dinner. "The sun sets on the south side of the island in the summer," he said as I rose to join him.

Earlier in the day, Kate and I had worked on the bikes, and I stupidly tracked chain oil through the house. As we stepped inside now, Pete greeted me with a living room laid out in newspaper pathways. "You're allowed to walk here, sonny," he laughed. Then Pete supplied me with wine in an unspillable baby's flask.

On Easter morning, Cheryl hid the eggs before the rest of us stumbled out of bed. Based on the fun these first-timers had coloring eggs, the hunt shaped up to be a doozy. The gun sounded and the search began. Did I say search? War is probably a better description. This Easter egg hunt was a contact sport, not for the timid or weak of heart. Pete, Nige, and I climbed over each other as we scoured the house. Couches were torn apart, beds and dressers flipped, shelves swept clear. A simple, "You're getting warm," sent elbows flying into rib cages.

When all the broken bones were splinted and nosebleeds stopped, Kate and I packed the bikes and said our goodbyes. Dead ahead loomed the Fletcher Challenge Marathon. As we were about to depart, the group produced two toy Easter chicks. We taped them to the top of the front bags, and they served as our hood ornaments for the coming weeks.

● ● ●

We pedaled north to Waikanae, then stopped so Kate could call home. In the ten days after Kim's departure, we had tried to set aside worries about Kate's grandmother. Yet daily Kate wondered aloud about "Mimi," and hurt for her Dad. When she dropped the phone and broke into tears, I knew Mimi was dead. Afterwards, we stood beside the phone box and I held Kate as she cried.

"What happens when all the old people are gone?" she sobbed.

Home felt very far away.

North Island

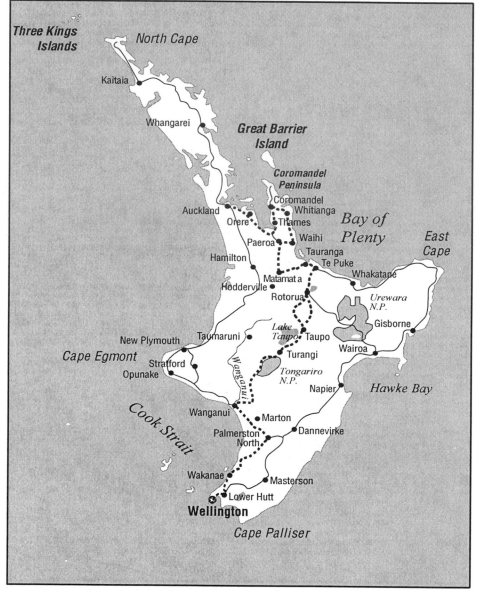

THE CHADEAU AND THE CHALLENGE

Chapter 11

Two bikers flew past as we continued to work our way north. They carried no gear. An hour later the bikers stood beside the road, waving for Kate and I to stop. The bloke was trim and square, with a dark mustache. The girl was also fit, wore funny glasses, and had short-cropped hair.

"Gidday," the bloke yelled as we pulled up. "Where you staying tonight?" We said we planned to camp somewhere up the road.

"Why don't you come stay with us," the girl asked. "My folks have a bach on the ocean at Waitarere." Phil and Sue introduced themselves, gave us directions, and in a flash were off.

In Waitarere, we met Sue's family, exchanged tales of our travels, and enjoyed a nice Easter meal. All of that was good medicine for the soul, considering the morning's bad news about Kate's grandmother. Phil and Sue, it turned out, were training for an impending bike tour of their own. They planned to work for passage on ocean freighters, buy bikes in Vancouver, then pedal through Canada, the US, and Europe.

As we departed in the morning, Sue's father assured us that the road to Wanganui ran flat. He was almost right. We bucked againsterlies much of the way and by Turakina, about eighty kilometers into the day, we felt worn. A woman in the dairy said that two big hills stood between us and Wanganui. She was right.

Both climbs hurt. Kate fell far behind but kept cranking without complaint. I waited at the top of the second hill...and waited. An occasional car broached the crest, and then finally Kate appeared, moving slowly. With every pedal her face grimaced and soon I heard an accompanying, "Ouch, ouuee, ouch...." Kate's cries and facial expressions signaled extreme pain. A cold rain started just as she reached me. We slapped on our garbage sacks and donned rain gear. Twenty minutes of hard biking passed before we found shelter under a grove of trees.

I leaned my bike against a fence as Kate pulled in and collapsed on the ground. Her left knee throbbed and with every pulse she cried out. The combination of sweat, wind, rain, and exhaustion had overwhelmed her system. Kate babbled incoherently. I persuaded her, manhandled her, into dry clothes. The rain continued beyond the shelter of our trees. We held each other and waited.

When the rains stopped, we pedaled into Wanganui. Kate used only her good leg. For the hundredth time, I marveled at Kate's strength and determination. She had biked every pass, run every rain storm, and bucked every wind that I had. Yet her muscle power was a fraction of mine. My bike trip was easy, Kate's often heroic.

● ● ●

A day of intense rain held us in Wanganui. Our unofficial gauge, the billy pot, measured the deluge at an inch and a half. The rain mattered little–with Kate's sore knee and my tired body, we weren't going anywhere anyway.

Clouds continued to threaten as we prepared to depart for Raetihi the following morning. We stopped in a dairy before leaving town to pick up groceries and ask about the road ahead. Another customer, an elderly woman, looked aghast. "Lord love, I couldn't imagine push-biking over the Para Paras. We came through there yesterday and I wasn't certain we were going to make it."

Kate and I wondered at her statement as we biked through the flats along the Wanganui River. A sign soon clued us in:

WELCOME TO PARA PARA - VALLEY OF A THOUSAND HILLS

This was not a super revelation for a couple of tired bikers. We laughed at the sign, trivialized it. What else could we do?

The billing rang true. Almost immediately, we climbed the endless hill that separates the watersheds of the Wanganui and Mangawhero Rivers. And that was just the start. By the end of the day, Kate claimed we must have climbed at least a hundred of those thousand hills. Individually, many of the hills are not imposing. As an aggregate, however, the Para Paras are awesome. Some short, some long, some steep, some gentle–but always, always, ALWAYS one more! When some malicious thunder heads and a cool breeze joined the party, we had the makings of a long day.

The Mangawhero Valley exuded bush and green. Few cars or homes disturbed the peace. Shepherds, driving their flocks down the road, waved and greeted us. We filled our water bottles at a country school where children at recess shouted "Gidday." That stop, lunch on a fencepost, and a tea break were our only rests in eight and a half hours and ninety kilometers. The rest of the day was up, up, and away from the river, back down, then up, up....

On some of the awe-inspiring hills, I biked to the top then trotted back to push Kate as she pedaled. The push helped her aching knee. Ten or fifteen kilometers from Raetihi, we felt sure we'd conquered the final hill. Then BOOM–dead ahead loomed the monster of the day, two kilometers long and perpendicular to the ground. Kate spotted a truck far above that had passed us twenty minutes earlier; the truck looked like a toy moving towards the skyline.

I pedaled hard one-third the way up, then jogged back to help push Kate's bike up to mine. We repeated the process for the middle third of the hill. This was one helluva walk, much less a bike ride. I pedaled Kate's bike to the top, then returned for mine while she finished the walk to the summit. As I ground up the final two hundred meters, a small red gremlin suddenly appeared out of the drizzle, jogging towards me with a big grin on her face.

"Could I be of some assistance, sir? Perhaps I could just jump in here and push." With that Kate jumped to the rear of my bike and pushed me the rest of the way to the summit.

From the top of the hill we looked back and laughed. The battle was over. We'd beaten it: the cold rain and endless hills. For a while we pedaled flats, then rounded a corner and plunged into a valley. Ahead rose another giant climb. We were so disheartened we didn't speak, just dropped our eyes and pedaled. I wished for a merciful death.

To our amazement, the road stayed flat the rest of the way. An icy headwind greeted us five kilometers out of Raetihi, but we were beyond caring. It all seemed too ridiculous, and we limped into town giggling like two crazed fools. As we passed the town cemetery, Kate quipped, "That must be where they keep all the dead bikers."

We descended on the motor camp with a couple quarts of brew and a strong desire to get out of the rain. The proprietor offered his children's playhouse for $12NZ($7.20US), a couple bucks more than camping. The playhouse contained one small bed, a light, and a table and chairs suitable for preschoolers. Still, it was clean, had a solid roof, and when a space heater was thrown in, we decided to splurge. Somehow we managed to get the gear and bikes inside and still find room for one sleeping bag on the floor, half under the bed.

Before dinner, we offered a prayer of multiple thanks: for weather that was not as bad as it could have been, for safe passage, for arrival before dark, and mostly for the health and opportunity to be on our journey at all.

● ● ●

Rain pounding on the doll house roof woke us. The previous day the rain came down in spurts; today it arrived in barrels. A two block ride to the dairy to drop off our milk bottle soaked me through. During a brief respite, we departed for the town of National Park, but thirty minutes later the clouds broke open. Painful rain drove us into a roadside barn. The barn was chockablock full of newly sheared wool, which looked incredibly

Waiting for a break in the rain near Horopito on the North Island.

inviting as my teeth chattered ferociously. Kate wasn't cold. While her Gore-Tex coat repelled the rain well, mine worked like a sieve.

We caught the next lull and pedaled on. At Horopito, the rain returned and we took refuge in a small, cinder block railway hut. I hung my coat up; drops rolled down the inside and splattered on the floor. Kate sat on my legs and tried to share her warmth. I shivered uncontrollably and worried that the shivering would soon give way to hypothermia.

In the town of National Park, we found hot food and changed into dry clothes. Rain continued to batter the road outside, so we made up things to do to avoid departure. We had biked along the western side of Mount Ruapehu and Tongariro National Park, but seen almost nothing because of constant low clouds. The road east toward the Chateau looked desolate and uninviting.

Kate and I pushed on during the next lull. Dark clouds looked down on us, circled, considered. The clouds granted us dry passage for nine kilometers to the Chateau turnoff, then unleashed. For twenty minutes we rode in cold sleet and a side wind that almost knocked us over. Kate lost all feeling in her extremities. "I can't feel my hands to steer with!" she yelled over the howling wind.

The clouds heard Kate's cries and recanted. The sleet stopped and a patch of blue sky appeared. We spotted the golf course ahead, and then the blue roof of the Chateau, New Zealand's second most famous hotel (behind Mount Cook's Hermitage). The Chateau's window framed a tuxedoed bloke standing underneath a chandelier. As we pedaled by, Kate looked down her nose, put on her best aristocratic airs, and intoned, "Yes dahling, we're staying at the 'Chadeau.'" Thereafter, we always referred to it as the "Chadeau," and always with the proper pomp.

We arrived at the Chateau at dusk. With the numerous stops to get out of the rain, we'd biked forty-eight "easy" kilometers in seven hours. The sleet and heavy cloud cover signaled snow. Kate and I had reached our misery quota for the second day running, so we took a caravan for the night. After wedging the bikes and gear safely inside, we turned on the electric stove for heat, then supplemented dinner with three quarts of beer. It was that kind of a day.

● ● ●

Snow and ice blanketed the ground in the morning. We read, caught up on letters, and worked on the journal. By early afternoon, the sun poked through and we both suffered from cabin fever. I took a run, Kate a walk.

I started up the hill to the Whakapapa Skifield. Part way up the first pitch, I glanced back and pulled up short. Ngauruhoe, one of the three volcanoes that make up Tongariro National Park, stood tall, alone, and visible for the first time since we'd arrived. Snow covered its cone; smoke wafted from its top. I jogged backwards up the hill until the corner robbed my view.

Past the Silica Springs trailhead, the wind started to whistle off Mount Ruapehu. Vegetation gave way to rocks and rubble and I imagined being on the moon after a fresh snow. The seal soon degraded to sharp gravel. I fought the wind and incline, hoping that this might be my one good training run before the marathon

Volcanoes Tongariro (left) and Ngauruhoe in Tongariro N.P.

in Rotorua.

After committing to "one more corner" four times, I reached the ski area. Skiing Ruapehu-style means no trees and no glitter, just a bunch of rocky slopes and modest ski club buildings. I made the turn back, happy to feel the help of the wind and hill. Below, dark clouds gathered their strength for an afternoon thundershower.

Kate and I sat in front of the stove that night and listed the toughest rides of the trip. In five months of pushing the pedals, seven especially trying days demanded recognition. Three of the seven toughest days had occurred in the week just past. We chewed on that thought for some time. Were we getting soft? Maybe the addition of cold weather was one stress too many?

A round of gin rummy eased our minds. Later, stepping outside for a communal moment with nature, I shivered and looked skyward. Finally, after days of rain and clouds, the sky stood clear. It would be a three-dog night for sure.

● ● ●

The ride away from the Chateau repaid us tenfold for our biking penance of the past week. We lost a thousand meters of elevation and, as if that wasn't enough, a strong tailwind rocketed us along. For an hour we hung on and screamed "WHEEE!" like a couple of kids. The sun took control and Kate and I rode in t-shirts for the first time in a week. We stopped in Turangi, taking a day to fish the famous Tongariro River, then continued north to Rotorua and the marathon.

In Rotorua we made our way to the Thermal Lodge, a budget accommodation that kept popping up in conversations with other travelers. The Thermal Lodge provided biking couples with grass to tent on, lockers for valuables, a garage for bike storage, hot showers, a modern kitchen, and a lounge–all for $11NZ ($6.60US). And the caretakers were nice, to boot.

Kate and I met four bikers inside. Scott and Karolyn lived in Davis, California. They had biked extensively through Australia and were now spending a few weeks in New Zealand. Scott was trim and hard, with bushy hair and a mustache. Karolyn was slim, blonde, and full of smiles. She leaned out the door as we approached and hollered, "Hey, you've got a bike like mine. All right."

John and Joan sported Canadian flags and maple leafs on all their gear. They hailed from Banff and were on a trip around the world. John and Joan caught the biking bug in Australia, then decided to bike New Zealand. The six of us spent the night eating pizza, swapping stories, and slipping into a comfortable friendship.

● ● ●

I jogged around town early the day before the Fletcher Challenge Marathon. Heavy clouds hung low in the sky. My legs, now comfortable in their role as pedalers, fought against the distant memory of running. Neglected muscles cried out, then subsided into an eerie tingling. Since Invercargill, on the southern tip of the South Island, I'd squeezed a dozen runs–only three over six miles–into the pedal north to Rotorua. Mostly, I'd tried to ignore the approaching race. The tingling in my legs carried with it a revelation that the marathon was real and soon.

When I returned to camp, the manager waved me in. Are you Scott? Are you a biker? Are you running the Fletcher Challenge? Three affirmative answers earned me a trip to the phone. As a marathoner who also happened to be a foreigner pedaling around New Zealand, I rated just freakish enough for the local paper to consider me "human interest" material. Ah well, just another ho-hum interview for a 3:43 personal-best marathoner.

Ten minutes later Simon Earle of the *Rotorua Daily Press* arrived. Simon tracked me down through my race form and a list of Rotorua motor camps. "Good bit of sleuthing," I told him.

"Not at all," he replied with obvious pride.

After pictures came the interview. I fielded questions philosophically. "My motivation? Participation is paramount. There is joy in winning, certainly, but being there, experiencing the rush of adrenaline and crush of pain transcends winning and losing." A couple tables away, Scott and Karolyn choked on their breakfast. With every question, Kate tried to jump in but my cruel looks stopped her cold. "Sure Boulder is a great place to be a runner," I said. "Me and Deke and Shorter...."

The pre-race pasta party that night lacked Americanisms. Few big signs or logo-covered t-shirts dotted the auditorium. Leather work shoes numbered equally with running shoes. Two beer servers smoked. A Maori group performed traditional songs and dances.

Walking back to camp through downtown Rotorua, Kate and I heard two nervous women chattering about the hills on the back side of the course. I worried more about cold rain compounding the next day's difficult task and rolled around the tent most of the night. Each time I woke I listened for rain, each time not a sound.

● ● ●

Marathon Day dawned clear and crisp. John and Joan and Scott and Karolyn shouted encouragement from their tents across the lawn. I ate some toast and jam, and drank some coffee, juice, and water.

The Thermal Lodge buzzed with runners. One older bloke told me, "I always reckon this is a four hour marathon, but I'm going to beat it this year, by damn, I'm going to beat it."

I'm praying for survival, I thought. Outwardly I said, "Good luck, mate."

I rode Kate's bike to the race while she jogged alongside. At the starting line, Kate warned me, "Don't even think about breaking four hours. Just make sure you don't kill yourself." I nodded in agreement, not hearing a word. We kissed.

HELP!

Watches everywhere beeped. The smell of analgesic rub hung in the air. A cannon boomed and the mob was off, shoes pounding, crowds cheering. The tide ebbed and flowed until we passed out of the Government Gardens. Kate pedaled alongside with words of encouragement for the first five kilometers. Distance markers passed quickly and I dreamed of a sub-four hour marathon.

Around me were the logos of running clubs from all over New Zealand: Massey, Auckland YMCA, Sunfresh Pakuranga, Wellington Marathon Clinic.... Typically American, I sported a t-shirt emblazoned with "SPECIALIZED," the manufacturer of my mountain bike. Countless times a spectator yelled, "Good on you Specialized!" then turned to his mate and said, "Specialized? Where the devil are they from?"

I hit the half in 1:59. Forget breaking four hours, my legs told me. Yet my mind toyed with the possibility. As we rounded the backside of Lake Rotorua a heavy headwind struck and the mind games ended.

Still, I managed the Mourea Hill, a windblock, and made the thirty-two kilometer mark on four hour splits. Ahead stood an ambulance, lights flashing, parked on the roadside. Two medical techs intently administered to a slight old man who was sprawled, face-up and unmoving, on the asphalt. Spittle drooled from the corner of the old man's mouth. His eyes were closed.

The heartless winds returned on the agonizingly long flats past Mourea Hill. The wheezer slipped behind me about then, and drafted me for two kilometers. I surged, he surged. I went left, he went left. Wheeze, wheeze, wheeze– he sounded ready to die. I jumped to a small trail off the road and finally shook the wheezer. I never did see his face.

By the thirty-eight kilometer mark, all hope for a four hour race vanished. I shuffled stiffly along, legs burning. Persevere, I told myself, don't walk. After forty kilometers on the slant of the road, my left leg began to throb. I searched out flat sidewalks whenever possible, but the pain did not subside.

Finally...down Fenton Street...where is that forty-one kilometer marker? Runners who had long finished made their way home. They shouted words of encouragement. I managed to return a smile, but it hurt.

Then the turn into the Government Gardens and the finish line came into sight. A race walker sprinted past in the final hundred meters. "There's Scott Bischke," the loudspeaker blared a moment later. "He looks like he'll be happy to cross the finish line." I wanted to hold off the race walker; I wanted to punch the announcer. I had strength for neither. Past the finish line I only had energy to look for Kate.

The result? A pitiful 4:19...but I didn't walk.

• • •

The following morning Scott and John, our friends from the Thermal Lodge, joined Kate and me for a bike ride to the post-marathon stretch out run. The run wound through the peaceful trails of the Whakarewarewa State Forest Park. I deemed the bike ride sufficient stretch out, handed my Rockhopper over to John, and took a seat in the grass. While John and Scott bee-lined for the backtrails of the Whaka Forest, Kate and I watched runners pass. Few showed any effect of the previous day's race. Running did not appeal to me.

The Rotorua Athletic Club supplied hot drinks and a hot mineral spa after the stretch out run. The four of us shared a spa pool with an older woman. Joan was full of smiles, rosy-cheeked, and vibrant. As the soreness melted away, Joan told us about herself. "I had migraine headaches for thirty years. Then I started running eight years ago, when I was fifty-seven, and the migraines disappeared. Now I'm completely free of them." Joan brushed the surface of the steaming water away from her face. "If I don't run for three or four days, though, the migraines return, even if I substitute aerobics for running."

Joan ran the marathon in little more time than I. She didn't run fast, she claimed, but she could run a long way. After we talked for a while longer, Joan recognized Kate and I. "Say, you're the two from the article in the paper, aren't you?" She had a funny way of tilting her head to the side and looking quizzically into your eyes. We said we were. "Well in that case," Joan continued with an affectionate smile, "you'll simply have to stay with me. Do what you want today, just pop in whenever."

We pedaled back to the Thermal Lodge and started packing. John and Joan, the Canadian bikers, departed before lunch. They had secured kiwifruit picking jobs in Te Puke prior to arriving in Rotorua. We promised to call a week or two later and try to join them.

Scott and Karolyn departed for Sacramento (via Auckland) that afternoon. Seeing them off at the bus did not leave Kate and I longing for the States. For us, New Zealand was feeling more like home every day.

● ● ●

The ride to Joan's neighborhood included one of the steepest hills we pedaled in New Zealand. Her driveway was the steepest hill we pedaled in New Zealand. Joan greeted us warmly. She wore running shoes, sweats, a marathon t-shirt, and a big black watch. Joan's eyes and smile sparkled with life and vitality.

Our plan was to bus to Auckland to meet Kate's parents, who were coming for a week's visit, then return to Rotorua and pedal back for a few days of fishing on the Tongariro River. We asked Joan if we might leave our bikes and extra gear in her garage. "Well don't be silly," she answered. "Of course you can. You two just think of this as your home and come and go as you please."

Joan took us to her favorite coffee shop in the morning before we caught the bus. When I tried to pay for the coffee, Joan slapped my hand and said, "Goodness, of course you won't pay. What kind of a hostess would I be?" Twenty- four hours after we met her, Kate and I stood outside the bus station hugging Joan goodbye.

We took Joan at her word and spent several nights with her in the coming weeks. Each time Joan welcomed us heartily. We shared friendship and good conversation, took turns cooking, and felt like family.

As part of that family, Joan shook us awake one morning at six fifteen to join her daily run through the Whaka Forest. Only a couple of weeks had passed since the marathon and I hadn't reclaimed my running enthusiasm. Yet there stood Joan, sixty-five years old, ruddy cheeks, great big smile, chomping at the bit to get out to the trails.

Clouds and mist hung in the trees as the three of us jogged off. Twenty minutes down Pohaturoa Trail, an icy rain started. Pre-dawn light barely penetrated the forest, but Joan slogged steadily onward. She talked continually, yet put out a pace that kept both Kate and I working to stay close.

● ● ●

A couple of mornings after Joan dropped us at the bus, Kate and I trudged into the Auckland Hyatt Hotel, where we were to meet Kate's parents, Giff and Ellen. They weren't yet checked in. As we stood at the desk the phone rang; the girl signaled Kate. Even in New Zealand, Ellen could make things happen.

Giff and Ellen had changed their minds and decided to stay in the Regent, Auckland's premier hotel. We beat them there. Two Rolls Royces and a couple of Jaguars sat in front of the Regent. Shiny marble pillars and tuxedoed doormen guarded the entry. Kate and I walked in carrying soiled backpacks and wearing tattered t-shirts, grimy shorts, and stinky running shoes. We passed the doorman and moved through the lobby without being challenged. The concierge and the receptionist appraised us sympathetically until we plopped our packs down beside the Grand Piano and sank into the overstuffed velvet couches.

The concierge walked over, hands folded in front of himself, and asked if he could help us. "We're checked in here tonight," Kate told him. A collective snicker passed through the lobby just as the Gibsons pulled in. After happy greetings, Giff straightened everything out.

The bellman came for our bags. He stood over my bomb-proof backpack, looking mystified, then turned to me. "Pardon me sir, where can I pick up this bag that I won't hurt it? Here?" I assured him that his selection of the shoulder strap was fine and off we went to the rooms.

Our rooms were nice, after a fashion: a marble bath with jets, a glassed marble shower, two plush robes for lounging, a stocked bar. It was nearly up to our usual standards, although I must admit the remote control for the sound system was a little difficult to master.

Later the four of us picked up a Maui Compas. The Maui, a Toyota van converted into a camper, had one hundred fifty thousand loving kilometers on it, left-handed column shifting, a stiff transmission, a sticky clutch, and the obnoxious habit of backfiring at the most inopportune times.

We toured Auckland, then returned to the Regent. Four cars waited in line: a new Honda, the Maui, a shiny BMW, and a Mercedes. A group ornamented in flowing gowns and stiff suits waited at the hotel door. I felt a surge of pride as we rocked and rattled up the drive. The attendant opened the door and we stepped out. Giff slipped him a couple of dollars. The Maui groaned and sputtered as the attendant struggled to start it. Finally the old beater submitted, coughing up black smoke all over the BMW behind, then jolted away with the satisfying belch of a backfire.

Kate and I donned our white Regent robes, sipped orange juice, and played with the stereo remote control. A knock on the door disturbed our reverie. Outside stood a chambermaid, complete with black dress, white hat, and lacy white apron. "Shall I turn down your bed for you, sir?" she asked.

"What?"

"Shall I turn down your bed for you, sir?"

I was appalled. Why should this woman want to fool with our bed? "Uh...no...er...I guess that won't be necessary."

"Fine, sir. Can I leave the complimentries with you?"

"Huh?"

Kate, who is infinitely more sophisticated than I, yelled from inside, "Let her in." In came the chambermaid to set mineral water on the nightstands and sweets on our pillows.

"You idiot," Kate said after the chambermaid departed. "I knew she had treats and you almost sent her away." I got pummeled with a pillow.

The next morning we ate in the Regent Brasserie. The food was good but we could have eaten for a week on the same amount of money. Afterwards we stepped out front to collect the Maui. The same car attendant stood on duty and cringed when we approached. The doorman and bellman rolled their eyes as the attendant departed to find the Maui. The concierge and receptionist peered innocently through the window. Everyone watched as the attendant repeatedly popped the clutch coming out of the lot. Stop...go...stop...go....

After dying three times, the Maui finally took pity on the attendant and made its way up the drive, welcoming us with a pleasant "Gidday" belch. The Maui stood tall in front of the marble stairs, but I could hear it breathe a sigh of relief as I climbed into the driver's seat. The concierge stepped out to wish us good-bye and, as we drove off, everyone waved at the strange Americans. The Maui saluted them with a final backfire.

The Maui purred contentedly as we drove north. We landed at the Pioneer in Paihia, a five star group of condominiums which look out on the Bay of Islands. Aside from morning runs and evening walks, the days that followed were filled with scenic boat tours, swimming pools, and shopping. It was a different side of New Zealand.

In Russell, we watched the weigh-in for a $25,000 marlin fishing contest. This was the final day of the contest and TVNZ was filming the weigh-in and awards ceremony for national release. A hundred folks gathered round the dock as a big marlin was hoisted. Ellen cajoled me through the crowd in hopes of finding an opening to get my picture near the marlin. A toothy

MC looked at the TV cameras and spoke into his microphone. "One hundred seven kilograms ladies and gentleman. That's not going to do it. Yesterday, you recall, a hundred thirty-five kilogram beauty was caught and that's going to be our winner. Yes ladies and gentlemen, $25,000 to...." Suddenly the mike went dead. I looked back and spotted Ellen tangled up in the cords, hopelessly trying to sort out which one belonged to the plug in. The MC fumed and TV people scurried about. I melted into the crowd.

Later, we traveled to Rotorua and joined the tourist crowds before the Gibson's deposited us back at Joan's house and returned to Auckland. It was a sad departure, the last time we'd see anyone in our families until we returned to the States. As Giff and Ellen rolled down the driveway, looking back and waving, the Maui belched and coughed up a final farewell plume.

BUG-EYED

Chapter 12

Kate and I pedaled into the town of Turangi twice: in late April, right before the marathon, and in mid-May. Our first stop was the day that we coasted from the Chateau to Turangi. Road signs along the Tongariro River announced, "Cliff Pool," "Red Hut Pool," "Boulder Pool," and the like. Fishing pools announced by road signs? This place, I reckoned, was going to be all right by me. A sign on the edge of town confirmed that we'd reached fishing's big time:

WELCOME TO TURANGI
TROUT FISHING CAPITOL OF THE WORLD

And trout fishing at Turangi means fly fishing, the only game on the Tongariro River. A hardware fisherman might as well look for a stretch of fishable water in Death Valley.

Fishing shops abound in Turangi; they are, in fact, essential to the local economy. One shop even stays open on Sundays, an unheard of event in New Zealand. Riches come to the shop owner who realizes that fishing knows no Sabbath, who doesn't laugh as glazey-eyed fishermen open their wallets and say, "Here, take whatever you need."

We stopped into one of the fishing shops to pick up a license and check the local fly patterns for the next day. Inside were a group of easy-talking American males. The group bounced around the shop, renting equipment, talking and laughing with a similar rhythm. A couple of them wore earrings.

The group soon discovered us and starting firing questions our way. When we mentioned Boulder, a tall, slim fellow wearing a misshapen baseball cap, interrupted. "You lived in Boulder? All right man, that's where we live! We're THE BLITZ GIRLS!" Kate was the only girl in the shop. "Yeah, we play rock and roll. You might of heard of us?" he asked hopefully.

"Sure," I said, not too convincingly. "I think I remember."

"We're touring New Zealand and Australia," he continued, eyes sparkling under the brim of his cap. "It's so hard to catch on in the States, so we decided to go for it over here. Kiwis are pretty dead, nobody likes to party. Got a few more gigs here, then we're jettin' back to Aussie." The speaker started bopping back and forth from one foot to another. "We're pretty hot in Aussie–cuttin' a record and everything."

THE BLITZ GIRLS had an hour to fish before hopping back in a van and heading for the night's gig. We wished them the best and left to walk along the Tongariro River.

An impressive number of people worked the river: a body in every pool, always a fly line in the air. Along about the start of May, spawning trout begin moving out of Lake Taupo and up the Tongariro. Fishermen follow the spawn with unbridled fanaticism. After a week without rain, anguished prayers echo down the river. Rain brings a "fresh"–the sweet smell of spawning grounds far upstream. A fresh triggers Lake Taupo trout into an upstream run and fishermen into a frenzy. Only in Turangi is cold rain greeted with smiles and slaps on the back and anticipation.

The trout in Lake Taupo are transplanted steelhead, a variety of rainbow trout that live in the sea and spawn in fresh water systems. Lake Taupo forms the trout's "sea" and the trout grow very large.

Kate and I tied flies at the motor camp, principally silly

looking things called muppets and bug-eyes that we learned about at the fishing shop. Muppets are bright orange and look like fish roe, a favorite delight of spawning trout. Bug-eyes are a nymph imitation. Both patterns include two ridiculous looking balls, links from a small silver chain, tied directly behind the hook eye. The result looks roughly like a small wooden toy with two oversized rollers attached. The proprietor assured us that these patterns caught fish. At first we balked, certain that he was pulling an old ruse on a couple of greenhorns. But the shopman persisted and, after numerous testimonials, we believed.

As we tied flies, the regulars returned from the river, checked us out, made suggestions. All lamented the lack of rain. Dave, a guide from Montana, joined us. Dave had a bushy blonde mustache and a healthy mountain appearance. His interest in our table companion, a Canadian girl, kept him at the table for an extended time and helped land some worthwhile advice. "This isn't like fishing the Bighorn," he said, referring to a river in Montana. "Here you can throw the damn tackle box at 'em, eight pound tippets, enough lead to make the nymph hit the water like a cannon ball. These aren't normal fish. I'll tell you this much—if you ain't on the bottom, you ain't fishin'."

Trout supplied dinner for many. For others, the talk of trout provided food for the soul. "Have you tried the Major Jones pool lately?"

"Lost a ten pounder today."

"I hear it may rain tomorrow. Lord knows we need it."

"Did you see that little kid pull in that seven pounder?"

"Tomorrow will be my day...."

The banter ran through me as Kate and I climbed into our sleeping bags. Outside the wind howled ferociously, almost ripping the tent from its anchors. I didn't care, I was about to step into the river of my dreams.

● ● ●

Kate and I walked an enormous chunk of the river the next day, exploring, fishing, watching others fight and land big trout. Neither of us got a touch. Above Cattle Rustler's Pool, I watched an old man work his nymph through a riffle. As I approached, he stepped slowly from the river. Then he stooped and lifted a big rainbow, maybe five pounds.

"Gidday," he said.

"Gidday. Looks like you're picking up a few there," I returned.

"Yep, got five. It's eleven though, so I think I'll go back home and have a nap." He was tall but bent, frail but life shone in his eyes.

"Where you from?" I asked.

"England. Come down to fish every year. May just buy a house and retire here someday."

"Say I'm a little new at this nymphing game," I said. "S'pose you could maybe give me a few pointers? Do you use those silly-looking muppets or bug-eyes? That's what they put me onto at the fishing shop."

"Sure, some use 'em" he answered, taking a fatherly posture. Then, indicating the end of his line, he said, "Hare and Copper–like this one here–is as good as any. Weighted, of course."

I thanked him for his help and walked up to the next pool, Hare and Copper firmly attached, confidence overflowing. Three casts later I picked up a two pound rainbow, almost as if by decree.

We talked another fisherman at the Red Hut Pool into hauling us back to town. He had four big fish. In the camp kitchen, others boasted of success or decried their misfortunes. Dave, the Montana fishing guide, told me not to get discouraged, "Takes everybody a few days to get onto it. Ya gotta pay your dues."

At that point we didn't have a few days; the marathon was less than a week away. I agonized over departing and vowed to return. A day on the river, however, satisfied Kate's fishing interest. Fishing became a bone of contention as we biked to the marathon.

"I could have just left you there," Kate said as she pedaled forward to bike alongside of me, "and you wouldn't have even missed me, would you?"

"Sure I would have...after a few days...."

Kate didn't appreciate my stab at humor. "I tried, I had fun, but that's enough. Then I heard you talking to Dave about moving to Turangi for two months! TWO MONTHS? This is not why I came to New Zealand, to watch you fish. I'm leaving. Have fun with your stupid fish!"

She pedaled off in a huff. When I caught up in Taupo, I found Kate engrossed in "her" new pastime, knitting. Typically self-starting, Kate had stopped into the library, copied a few pages about casting on and stitches, then dropped into a wool shop for a short primer.

Knitting helped maintain Kate's sanity when we returned to Turangi. Oh yes, we did return in mid-May, after the marathon and Kate's parents' visit. Kate fought our return tooth and nail, lost, and eventually protested by not fishing–though that wasn't a great sacrifice. Instead she spent the days reading, running, or holed up at the motor camp knitting. I was a heel and knew it. The resolve of a crazed fly fisherman, however, should never be underestimated.

● ● ●

On pedaling into Turangi the second time, we found things little changed. We stopped in at my favorite fishing shop and I dropped thirty or forty dollars on wader rental, fly tying gear, and a license. At the motor camp we ran into Dave, the Montana fishing guide. I voiced my frustration at our first stop on the Tongariro and vowed success in this round. Dave repeated his earlier statement, "Just remember– if you ain't on the bottom, you ain't fishin'." He walked off muttering something about us needing a fresh to get the fish moving.

I slept fitfully that night and, at five thirty, could see no reason to continue the charade. The morning chores exercised themselves effortlessly: knife, license, boots, coffee, bathroom stop, set up the rod.... The routine had played itself out sixty or seventy times in my sleeplessness.

At six thirty I threw on my backpack, took rod in hand, and jogged off to Admiral's Pool. As I ran, dangling waders kicked me in the rear. Each breath materialized as a small puff. The promise of the sun glowed in the east, but darkness gave ground grudgingly. On the highway, bleary-eyed fishermen drove past, turned around to look at me, then shook their heads.

It was about a two mile run to Admiral's Pool. If justice prevails in the world, I reckoned, my first fish will certainly go over ten pounds. I hoped to arrive before anyone else, but no such luck; two wetliners worked the pool as I struggled into my waders.

Two hours later...no fish...not a whisper. A Maori stepped into the pool and caught two big trout. "Try a small dry fly," he said. A what? Everyone knows that the fish are only hitting nymphs or wet flies. "A small dry fly," he repeated. I did and caught a two pounder. The Maori grinned.

In three days I had little else to cheer about. Neverfail Pool failed me. In Kamahi Pool, I spotted three big fish, deep. If you ain't on the bottom, you ain't fishin', he says, does he. I tied on two heavily leaded nymphs, then added a nice hunk of split shot for good measure. The casts that didn't plunk off the back of my head splashed down like an Apollo landing. Yet the fish didn't move. Nor did they strike.

One day Kate joined me for lunch and we decided to bike out to the Tongariro Fish Hatchery, where a kids' fishing day was underway. Beaming kids passed as we walked towards the frothing concrete pool. Each proudly carried their catch on a grass stringer.

I carried my rod as I planned to try the Birch Pool after our hatchery visit. A lad stopped me, "Hey mister! They won't allow you to use your own pole." Thanks kid.

A moment later, we ran smack into the shopman from the fishing store. He surveyed my rod and waders, looked to the kids' fishing pool, then commented wryly, "My God, is it that bad on the river today?"

Kate doubled over in laughter as I turned beet red. I could read her mind–maybe there is justice for my sacrifice.

I escaped into the visitors' center where old photos spoke of past glory days. One picture showed a fisherman with seventy-eight trout, all big. Another showed a bloke with ten fish, each over ten pounds.

And me with little yet and no improvement by the end of the day. I biked back to the motor camp at dusk, rod flailing in front of me. Some of the same fishers who'd seen my early morning run drove past and again shook their heads.

● ● ●

In the evenings at the motorcamp, I added my laments to the others whom luck had sidestepped. We all cried for rain and a new fresh to get the fish moving.

After my second less-than-successful day, I talked with a fishing guide from Auckland. Tony was stocky, like a pitbull, with black hair and a bushy mustache, big jowls, and an olive complexion. I'm not sure of Tony's last name, but his middle name must have been "TimeBomb." Tony was half Italian, half Iranian. By his own reckoning, he was the only guide in New Zealand who spoke Farsi.

"I get all the rich oil bastards from the Middle East," he told me. "I never advertise. I'm the only one who can talk to them, eh? They find me. And when those boys come it's the Chateau, not this dumpy camp."

Tony's clients had departed and he planned some non-professional fishing on the Tongariro's upper pools in the morning. He invited me along.

Sometime that night the rain started. Fisherman and fish heard the noise overhead and neither slept; a fresh was in the making.

We left camp at six. Tony raged about his latest clients, a man and his son. "Two days with that little bastard—never had a rod in his hand before. I needed that like a hole in the head, eh?"

Five fishermen waited in the rain as we approached the Whitikau Pool. At the first hint of light they stepped into the pool, one-by-one, and started moving slowly upstream. For ten minutes Tony mumbled that the fishermen weren't moving fast enough. Finally he stepped into the water and waved his hands, shooing them along. "Hey, the rules say that you must move THROUGH the pool. The rest of us want a chance."

The "rest of us" consisted only of Tony and me and, as it wasn't even light yet, I was in no hurry.

The man in the lead answered, "Listen, I was the first one here. That gives me the right to move through any way I please on the first pass."

"But you MUST move, you bastard, the rest of us want to get in."

A second man spoke. "Sit down and wait, asshole. If you want in first, then get up earlier and get here. We've been waiting a half hour."

I sat on shore in wonderment, watching the exchange get increasingly ugly. TimeBomb grabbed his rod. "Come on Scott, let's go in."

"No thanks, Tony, I can wait," I returned. "I think I'll just sit here and watch for a few minutes."

Tony plowed into the bottom of the pool and began to cast angrily. The other fishermen stood about eight or ten feet apart, but Tony stood back-to-back with his neighbor. Tony cast left-handed, his neighbor right-handed. Soon the two were touching and, as he cast, Tony physically assisted the other fisherman upstream. "Hey you stupid asshole, quit pushing me."

"Who are you calling..."

I was in the water fishing by this time and, just as a shoving match commenced, I hooked up with Tony. Everything stopped as he untangled our lines, but five minutes later the back-to-back waltz started anew. Again I hooked up with Tony. He muttered to himself–something, I think, comparing me with the kid from the previous days. After the third hookup, TimeBomb exploded. "Listen Scott! You organize with me, I'll organize with him, and we'll all be happy, eh?"

My nerves were shot. Aside from the near fights, I'd never fished in a picket fence before, and in a lefty's pool to boot.

Tony stopped part way through the rotation. The first man in had exited the short pool and returned to the bottom to find no room. "Hey idiot," he hollered at Tony, "KEEP MOVING!"

"I'm just answering you back, Mister," TimeBomb shouted with a sneer. "How does it feel to have to wait? Not so good when your out on the bank, eh?"

"Why you stupid asshole!" The man yelled back. "First you bitch and whine, then you start pushing me mate up the stream. Why don't you get the hell out of here!"

Who's in charge? A North Island brown trout gives Scott a workout.

I abandoned my position in line and climbed out on shore. Contact fly fishing is not my bag.

Along about then, Tony hooked into a good fish and the altercation ended. Line ripped off the reel as the trout ran downstream into heavy water. Tony pursued to the pool fifty meters below.

"Maybe that will improve his disposition," I remarked to the others, hoping to distance myself from TimeBomb.

Soon Tony returned with his fish, a beautiful five pound hen rainbow, and sat with me on the bank to plead his case. I just shook my head. Grown men acting like three-year-olds; this was an ugly side of fly fishing I'd never seen.

The tension eased a bit after that. The rain continued to fall as lines rhythmically flew upstream, snapped straight, then fell like oars on a scull. And the fish started to bite. In the next two hours, fifteen fish over five pounds fell to the nymphers, the biggest nine pounds. I hooked into two monsters; one broke me off immediately. I followed the other through rapids to the pool below. After a ten minute battle I had the fish to shore, but a last surge snapped my trace. I collapsed on a rock and wanted to cry.

On the drive back, Tony continued to relive the argument. "They get mad, I get mad, and then we just start going at each other. It is all stupid, eh? Luckily, I always cool down first in these things. I'm big enough to let him go on thinking he's right and we don't get in a big fight."

Bullshit, TimeBomb.

The following morning brought more rain and heavy withdrawal. Kate and I had to depart. We had a date to keep with Gavin and Sasha, tramping friends from the South Island. Besides, I couldn't ask Kate to spend another day sitting at the motor camp.

A final stop at the fishing shop didn't ease my pain. "Big fresh coming down, mate," the shopman said. "They'll be running again today. Boy is the fishing gonna be good!"

I winced.... We pedaled north in the rain.

● ● ●

Gavin and Sasha met us at Lake Rotoiti, near Rotorua, where they had access to a comfortable bach on the lake's edge. Months before, while tramping in the Caples Valley near Queenstown, Gavin and Sasha had invited us to spend a few days at the bach relaxing and fishing.

When we pedaled up to the small cottage, Gavin stood outside replacing the line on his fly reel. Gav greeted us heartily. He is of medium height, slim, with handsome, chiseled features that strongly hint of his South African homeland. Gav wore a plaid wool shirt, sweat pants, and leather sandals. Shortly, Sasha returned from a walk. Sasha is fit and feminine, has long golden hair, vibrant eyes, and a smile that needs no coaxing. Sash wore a pink wool jersey, which she'd knitted, and jeans.

Soon the wine and conversation flowed. We relived adventures since our last meeting and talked of the marathon. Sasha had also run the marathon, her first, in 3:25!

Eventually the conversation became nationalistic. Kate and I recited our list of Kiwi grievances: lack of variety in food and consumer goods, backwards bush ethics.... Sasha jumped on us about Americans always thinking they're superior, playing ruler to the rest of the world, and so on. Back and forth we went, in good humor, warmed by the wine.

"Just because we're small, America thinks it can kick us around," Sasha lamented. "Even worse, the Aussie's treat us like their little brothers. That makes me so mad!" She shook her head in disgust. "Everybody's always picking on us."

"Picking on you?" Kate exclaimed, almost coming out of her chair. "Try being American. People are always telling us, 'You're too big, you're too rich, you're stuck up....'"

"We get an earful!" I took up the charge. "We're just lucky we pass as Canadians sometimes so we don't have to listen to that abuse."

Gavin, who quietly listened through most of this good- natured belly-aching, took a long pull on his pipe and sat forward. "If you think you catch a lot of heat, try being a white, middle class South African."

Sasha, Kate, and I looked at each other and cracked up. Gav had a point.

We lazed around the next morning until Sasha departed for Auckland and work. Then Gav, Kate, and I loaded the fishing gear in the car and headed for the Horomanga River. The Horomanga runs out of the western side of Urewara National Park and dumps into the Rangitaiki River. The Horomanga doesn't hold much of a native trout population, but it is a spawning ground for Rangitaiki trout. There wasn't a fisherman within fifty kilometers, no mad Italian/Iranians, no picket fence of casters–just the river, the rod, and a cool breeze.

For the most part, the Horomanga wasn't more than a foot deep. Gavin lost one nice fish almost as soon as we started, and soon lost another. Kate and I traded off with a pair of borrowed chest waders. I took three small trout. Finally I hooked into a three and a half pound rainbow that danced across the stream before succumbing to Gavin's net.

On the way to lunch, Gavin missed another fish. He kicked himself mercilessly for being slow on the strike. Gav felt a bit frustrated about being out-fished by a Yank, though I certainly didn't needle him...much.

After lunch we crossed the highway and started upstream. I watched Kate fish a nymph while Gavin worked a side channel. Suddenly Gav whooped! At once the water in front of him exploded, his pole bent double, and he set his feet as if in a tug-of-war. The side stream was only fifteen feet wide. An angry trout shot straight across the top of the water and right up onto dry land! For a moment, time stopped. The fish was magnificent. Then the trout looked down, realized its embarrassing predicament, and flopped back into the water.

The giant submerged and flew past Gav going downstream. "WHAT THE HELL AM I GOING TO DO?" Gav yelled. "SHIT! I KNOW WE'RE GONNA LOSE HIM!" With one hand Gav ripped the net from his side and tossed it into the stream. I raced to retrieve the net as Gav stumbled downstream. By now, the fish was thirty meters below us in the heavy current of the main channel. Every time Gav tried to hold the monster, more line just zipped off the reel.

Kate and I hit the shore running. Two hundred meters downstream I finally got in front of the fish and climbed into the water. Gav tried to work the fish to the bank, but one glimpse of me sent the monster back into the current and off on another tear. A hundred meters further along I climbed in again, this time at a small backwash. Gav steered the fish towards my submerged net. Slowly the tail and dorsal fin became visible and I lunged. "I GOT HIM!" I screamed, lifting the heavy fish from the stream.

Then the net broke.

Everything plummeted into the water, including me. I landed on my knees, dove for the net, grabbed both sides and shoveled the entire wet mess, fish and all, skyward. We landed in a heap on shore. Gav and Kate were soon on top the pile laughing and shouting.

Gav beamed. "God is it a trophy? Is it? Do you think it's a trophy?" A hundred times he asked. The deliar told the story later that night: seven and a half pounds of mouth-watering trout.

● ● ●

Kate and I fished another day with Gavin, with a bit less excitement, then got ready to move on. Joan and John, our Canadian biking friends from Rotorua, had signed us up for the final two weeks of the kiwifruit picking in Te Puke. May holidays were just ending and we would fill jobs vacated by the local school kids. The orchardist expected us the next day.

We loaded up and said our thanks. Gavin took my backpack and some extra gear that we wouldn't be using for a while. He planned on staying at the bach for some quiet time before returning to the fast pace of Auckland. "No fishing today," Gav claimed. "I'm just going to read, relax, and gather my thoughts."

Gav's rod, however, waited in the corner, assembled, ready, and half-hidden. Kate and I both laughed as pedaled away from the bach. Kate guessed Gav would be fishing within the hour. I gave him twenty minutes.

WHAT'S THE GUTS?

Chapter 13

The ride away from Gav's bach, past Okere Falls, and down to Paengaroa was mostly easy and uncrowded. Outside Te Puke, however, a stream of cars poured onto the road. Closer inspection revealed another unlikely sight: a metallic slice of kiwifruit that must have stood four stories high. Beside the enormous kiwi was a visitors' center. Golf carts, made up to look like the fuzzy fruit, carried tourists through a small orchard nearby.

New Zealand produced almost seventy percent of the world's kiwifruit in 1985. The majority of that was grown in the area around Te Puke. Te Puke's mild, moist climate and volcanic soils are perfect for the kiwi.

With the harvest come the pickers, mostly itinerants like Kate and I. The town's population of six thousand almost doubles during the month of May. John and Joan, the Canadian bikers we met in Rotorua, arranged the job for us. They'd been picking for the three weeks since the marathon. Only two weeks of the harvest remained. That suited Kate and I fine. In two weeks we could rejuvenate our finances, work on the bikes, and gather momentum for our impending pedal to the Coromandel Peninsula.

We rode through town, then turned up a country lane into the orchards. Everything turned deep green. Tall shelterbelt trees cordoned off huge blocks of land. Pallets, bins, and shiny tractors sat in the yards next to corrugated metal sheds. Small drives led to beautiful houses. Out front, fancy signs with script writing announced the names of the orchardists. Below hung hand-painted signs which proclaimed, "Pickers wanted" or "No help needed." Broken kiwifruit lay rotting in the road. And everywhere were the kiwi vines, held aloft by wooden supports, row after row after row.

Ahead, the road suddenly filled with the approach of a small, green tank. The tank swerved into the gravel opposite us and out jumped Joan and John. John yelled, "Howdy mates!" and the four of us exchanged excited hugs. Three weeks in the orchard hadn't changed their appearances. John wore hiking shoes, faded sweats, and a blue bunting pullover with two patches: a Canadian maple leaf and one that said "Sunshine," where he taught telemark skiing. John was slim and blond; the beard that surrounded his smile hinted at a red. Joan wore jeans and a Beaver canoe t-shirt. Her long, dark hair was brushed back from a face that radiated health and vibrancy. Joan's voice carried a tinge of Canadian brogue.

We stood in the middle of the road laughing and joking while Joan and John raved about hot tubs, swimming pools, and fishing on The Boss's forty foot boat. "And to top it all off," Joan exclaimed, "we get the NIVA!"

"Niva?" we asked dumbly.

"Not Niva...NIVA!" John said NIVA! like a basketball announcer introducing the star player. "It's a Russian four wheel drive. Ain't she a beaut'?" John ran his hand lovingly along the top of the vehicle.

I didn't even know Russians made cars. I would soon learn, however. The Russians had designed the NIVA! in the Sherman tank tradition. Shocks and seat padding had been left out–biking on washboard was cushy in comparison with taking the NIVA! into town. The car required, no, demanded, two people aboard. It took that much muscle to depress the accelerator and fight with the steering wheel.

Lord, how we would grow to love that car.

"One thing," John warned us, "The Boss drinks Lion or DB beer. He thinks Waikato is 'rotgut river sludge!' We told him that you're the ones that introduced us to Waikato, so your standing is already in question."

Joan and John gave us directions to the orchard, then piled back into the tank and sped off with a cry of "NIVA! RULES!"

● ● ●

We pedaled a couple more kilometers through the orchards and then turned up a single lane drive. Kiwi vines pressed up to the drive on one side, shelterbelt trees on the other. A nice house, white with a big deck, sat at the end of the pavement. Behind that was a two-story metal shed.

We met The Boss and The Bosslady in the house. He was a big fellow (at least in the stomach area), with gray hair (a bit thin), ruddy cheeks, and a jagged smile. The Boss grunted a lot and acted surly but was a pussycat at heart. The Bosslady was slim, with white hair, and quiet. She smiled a lot. For a month every year these two opened their house to a motley, rag-tag group of international pickers.

The Boss and Bosslady jumped into kiwi at the right time. In the 1950's, some far-sighted marketeer changed the fruit's name from Chinese gooseberry to kiwi. The industry hasn't looked back since. Big money has been made in kiwifruit in the last fifteen years, witness the rapid conversion of dairy farms to kiwi orchards.

Kate and I moved on to meet the crew, self-dubbed the "International A-team." We found David and Andrew, the POMEs (Prisoners Of Mother England), in the hot tub. David was tall and round, Andrew slim and wiry. Both had pale skin and thin mustaches. The POMEs were a couple of overgrown kids looking for a good time. As Andrew said, "We're not travelers or students, just a coupla' thugs from Birming'am."

David concurred, "Yep, that's us, just a coupla' 'ooligans."

In sharp contrast to the POMEs were the Israeli's, Hanna and Oded. Hanna had dark, kinky hair and a pleasant smile. Oded was tall and strong, clean-shaven with close-cropped hair. "Dedi," as we were fond of calling him, always looked like a military man on leave. Hanna and Dedi understood close living and community work; they lived in a kibbutz in Israel.

Doug, a Californian, sat in the living room with his feet up. Doug was filling the void of his football fetish with World Cup Rugby. He was the only A-team member who could–or wanted to–keep up with the POMEs' nighttime escapades.

In the kitchen preparing dinner were Yoshiko, a pretty biker from Japan, and round Birgette from Germany (the Pomes liked to call her "Beergut"). Finally, there was Rolf; we were always forgetting Rolf, the semi-nerdish Austrian with ultra-short hair and John Denver glasses.

That, along with Joan and John, rounded out the International A-team. We were the roughest, toughest bunch of pickers and packers ever assembled in Te Puke. And we were illegal, all but one.

The kiwifruit harvest survives on itinerant labor. Our orchard was no different than any other. Cries ring out that the illegals steal jobs that rightfully belong to unemployed Kiwis. There's a problem, however. The unemployed Kiwis might live hundreds of kilometers from the orchards. Few wish to leave their homes and families for six weeks worth of work and life in a motor camp. Illegals step in, eager for short-term employment. The law looks the other way; the harvest is the most important thing.

Te Puke does not reach out with open arms to embrace the vital itinerant pickers. Aside from the West Coast of the South Island, Te Puke was the only place in New Zealand we were treated poorly by Kiwis. Every time we went into town, shopowners, clerks, and postal workers verbally abused us or simply ignored us. To be fair, they were descended on nightly for weeks by throngs of screaming idiots. We, on the other hand, were so tired that we just wanted to buy our goods and go home.

● ● ●

On our first night at the orchard there was a party for Joan's birthday. Beer flowed freely. The Boss offered me a DB. Remembering his distaste for Waikato, I replied, "DB? C'mon, that's beginners beer. Don't you have any Waikato?"

The Boss's face turned red as the crew joined in laughter. He yanked back the beer he was offering and bellowed, "No beer for this joker while he's in my house."

After the party, Joan, John, Kate, and I loaded into the NIVA! for the drive home. Most of the internationals stayed in the main house, but we were two kilometers up the road living next to a kiwi orchard. Joan and John bunked on ground cots in a cement floored she-ed (we quickly learned that in the kiwi industry, "shed" is pronounced "she-ed"). Two old chairs, a rough wood table, and a campstove rounded out their furnishings. Also included were a sink, a hot-water Zip for tea, and an inside flush toilet. The Boss dragged up a neighbor's caravan for Kate and I. The caravan added a guest room and a dining room to the she-ed.

We had everything two biking couples could ever hope for.

● ● ●

Thus began two weeks of kiwifruit saturation: we picked kiwis; we packed kiwis; we ate kiwis; we talked kiwis; we even slept amid the kiwis.

The days fell into a routine. Every morning at seven we struggled out of our warm sleeping bags, lit the burners, then donned wool socks and sweaters to battle the cold. Outside, the sun rose over the Bay of Plenty. From our vantage point on a hill, we saw a checkerboard of orchard blocks sparkling with dew and, farther off, green paddocks in front of blue ocean. Breakfast was usually a mug of hot chocolate and homemade muesli with–what else–kiwifruit sliced on top.

About seven forty-five we rounded up Joan and John and threw the lunch and gear into the NIVA!. The NIVA!'s rear door, which must have weighed six hundred pounds, had conveniently been designed without a catch. Two of us struggled to lift the door while a third blocked it up with a two-by-four. After loading, everyone stayed out of the car until the two-by-four was successfully extracted. Being inside meant risking permanent hearing loss.

With a cry of "NIVA! RULES!" John would spin out through the dew-soaked grass and up onto the road. Workers carrying

Kate and Joan picking Kiwifruit in TePuke

lunch pails walked along the small lane as we pulled up to the house. Most of them wore wool jerseys and long pants. We greeted each other with slaps on the back and waves. The workers slowly circled in on the packing she-ed, where one of the permanent hires usually had a tractor fired up and was already moving pallets about.

The Boss stood in front of the packing she-ed greeting people. He frequently shouted "What's the Guts?", meaning what's happening, or "You know the rules," for a set of commandments he'd supposedly laid down and we were supposed to obey. Everyday he broke the A-team into groups for the she-ed and the orchard. Around eight, The Boss started clapping his hands together and banging things. The pickers yawned and stretched, hopelessly trying to clear the cobwebs. "Let's get to it," The Boss would bellow. "C'mon, you know the rules!"

After a little more grumbling, the pickers struggled to their feet, collected white canvas aprons, slipped on cotton gloves (to protect the fruit from rough handling and fingernails), and ducked into the orchard, heads down to avoid the heavy vines.

Most mornings started dewy and cool. An endless expanse of fruit stretched before us, the vines supported by wooden frames seven feet high. Snip, snip, snip–the sound of kiwifruit stems popping off the vine. "Two handed picking," The Boss yelled our first day. Click, click, click.... The apron slowly grew heavy; the bins beckoned. Snip, snip, snip.... Time became a series of five minute cycles–pick, fill, dump, find a new position. Click, click, click.... The fruit were hard, unripe, easy to palm. Snip, snip, snip.... Hey, careful! You know what The Boss says, treat 'em like eggs. Click, click, click...snip, snip, snip.... No flats or doubles. C'mon, you know the rules! Click, click, click... Everybody else seems to be doing two to my one. Didn't I go to the bin at the same time as Doug a few minutes ago? He's there again and I'm only half full. Snip, snip, snip.... Oops, they're spilling out the top, time to dump again. Click, click....

SMOKO!

Aprons flew through the air. Tired muscles suddenly came alive. The smokers quickly rolled cigarettes. If they hurried they could smoke a couple during the break. Fifteen minutes of life–just time to grab morning tea and a biscuit back at the she-ed and doff some clothes. The sun was high now and the dew almost gone.

The Boss circulated among his serfs at smoko. "Hey, what's the guts? Pretty wet out there? Want you to go out back when you finish the block you're on. Hey Joan, you'll be inside packing 'til lunch."

The Boss got restless again about ten fifteen and started clapping, kicking garbage cans, and making guttural sounds. With a final swallow of tea, the pickers moved back to the orchard. From the she-ed came the rumble of the conveyer line grinding into action.

Snip, snip, snip.... Now the work began in earnest. Click, click, click.... Tired muscles were loose, the air warmer, the sun climbing. Snip, snip, snip.... The apron bulged almost as soon as it was dumped–the feel of a thousand golf balls wrapped around the stomach. Click, click, click.... Somebody crank that music.

Snip, snip, snip...click, click, click.... Another row done, the block almost complete. Move! Snip, snip, snip.... Bins full. Take that tractor to the she-ed. Somebody drive the other one up. Let's go! Click, click....

LUNCH!

Hop on, we'll drive in. Some folks climbed right into the fruit bins while others balanced precariously on the edge of the trailer. Everyone ducked low to avoid the dangling vines. We imagined ourselves riding in golf carts decorated to look like kiwis, just like at the Big Kiwi tourist park.

"...And on your left, ladies and gentleman, you'll see our national fruit, the kiwi. Highly skilled pickers carefully gather this docile fruit, the first step on the way to the packing she-ed and eventually your table. Thank you, that will be five dollars, please."

The half hour lunch seemed to last ten minutes. Doff more clothes and eat a sandwich. "Here's a ripe one I picked, anybody want it?" Amidst the groans, one hand always emerged. The internationals needed sustenance and kiwis were free.

Soon pallets slammed to the ground and garbage cans rolled down the drive. All right Boss–we're going, we're going.

Snip, snip, snip.... After lunch the sun stood high but still the thick vines let scant light penetrate. Click, click, click.... With both hands overhead you could come down with four of the fuzzy balls, six if inspired. Snip, snip, snip.... Eighty-six maximum without moving your feet, three hundred maximum per apron, sixteen thousand fruit per picker per day. Click, click....

SMOKO!

A kiss between couples was always frowned upon. "Hey, what's the guts? You know the rules." Old women from the she-ed, feeling their oats at afternoon tea, spoke just loud enough to be heard, "If I was only thirty years younger" or "Look at those legs," and then giggled at their wickedness.

Garbage cans whistled through the air–back to work.

Snip, snip, snip.... The final push. Thank God for World Cup Rugby. Who's playing today? Click, click, click...snip, snip, snip.... Will somebody tell those POMEs to speak English so we can understand them. Click, click, click.... Damn it! Who's throwing fruit? Snip, snip, snip.... Gotta finish this last bin before we call it a day. Click, click, click.... Quitcherbitchin', you know the rules! Snip, snip, snip.... We didn't even make a dent today. Look at all of 'em. Tomorrow, we'll worry about them tomorrow. Click, click....

THAT'S IT!

Day's end meant a quick shower to clean off the grime, then a short ride home in the NIVA!. Dinner was usually a hearty soup, pasta and sauce, or curried kumara and rice. Kumara is the Maori name for the local variety of mouth watering sweet potato.

After dinner and a brief wind down period, Joan and John often joined us for Waikato beer and popcorn. We relived past travels and talked of Banff, Montana, and Colorado. We became good friends during those two weeks and soon confided our fears and dreams. Most often we discussed the strains associated with constant companionship and the uncertain future waiting at the end of our travels.

Later, we returned to our own homes to read, write letters, and work on journals. Outside the Southern Cross rose in the night sky, and cool Bay of Plenty air fell over the orchards.

● ● ●

Our relationship took a beating during the weeks of kiwifruit picking. Kate and I were on shaky ground and rapidly heading for a fall. Nothing we did together worked. In truth, we were happy to be separated for most of the day: Kate in the packing she-ed, me in the orchard. Our psyches had become too closely intertwined. We were sensitive to every detail of each others' personality, every bad habit, every quirk. Almost nightly we had an argument that would leave Kate crying and me fighting mad. Tears frequently had to be dried in mid-drop when John or Joan popped their head into the caravan. Having them around was a great help, almost like built-in group therapy, as they understood the problems we were going through.

Kate and I tolerated each other through the weeks of kiwifruit picking. We were not happy to be together and frequently spoke of biking separately for a few weeks after the picking was over.

● ● ●

. The Boss sent everybody into the orchards one day because of approaching rain. Wet kiwis can't be packed, so we needed a stockpile of dry fruit. For two days after that it rained and everyone moved into the she-ed.

The she-ed is the antithesis to the orchard: noisy, fast, continual. Workers and machines team to sort and pack the fruit. First comes the grader, a mind-scrambling machine where an endless stream of kiwis roll over and over while graders frantically search for imperfections. Fruit with stems, water spots, or almost any small blemish are deemed unsuitable for export. Some of the rejects make it to local market, some are made into wine. Most rot. The graders were always easy to spot at smoko–they were the ones rubbing their eyes and stumbling into each other.

Farther along the line, a machine weighs and sorts the fruit, then jounces them down rubber belts to waiting packers. Each packer handles different size fruit: 27,33,...46; the numbers describe how many fruit fit into a tray. Tuckers cover the fruit, crease the cellophane into the side of the trays, slap a cardboard lid on top, then stack the finished trays thirty high, six per level, on pallets. Loaders secure the finished pallets with strapping tape and wheel them into cold storage. Kiwifruit are a distributors dream. Picked hard, they don't ripen if held at zero degrees Celsius. Thus they can be stored through the year and released to meet market demands.

All this, of course, is how the she-ed is supposed to work. In practice, there were problems and comedies. Graders with bad aim frequently missed the waste bins and kiwis skittered across the floor. Bushels of thirty-nines suddenly appeared, leaving the thirty-nine packer standing knee-deep in fruit and crying for help. Tuckers jumped back and forth between packing lines; soon trays piled toward the ceiling. As the trays teetered and made ready for a swan dive to the floor, someone leapt to the rescue. All around workers cheered.

The Boss moved through the she-ed confidently, almost arrogantly. He shifted people around, gave a hand now and again, and toyed with the speed on the conveyer belt. Mostly, though, The Boss simply looked down from above and smiled. The Bosslady, meanwhile, bustled about, pulling trays for quality checks. On the best days, she passed out pay and then we smiled.

● ● ●

Friday brought an end to the long week. Funny how tough it was to actually have to work again. Still, our timing was impeccable; by showing up for the last two weeks of picking, we got to partake in all the season-ending parties. The first was in town at Roz's. Roz, a local, was the head grader in the she-ed, though she could as easily been one of Santa's elves.

As the International A-team worked its way through a fine meal and good Kiwi wines, the conversation turned to Israel and Hanna and Oded. Everyone wanted to know how it felt living under the constant threat of Arab attack. "Sure we think of it," Dedi said, sitting back from the table, "but our lives continue." Dedi gestured towards me. "You tell us that not everyone gets shot in the States everyday, that we just hear the bad news. It is the same for us. Months go by where nothing happens, but you do not hear of that."

"What about being in the military?" Kate asked. "Isn't it mandatory?"

Dedi spoke philosophically as he rolled a post-meal smoke. "I spent my time in the military, as every young Israeli must. If I had to choose, of course I would not have done it. I do not desire war. But if our country is to be strong and safe, we must learn to defend ourselves. It is our duty."

The group separated after dinner, some working on the dishes, some making coffee and tea, others preparing dessert. Later, we moved into the living room. The talk of Israel continued, directed particularly towards Hanna and Oded's kibbutz. A kibbutz is a collective farm, but even more, it is a philosophy of communal social order. The kibbutz system started in Israel in the early

1900's to provide a safe, structured society where Jews could practice their religion, raise families, and grow crops.

"We love the kibbutz," Hanna said as she showed us pictures of an irrigation project. "We can talk about it for hours, so you must stop us if you are bored."

Dedi was in charge of peanut farming for the kibbutz, something he knew nothing about when he started. The fruits of individual labor go to the kibbutz and, in return, kibbutz members receive the bounty of the group. Each family has a small house, food, and pocket money. Children are cared for en-masse, a system which builds a sense of bonding between young kibbutzniks. The kibbutz frequently sends members abroad–like Hanna and Oded–in hopes of expanding the groups' horizons. "Next time," Hanna said as she reached out to feel the warmth of the fire, "it will be someone else's turn."

Hanna originally lived at a nearby kibbutz before Oded spirited her away. I asked Dedi what he would do if he ever desired to live at a different kibbutz. "It is never done," he said, as if shocked by the idea. "Only through marriage. I have a commitment to four hundred fifty people in my kibbutz, like a marriage commitment. I could never leave."

Hanna and Oded invited us to come live and work with them for a year. "Come visit five, ten, twenty years from now. It doesn't matter. We will be there."

• • •

Sunday was a busy day–books, letters, knitting–all in preparation for The Boss's season ending blowout at Mount Maunganui. Rumor had it that the annual Chinese dinner might get a bit out of hand; we were all expectant. The NIVA! delivered John, Joan, Kate, and I to the gala in style. We stepped out in our least holey t-shirts and our cleanest shorts and sweatpants. With the crowd gathered and the first beers tossed back, the food arrived. The pickers mostly sat together which, in an eating sense, proved to be a major mistake. Fried rice, sweet and sour pork, and chop suey all seemed to sublime straight into midair.

Lack of food, however, did not mean lack of drink. The crowd floated freely about on an ocean of wine and beer. Soon old women, loosened from their inhibitions, kissed the cheeks of the young pickers they admired. The Bosslady crawled under the table, only coming up long enough to babble, "I'm sorry, I'm really sorry."

Following dinner, the time came for the dirty laundry to be trotted out. The first to catch it was Doug, the Californian. Doug had brown hair, glasses, a sharp wit, and an infectious smile. His shoes had been pinched while he and the POMEs partied and danced at the local pub. We'd riddled him about his shoes for days and this night was no different. Rather than taking it lying down, Doug surprised us all by jumping up and pulling out a harmonica. He started pounding out some sweet blues and soon everybody was clapping and yelling, "YEA, DO IT DOUG!" Then Doug got wound up and laid out some soul searching vocals to accompany his vibrating harmonica:

I got those kiwifruit picking blues....
I got those kiwifruit picking blues....
and right now you know the big news....
somebody done run off with my shoes....

The crowd hit the floor and applause hit the roof. But Doug was just getting warmed up. There were more verses– something for every memorable event of the past weeks. In between each line, Doug wailed on the harmonica, dipping down at the waist, face contorted, veins on his neck standing out. When Doug wound down with a final, "I got those kiwifruit picking ba-loo-ooz!", the crowd broke into raucous applause. The few diners not with our party looked amongst each other and wondered if the night might better have been spent at home.

● ● ●

No one moved the morning after the party. Even if anyone felt physically able, it didn't matter. The orchards dripped with the previous night's rain. The A-team convened at noon and picked for a half day after things dried out a bit.

Tuesday was Hanna and Oded's last day, so we gathered at Roz's again for a massive potluck. Aside from Rolf, it was the first official departure of an A-teamer. We all knew that things were rapidly winding down. It had been quiet picking the past few days, almost deathly quiet after the big party as everyone considered where their travels would take them next.

Two rugby players from the Arizona Wildcats, house guests for Roz, showed up and joined the party. They were on a rugby tour playing club teams throughout the North Island. Neither displayed much of an appreciation for New Zealand and they reminded Kate and me of how far removed we'd become from life at home. We talked rugby, kiwifruit, and biking, finding little common ground, then finally hit on Vegemite. Vegemite is a national passion in both New Zealand and Australia, much like peanut butter in the States. It has the consistency and taste of axle grease. "God awful stuff," one of Arizona players groaned. "Every time one of us screws up in practice, the punishment is to eat a slice of bread with Vegemite. Some of the guys can't keep it down."

● ● ●

The Boss exuded good will on curtain call day. The harvest was done and soon the profits could be counted. We were all in the she-ed by mid-afternoon and made bets on when the last kiwi would bounce down the line. It all ended at three forty-five. Brews were passed around, pictures taken, goodbyes said. The Boss took a few golf swings, bashing helpless kiwis into pulpy messes.

The following morning we loaded Joan and John, and their bikes and gear, into the NIVA! to give them a head start away from Te Puke. They were nervous. Five weeks had passed since they last biked. Also, they were starting south just as the jaws of winter were about to close on the North Island. Kate and I, on the other hand, planned to pedal north, to the Coromandel Peninsula.

We ate dinner at The Boss's house our final night at the orchard. Dinner consisted of roast hogget, spuds, kumara, cauliflower, and parsnip. For dessert, there was pavlova topped with kiwifruit. The kiwis weren't all ripe, much to The Boss's chagrin.

GOOOOD BUZZZZ!

Chapter 14

Kiwifruit season was done, Joan and John were gone, the NIVA! was back home, and we found ourselves alone with the bikes again. Between Kate's parents' visit and fruit picking, we'd only done a week's worth of serious biking in the month since the marathon. The easy life disagreed with us. I'd gained ten pounds, all around the belly, and felt like an over-ripe kiwifruit ready to burst. Kate remained her usual slim self, but felt a bit hesitant about readjusting to the rigors of the road.

Still the thought of traveling again excited us. We happily dusted off our bikes, cleaned and lubed the drivetrains, adjusted the brakes, trued the wheels. Gear fell into familiar nooks in the panniers, and soon we were ready.

After a thorough cleaning of the she-ed and caravan, we closed up shop and rode down the hill to bid our farewells. The Boss and Bosslady looked exhausted but happy to have another picking season done. Sanity stood a reasonable chance of returning to the house now that the pickers were trickling away.

We made a final stop, at the POMEs' caravan, before pedaling out. The thugs were sleeping off a night of recreation and only grunted when I banged on the door. Inside, Andrew slept with his mouth agape; Dave was wrapped in a Union Jack. A toxic aroma emanated from the caravan. I quickly rapped each of them on the noggin and said goodbye. Neither stirred.

• • •

Kate and I rode happily away from the orchard, testing old muscles and reacquainting ourselves with the bikes. The sky was cloudless, the sun bright. The air, however, held a coolness that would not disappear with the morning. The first day of winter was only fifteen days away.

I stopped into Tauranga to pick up some riding gloves; mine had disappeared during our weeks of inactivity. Kate rode on to get a head start towards Matamata. Earlier we called Stephen and Rachel, friends we'd made on the South Island, and Stephen expected us at his two o'clock rugby match.

When the bike shop owner found out our destination, he said, "Matamata, mate? You're gonna hate The Hill." My map showed "The Hill" to be the Kaimai Range. I wasn't particularly concerned about making it to the top, we'd long since passed that point. Rather, I wondered about making it to Matamata on time. Combined with underused muscles and ninety-plus kilometers from the orchard, The Hill might eliminate our chance to see Stephen's rugby match.

I pedaled out of town, then stopped at a roadside 4-Square grocery shop to pick up a morning snack. "Is that the lot?" the shopkeeper asked.

"Yep."

He rang up the goods and said, "One dollar, thank you."

"Have you seen another biker come by in the last half hour or so?" I said as I paid.

"Ta," the shopkeeper said, accepting the money. Then, looking up from the cash register, he asked, "Blonde-haired lass?"

Not my Kate, she's a brunette. "Was she wearing a yellow helmet?"

"Rightio, mate. Blonde-haired lass with a yellow helmet. Stopped through on about twenty minutes ago. Told her I reckoned she was gonna hate The Hill and that maybe I could find her a lift to the top."

It was Kate all right. The months of constant outdoor living had bleached her hair until people thought of her as a blonde. The change took place so gradually, I hadn't even noticed.

I worked myself up the first long section of The Hill before catching the blonde. A local had stopped and asked Kate if she wanted to throw her bike in the back of his ute for a ride up The Hill. Everyone seemed worried about our welfare this day. Admittedly, the last vestiges of the summer bike travelers had long since disappeared and we probably looked a bit odd. We laughed at this sudden epidemic of maternal instincts and continued to climb The Hill. Crest after crest fell to our pedaling, but soon it was obvious we'd have to give Stephen's rugby match a miss.

A van passed and pulled to a stop up the road. A stout, smiling bloke climbed out and waited. His face was square, its features strong. As I pedaled up he yelled, "Gidday! How ya goin', bro? Saw you working your way up The Hill and thought you might like a lift the rest of the way. Name's John." John wore a sweatshirt with the emblem of a Christian camp across the chest. His smile and goodwill were downright contagious.

After introducing myself, I said I wasn't sure about the ride and would ask Kate when she arrived. Would she feel guilty? Would I feel guilty? We were there to bike, not to get toted around. Yet in a couple of instances, the moment was right. This was to be one of those moments.

We crammed the bikes into the van, met John's wife, Linda, and set off to complete The Hill. John and Linda worked in Hodderville at a Salvation Army home for kids with drug problems. "Hey, brother," John said, an idea forming, "have you got wet suits along?" C'mon John, wet suits? "Doesn't matter. I'm taking the lads canoeing down the Wanganui River tomorrow. We got heaps of gear. How'd you like to join us?"

How? We'd been dying to canoe the Wanganui. Now out of the blue, after knowing us for five minutes, John presents the idea on a silver platter. "You bet we'll go!"

The ride to the summit took about ten minutes, an hour if we'd biked. A motorcyclist sat on the railing at the summit overlook. "Looks like the local Filthy Few are out today," John lamented. Snow-covered Mount Ruapehu shimmered far to the south, endless green dairy land spread out below, but the biker dominated the scene. Twenty stones of him struggled against torn leather riding pants and a jean jacket which bore the colors of the Filthy Few. A dusty leather hat covered his matted tresses and oily boots anchored his bulk. His gloves had no fingers, his coat no arms. Tattoos graced both massive biceps. Around him were greasy underlings and miscellaneous women.

We unloaded the bikes right in front of their choppers. The biker stood up from the rail and crossed his arms on his massive stomach. The underlings glanced among themselves.

John drove off.

"Gidday," I said.

Surprisingly, he replied. "Where youse headed on those puny bikes?"

"Matamata...well...er...gidday."

• • •

We coasted into Matamata in time for the second half of Stephen's rugby match. I don't remember who won. What I do remember is that Stephen wasn't playing and I couldn't understand why. To see Stephen is to know what I'm talking about. He's a big bloke, probably six foot four, two hundred thirty pounds. And strong. Every inch of him screams, "Rugby!"

After the match Kate and I biked five kilometers back to Stephen's dairy farm, met the family, and cleaned up. Later Stephen took us to the rugby club to find Rachel and join in the post-game activities. Rachel hadn't changed a lick since the enjoyable nights we'd spent together on the South Island. She's robust and cheerful, with a beautiful smile, kinky auburn hair, and a fair complexion. Rachel greeted us each with a happy kiss on the cheek and suddenly we had an identity in the mass of rugby-crazed Kiwis.

Kiwis are sporting fanatics and sporting clubs are a manifestation of that fanaticism. Almost every town boasts a cricket club, rugby club, squash club, tennis club, bowling club, running club.... Clubs provide a forum for gathering to celebrate or wake. Friendships are renewed and community pride is forged over the post-competition beer.

In New Zealand, most folks participate; sports are meant for the common man and woman. Even the rugby All Blacks, New Zealand's closest brush with the hero-worship market, are unpaid amateurs. It's refreshing to tune in the network sports and hear first and foremost the results of club rugby, club netball, and club cricket–folks long out of school but still participating.

The Matamata Rugby Club was rocking on this night. We eventually took our leave and returned to the farm. Steve let Kate and I use his wonderful, warm water bed and we fell asleep dreaming of canoes, wetsuits, and whitewater.

● ● ●

"C'mon and we'll get a good feed into you before we send you down the river," Rachel said, waving us into the kitchen. And oh what a feed: roast lamb, pumpkin, kumara, silverbeet, cauliflower, and potatoes.

When we could eat no more, Rachel picked up our plates and said, "Hope you left room for some pavlova. Nana made it and you're gonna love it." She dished us a couple of big pieces. We wouldn't need to eat for the four days we'd spend on the river.

"Hey, how about a little cof' to wash that down with?"

● ● ●

Stephen and Rachel drove us to Putaruru, some thirty kilometers to the south, where Linda, from our ride in the van, picked us up in front of the post office. During the short ride, Linda explained that the Salvation Army owns a block of land at Hodderville. The land is split into a sheep ranch, several dairy farms, and a teen center. The latter was previously a boys' home, but recently redirected towards helping kids with drug and alcohol problems.

"We put the kids through six week courses that stress outdoor skills," Linda said. "The hope is that we can stretch them into new areas, help them gain new confidence in themselves, and show them that life can be exciting and fulfilling without drugs."

We were driving on a narrow road through open, rolling country. When another car approached, Linda pulled far over to let it pass. "The problems almost always involve the family. It's hard to see that you've made progress and then realize what sort of atmosphere you're sending them back to."

Houses, garages, and dormitories lined the large rugby paddock at Hodderville. The group waited; everyone eyed us without looking. A rugby ball sailed back and forth....

Then John came bursting forward to meet us. He'd lost what little hair he had when we first met, right down to the bone. The lads had been turned loose with shears and the freedom to design his coiffure. John wore a blue one-piece jumpsuit and wire-rimmed sunglasses. I thought of Chuck Yeager.

"Gidday Katie, gidday Scott!" John exclaimed. Then, turning, he yelled, "Hey you monkeys, quit mucking around and circle up. I want you to meet our two American friends that will be joining the team."

The group filed by. First came the leaders. Lyle, with silver hair, a furrowed face, and medium build, was to be the driver of the sag wagon. "Just call him Honk," John said. Honk was John's Dad. The young adult leaders, both filled with the spirit, were the go-betweens. Guy was pudgy, had short hair with a tail in back, and was just a bit too serious for the lads. Ned was the lad's man, the undeniable leader. He was a Samoan who had come to the Lord out of inner city Auckland. Ned was forever singing Christian songs. Frequently the lads sang along.

Next came the lads. The common uniform was a black wool stocking cap and wool gloves with the fingers cut out. The operative piece of vocabulary was wicked, pronounced "wick-eed!" Of the lads, three–Mark, Rodney, and Jeremiah–were at least part Maori. Mark was tall, friendly, inquisitive, and easily the most mature. Rodney was wiry and slippery. He took up Ned's habit of constantly singing but forever dawdled in hopes of gaining attention. Rodney was a constant thorn in Guy's side. Jeremiah, the thinker, often walked quietly off by himself. Next was Steve, Mr. Negative, yet he was always ready to request another song. Finally came little James, "Baldy" as the lads were fond of referring to him. James's earring, lack of brainpower, and incredible flatulence earned him the whipping post position in the group.

We piled bags, buckets, and bodies into the van. Five yellow canoes followed on a trailer. James got tapped to sit with us as we drove away from Hodderville. Soon we pulled over. "Ok, quiet down back there," John yelled from the drivers seat. "Let's have a prayer.... Lord, we just ask that you grant us a safe trip and that we have lots of fun in that glorious river you created. We ask that you help us act responsibly. Most of all we thank you for our new friends. In Jesus name we pray, Amen."

The drive took us straight south, through Tokoroa and along the west coast of Lake Taupo. Ned shouted potato chips and coke along the way. In the front, John, Honk, and Guy talked about scripture and a seven-headed serpent. James frequently reached for the window to air us out, then claimed a stinky innocence while being pelted with life jackets.

The lads soon discovered Kate and I, and questions about the States filled the van. "Have you ever been to Disneyland?"

"What about the Grand Canyon, what's that like?"

"Youse ever see a grizzly?"

"There's murders everywhere in the States, huh? I heard in New York City...."

As the evening wore on and we began to fit, the van slid into Taumarunui, where the Wanganui River meets the Ongarue River. We set up camp in the sheep-dirtied park at the confluence. No other groups joined us. For most the lure of whitewater fun diminished with the late fall cold. The lads played rugby in a nearby paddock while Kate and I went for a walk. Smoke from coal-fired furnaces blanketed the valley.

John and Honk returned to camp with fish and chips. We had a prayer and everyone hopped from foot to foot, trying to stay warm while they ate. James got yelled at for eating more than his share. Guy chased Rodney around camp for not helping with the dishes. The night was cold; the moon shone from between the clouds. We all spotted the Southern Cross, then turned in. It was six forty-five.

● ● ●

With John and the lads ready to run the Wanganui River.

The next morning we rose early. John sat alone at the picnic table, bundled against the cold, reading his Bible. Kate and I walked into town for groceries, then returned and got suited up. The wetsuits felt marvelous in the cold morning air. John gave us a pep talk about rapids and rocks and safety. We had a prayer, then climbed into the canoes and pushed off.

Kate took the stern based on her prior experience canoeing in the Quetico of Canada. She hadn't lost her skills and I was quickly tutored in the J and C strokes. "No ruddering under pain of death," she threatened.

Shortly after we put in, the Wanganui twisted and turned into a steep gorge. Wanganui National Park was created in 1986, largely to protect the Wanganui River and the unspoiled lowland forests which enclose it. The Wanganui is New Zealand's second longest river, over three hundred kilometers from the headwaters on Mount Tongariro to the ocean mouth at the city of Wanganui. Thick, emerald bush borders the river for much of its length.

Along the way are some beautiful stretches of whitewater and liberally spaced campgrounds. Road access is practically nil.

John and James led the pack through the first good white water. John's voice echoed down the gorge, "Gooood Buzzzz!" Answering whoops went up from every boat. Kate and I hit the first white water timidly, but survived. A check of our river charts showed that the big rapids would come that first day.

Rapid after rapid fell to our bow and we soon began to feel comfortable and confident. Not dry, however. With me in front we nose planted into every monster wave. Icy water shot up and out, drenching me and filling the bottom of the boat. Kate and I had only a single pair of shoes, so we wore plastic bags in hopes of keeping them dry. This setup proved to be a big success for three or four milliseconds.

Steve and Mark succumbed to a big standing wave and floated a half kilometer downstream before we could fish them out. Ned and Jeremiah got turned sideways in another stretch of big rapids and flipped. As they extracted themselves from the river bottom, Jeremiah yelled, "Wicked man! Wick-eed!"

Kate and I lost touch with the river while watching the carnage and ran smack into an enormous wall of water that filled the gunnels. Kate screamed at me not to rock the boat–the inertia of the on-board water would tumble us over. All I could do was laugh; drenched as I was, in the water or out didn't seem to make much difference. We still had a hundred meters of rapids to negotiate before the next flat. Somehow, half sunken, we worked our way in slow motion through the waves. Once to shore, we dumped our canoe out as John and James maneuvered through the last of the tough stretch. "Gooood Buzzzz!" John yelled. "Yea! Gooooood Buzzzz!"

The sun, which had been absent, came out in force as we pulled in for the day. We set up camp and dried out. Dinner was a delicious, dehydrated concoction. With only one pot and eleven hungry mouths, meals required real patience. First a hot cuppa for the crew, then the main course, then some pudding and another hot drink. Each of us had only a plastic cup and a spoon, but that was sufficient. Dinner was a two hour undertaking.

While the lads set to work on dishes, Honk busily tended his fire. The nighttime fires were Honk's pride and joy, his contribution to the group. And he was possessive about his fires: every log had its niche, every article of clothing a special pozzi for optimal drying. Never mind that they were your clothes, to dry them at Honk's fire was to give up all ownership rights. As the lone female in the group, poor Kate took the brunt of Honk's special treatment. He fussed endlessly over her.

Honk was a good man. Eight months earlier, a massive heart attack struck him and necessitated a multiple bypass. Honk looked fit enough, but still hammered down greasy fish and chips, wore few warm clothes, and lifted heavy canoes. Kate and I worried about Honk.

It was far warmer on that second night and we stayed up later. Talk around the fire turned frequently to the caving expedition planned for the end of the canoe trip. I went to bed with a gremlin gnawing at my stomach and dreamed of being trapped under a thousand tons of dirt and rock. I don't do well in small spaces.

● ● ●

In the morning we loaded the van for Honk, collected the fire-dried clothes, and set off. Kate and I opted to wear sacrificial wool socks and no shoes. At least that way we would have dry footwear at the end of the day.

I took the stern and that made Kate nervous. No worries–on day two the river more closely resembled a bath tub than a whirlpool. Still, I got plenty of free advice and even managed to learn a little. The river continued to wind through the gorge but deepened and slowed ever more as the day went on. We did hit one big stopper that held us in mid-air for what seemed like a minute before slapping us into the froth below. Gooood Buzzzz!

"RAFT UP!" John frequently called us together, sometimes to talk about a rapid ahead, usually to break out the skroggin. Skroggin is the Kiwi version of gorp; each letter in "skroggin" stands for one of the ingredients. We never made it through an entire raft-up session without hearing, "Rodney! Leave some skroggin for other people, mate!" or "James! Put some of that skroggin back, son!" We linked up, five boats abreast, hooked together by dangling legs. The folks in the outside canoes paddled us along. Even short, choppy waves bounced off the hulls of our quintamaran and sent cold spray flying.

Along the way we spotted a stag high on a bluff, and also numerous goats. Goats, the domestic variety, frequently escape into the Kiwi bush and become wild. A goat in the bush is fair game for anyone. The kids on John's last trip down the Wanganui bagged a young goat, put it in their canoe, then took it back to Hodderville in the van. The lads were all worked up about doing the same.

"GOATS! GET 'EM!" One hunt took the lads high up the gorge wall and out of sight. Suddenly the bush rumbled and two enormous boulders tumbled into the river. Fast on their heels was Rodney, also tumbling, but spared the cold plunge by a tree, which he took head on. The only good opportunity to trap a goat ended with Guy and a black billy in a standoff. The billy juked right then cut left. Guy dove face first in the mud while the goat skittered up into the bush and disappeared.

Our paddling for the day ended at the confluence of the Ohura River with the Wanganui. We unloaded at an old houseboat mooring which was used in the early nineteen hundreds by tourists coming up the river. A water fight broke out. Guy sought revenge on John, who had dumped him earlier in the day. Everyone took the plunge except for the Americans.

Our camp sat on a bluff overlooking the river. We pulled the canoes safely ashore, then made for the van to get our gear. The closest road access to the camp was a twenty minute walk through the bush. Just up from camp, the track crossed a vast swinging bridge over the Ohura. Below a five meter waterfall spanned the river. John walked with Kate and me and told about first meeting Ned, his helper, while serving food to homeless street kids in Auckland. Years later they met again, and Ned remembered John's kindness.

The afternoon slid slowly into evening. Ned and some of the lads headed for the river to try some eeling. A barefooted Jeremiah padded through the open hills behind us in a futile effort to catch up with a herd of goats. Meanwhile, the war between

Rodney and Guy continued. "Rodney! Get back here and help put up the tent!...Rodney, c'mon mate, pick up your shoes...."

Our camp sat on the site of a former Maori pa. Pas provided safe haven for the Maoris of old. They were built on high, secluded, easily defendable sites. This pa had two historic poles, one representing good, the other evil.

After dinner, everyone migrated to the fire. The moon rose and grew large. Dew began to settle out. Then Ned started to sing and the rest of us joined in:

I've got a river of life flowing out from me...
Makes the lame to walk and the blind to see...
Opens prison doors, sets the captives free...
I've got a river of life flowing out from me....

For an hour we sang, mostly fun, spiritual songs and then later "Hey Jude" and other hits from the past. John beat away at a plastic bucket; the rest of us swayed back and forth and clapped our hands. Happy, bawdy voices filled the still of the night.

Firelight illuminated the faces around the circle. Clothes dangled everywhere, shielding most of the fire's heat, but the night was warm. In a quiet spell, Honk witnessed his conversion. "I know where you all are coming from. I had a lot of problems with alcohol years ago, but then I found The Lord. The Lord removed the scourge of alcohol from me. I have given it up and he has set me free. It says in...."

The lads looked impassively about. They sang Christian songs fervently and sometimes even mumbled "Amen" and "Yes Lord" while prayers were being spoken. Yet I couldn't help but feel this was a reflection of what was expected of them.

For the first two days, the lads said little that set them apart from other teenagers. The only exception was that they all craved cigarettes. Then, as Honk wound down, Mark moved deeper into the firelit circle and said quietly, "Yeah, I was into Christianity and church and all that until I was fifteen. Then I started to go to the bars and drink and smoke pot. And youse know why? 'Cuz I like it. I mean I really like it, man. Me old lady used to always be on speed. I didn't have to go out lookin' for drugs, I'd get my drugs from her."

An uneasiness settled over the camp. Several minutes passed before the singing resumed.

• • •

The final day of the canoe trip was short and docile. Steep, bush-lined gorge continued to surround us, but the river went board flat. Speed and excitement existed only in the paddle.

Three quarters of the way to our final campsite, we stopped at a beautiful waterfall. This one, on the Waipahihi Stream, had eroded a narrow cleft twenty feet into the side of the gorge. The waterfall pounded deep within the crevice, hidden by rounded stone and dense mist. A frigid stream four feet deep flowed through the cleft. At the base of the gorge wall, the stream fanned out over flat shale before entering the Wanganui.

Here I knew I must go in. Up to this point, Kate and I had avoided the water fights and dunkings. As outsiders, no one was quite sure how to treat us, how far they could push in good fun. Growing into the group meant losing guest privileges. I heard the enemy plotting quietly, "Wick-eed man, let's throw him in the ice water." With the odds eight to one, I was definitely going in; it was only a question of how.

I opted for the offensive, grabbed John, and we tumbled into the breath-robbing water. As soon as John knew that the game was up, he flipped me like a wet rag. My body heat evaporated instantly. We shrieked hysterically as we grappled. The lads quickly joined the fracas and uncontrollable hoots mixed with the pounding of the waterfall. We swam and climbed over each other to the back of the cleft, nine goose-bumped, white-faced ice cubes. Then we gingerly shimmied up the slippery rock sides and cannonballed into the pool at the base of the waterfall.

When we emerged from the crevice, sixteen hungry eyes turned on Kate. She backed away and hid behind me. I pleaded for her life knowing that she would surely die if subjected to the frigid waters. The mob retreated and Kate was spared.

After a shivery lunch, we canoed through the final section of river, then paddled up a small tributary, the Retaruke, to our take out point. Far behind, Guy squawked at Rodney, "C'mon mate, paddle! BOTH HANDS, Rodney!" Honk pulled in at the same instant we arrived. To travel the same twelve kilometers, Honk had to return to Taumarunui, then worked his way through a couple of hours of winding backcountry roads.

We camped near Whakahoro Hut, high above the Wanganui River. Everyone hung their clothes on the fence to dry and Honk soon had a fire roaring. The rugby ball came out and was punted across the paddock. Some of the lads tried eeling. John alternately cooked and attempted to convince me that caving the next day would be good fun.

After dinner, we again joined in song around the fire. The atmosphere quickly grew festive as we played silly games like "Bizz-Buzz." The climax of all the games came when someone botched the order of noises or words and was jeered into the group's center. Typical punishments included doing a dance, performing a Maori haka, or giving a thirty second talk on the merits of toilet paper. Pitiful little James put in untold center time. He simply couldn't comprehend that in "Opens prison doors, sets the captives free" the word was "captives," not "captains." James went to the center forty-eight times for the same mistake.

One by one the lads retired to their tents. I decided to take a walk around the paddock before turning in. Cold dew quickly soaked my feet. There was no sound. The moon was full and high. A hundred meters from camp, I stopped and looked back. The enormous tree hanging over our tents cast a dark shadow. Elsewhere the paddock was brightly illuminated, even blades of grass discernable. Across the valley, dark silhouettes of trees and branches lined the ridge like cutouts from a paper shadow. Moonlight transformed wispy clouds into huge, cold snowflakes. One cloud drifted directly in front of the moon, softening but not diminishing its glow. Hungry fog rolled up the valley and licked its way slowly towards our paddock. Trees became ghosts and then disappeared.

I watched until the chill overcame me, then returned to the tent and shivered into my bag. Kate rolled sluggishly over and murmured, "How is it out there?"

Only one answer seemed appropriate, "Wick-eed!"

• • •

From the moment I'd learned about the caving expedition at the end of the trip, the knots in my stomach had multiplied. Whenever caving came up, I only grunted, smiled, and said, "Probably not." With the day for caving upon us, the knots tightened relentlessly.

John started to lay it on thick as we left the river and started for the caves. "We're going into the caves, mateys, hee-hee-ho-ho-ha-ha. Down where it's deep and dark and cold." Aside, John told Kate and I that he liked to make it sound scary to prepare the lads for the worst. By comparison the real thing hopefully wouldn't be that bad. I would have been happier without the theatrics.

Guy kept praying that the caves would be flooded. He'd already been down once while helping on a previous trip. I asked Guy if we'd have to crawl through tight places and he said, "Yep. Not only that, but we also walk through thigh deep water–cold water." Guy didn't help my enthusiasm much.

We stopped at the Outdoor Pursuits Center, on the northern end of Tongariro National Park, to find out if the caves were flooded. They weren't. The van stalled twice on the way to the caves and I was overjoyed that we'd run out of gas. We hadn't.

John told more stories around the lunch table. "We call this the Last Supper, lads...whoops, lads and lasses. One good thing, there's no wind down there. Bit like a chilly bin though, eh? Hee-hee."

Kate struggled with the decision of whether or not to go while the rest of us donned helmets, headlamps, and rain gear. I'd finally decided I could do it, almost had to go given such a golden opportunity. I quietly confided to Kate that the thought of crawling through tiny spaces and being trapped under dirt scared me to death. "That doesn't bother me at all," she said. "It's just the thought of being so wet and cold."

"Well, at least I can tell you what it was like," I said with hollow braveness. But at the last moment, Kate decided to go.

We followed a windy dirt road to an unremarkable turnout. Ten little miners filed out of the van and plunged down into the bush. We came to a stairway and, at the bottom of that, a small stream. Kate pointed to a hole that John told her we would exit the underground from. The hole was narrow and dark. A pile of rubble stood above the opening and when a pebble rolled off into the depths, no sound returned.

Packs and gear littered the ground around the exit. "Who's all this stuff belong to?" Kate whispered to me. "Cavers that didn't make it back?" Kate's voice was nervous, yet filled with excitement and anticipation. I couldn't even reply. My chest was tight, my stomach fully knotted now, and my breathing hindered by the heart in my throat.

Ten steps farther we came to another opening–the entrance. This hole was larger and we peered twenty feet down into the bowels of the earth. John stopped.

"Circle up mates," he said. "Time for the proverbial before picture. We may never have this group assembled together again, hee, hee." Nervous laughter. BING! something in my stomach snapped.

John continued. "OK lads, listen up here. The Lord made this fine cave at the beginning of creation knowing that we'd be here to enjoy it today. Now it's going to be dark Down There (BING! another snap in my stomach), so I want those of you with lights to help the others. I don't want anybody mucking around down there and going 'oooeeeooo' or like that 'cuz some people might be a bit anxious and that might bother them. I know, I was really scared the first time I went Down There."

I looked between the group and the hole and turned white. I mouthed to Kate that I couldn't go down. She nodded.

"And I don't want any of us separating," John growled. "Stay right together, you little monkeys. Last time part of the group got into a different tunnel and we were split (BING!). We got together quick enough, but none of that! All right, who's feeling a little bit nervous?"

My hand shot straight up. Kate said, "We got one here." A few giggles passed among the lads but the rest of the hands stayed down.

"C'mon, there's nothing wrong with admitting you're afraid.

Once we get Down There (BING!) you'll bloody well love it, but man I was anxious, too." Little James's hand went up. "Ok James, you'll go after me, then Scott, Kate, Steve.... Ned, you bring up the rear."

"Oh no bro'!" Theatrics. More laughter. That Ned.

"OK, let's go!" (BING!)

Why is it, I wondered, that of all our activities we aren't having a prayer before caving?

"No, no, no," my mind cried out, but still my legs took me down. Somewhere about three minutes earlier I had realized that this wasn't anything like the Lewis and Clark Caverns back in Montana. There would be no doorways, no stairways, NO LIGHTS! This was a real cave: no glitter, no commercialism, no polish that guaranteed we wouldn't have to squeeze through tiny cracks, no entry fee that said the roof wouldn't collapse.

We stopped at the bottom of the opening to receive final instructions before descending into the darkness. John had spotted me turning white back on the surface and knew that I was the only one likely to be a problem. I knelt at first, then stood up to better see the light from the surface. Honk's silhouette hung twenty feet above.

"Now I know some of you (he meant me) are going to be a bit nervous. Don't worry, we all are our first time. We'll turn out the lights when we get Down There and see what it's like in the total dark (BING! BING! my stomach was being torn to shreds), but just stay calm. If you feel tough just call out and we'll stop and let you get your wits back. You'll find she comes in waves, first you'll be OK, then she'll hit you (BING!) and you'll be scared. Just push her through and you'll be fine."

I was near fainting. I kept looking at Kate and mouthing that I couldn't do it. John watched my antics and kept feeding the group (me) words of encouragement. He even asked me to name the ceiling growths in an effort to calm me.

I could step outside my body and see what was happening: my fears, John's reactions. I know you're trying to calm me John, I thought, but it's not going to work. My rational mind no longer held control. All I could envision was being trapped under tons of dirt and rock, down farther and farther away from the light, people in front, people behind, trapped with no where to go, deserted, air running out, water rising, roofs collapsing, squeezed tighter and tighter.

John continued, "Now one other thing–this cave here is made of limestone, not lava or something volcanic. She was hollowed out by water so youse don't have to worry 'bout no earthquakes or nothing. I must admit we heard one 'crack' last time we were here (BING! BING! BING!), but it weren't nothing so don't worry. You may just be hearing your helmet hit the cave wall, 'specially in this one spot that's a particularly tight ol'' squeeze (BING! BING! BING!)."

The black hole sucked at me like a vacuum and I only wanted to escape. Inside, my ego and sense of self- preservation battled. "Thousands have been through safely, you know."

"Tough."

"All these kids are going down."

"Tough, I'm not going."

"You'll look like a coward if you don't go down."

"Tough, I'm NOT GOING!"

John stood up. "OK, let's move in."

"Th-that's it John," I stammered. "I'm going back. I can't do it." The decision made.

"C'mon, you'll be right mate."

"It's no good John. I feel terrible."

"Wait, have a look here, mate." John shined his light into the abscess. "At least see where we're going."

"Sure, great John," I said. "It's just not right for me."

Kate smiled and squeezed my arm. I gave her the headlamp and started moving past the lads towards the climb back to life. None looked at me. "Sorry guys," I said for some reason.

"You're all right mate, no worries." Guy put his hand on my shoulder as I passed.

Finally past Ned, "Don't worry about it bro." God, I just wanted out!

I scrambled fast up to the light. Five feet from the top, my heart jumped right out of my throat and I started to sob. My chest, suddenly released, sucked in heaping volumes of sweet air.

Below, I heard John trying to calm everybody. "That's all right. Some people just have an abnormal fear of caves and it's best they admit it up front." I wondered how the group reacted to my sobs–certainly not a morale booster to the first timers.

I sat at the cave entrance in tears, my body shaking. Honk stood by telling me that it was OK and not to worry. The group started off. Soon Honk and I climbed back up to the van. I felt ashamed, relieved, but mostly just plain scared. Honk put his arm around me.

Half way up the hill, Honk started to breathe hard and I worried about his heart. I pulled him up the last incline, then left him at the van and went for a walk. I had to be alone.

Honk had a biscuit and cold drink waiting for me when I returned to the van. I asked if the color had returned to my face. He laughed and answered, "You look fine, mate. You'll be right. Just don't be surprised if the others razz you a bit." We stood by the van and watched a colorful wood pigeon sitting high in a tree. I continued to rattle inside and realized I needed to walk some more and try to make sense out of something senseless. Part way down the road I looked back; Honk sat on a railing by the van, still watching the pigeon.

"Hey Honk...thanks."

"No worries mate."

● ● ●

Whoops and whistles signaled the return of the nine little miners. Kate, wet and muddy and flushed with adrenaline, pulled me aside and exclaimed, "You're lucky you didn't go. We crawled through this one spot that was only twelve inches high with a four inches of water running through it. I couldn't lift my head because it would hit the roof, but I couldn't lower it 'cuz my mouth would be in water. You would have hated it."

THE QUIET
COROMANDEL

Chapter 15

Soon after we landed back at Hodderville, Stephen arrived to take us to his dairy farm at Matamata. John looked at me kind of funny as we prepared to say good-bye. I don't think he ever really figured me out. The same guy he found pounding up The Hill and fought with under a waterfall, also failed at caving and admitted to being half the canoeist that his girlfriend was. Still, as we shook hands, John said, "Good to know you, mate."

"Good to know you, mate," I returned. I had grown to respect John and his deep convictions. His work with the lads and love of God was inspiring. Mostly I appreciated that even with those qualities, John could be just another bloke.

● ● ●

Kate and I helped Stephen and his brother Simon shift the cattle in the morning. Movable electric fences kept each mob in a small portion of the paddock. Once the cattle cropped that area low, the fence was moved, leading to a minor stampede of hungry Jerseys. Stephen orchestrated the mob shifts while Simon drove the tractor and fed silage. Kate and I carried stakes, rolled up wire, and shooed cattle.

We shifted the cattle after the frost disappeared. Frost induces stomach bloat, a potentially fatal disease. Stephen showed us an arrowhead-shaped razor used to pierce the hide and stomach of a bloated cow. Without this pressure release, the stomach grows and grows, eventually suffocating the animal. A couple of Stephen's cattle had recently suffered such a fate.

Steve and Simon owned over two hundred Jerseys. They knew each cow personally. "Number one thirty-four over there is a great milker," Simon told me. He leaned on a gate while pointing out the cattle and their identifying ear tags. "Her mother is seventy-six. That one twenty-two is a real problem, always knocking down fences. Fifty-eight is almost a family pet. Watch this, she'll come right up to me."

The younger cattle, those not milking, were fenced in a separate area from the others. In the spring most young males, called "bobbies," are put in a roadside box to be collected for the slaughter house. "That's where your veal comes from," Stephen yelled over the roar of the tractor as we rode back to the house. "Bloke picks 'em up every day during calving and gives us credit. We might hang on to a bobby or two, but with artificial insemination, we don't really need any bulls. Another bloke comes around with the Bull of the Day–got a picture, bloodlines and like that–and we pick out the one we want to be used in our mob. Better the bloodlines, the more you gotta pay."

We spent the afternoon at Field Days, an enormous farming extravaganza. Tractors, pumps, trucks, breeders, troughs, irrigation systems: everything imaginable dealing with farming was on display. Farmers and their families questioned salesmen, waded through the equipment, and licked ice cream cones.

One of the local agricultural universities directed a tractor pull. Two four-wheel drive tractors squared off against a lowly two-wheel drive. Excited college kids hooked concrete sleds behind each tractor. Another tractor smoothed three lanes and then the gun sounded. The two-wheel drive tractor jolted off the starting line and pulled steadily away for an easy victory. "There ya have it folks," the announcer boomed to the crowd. He paused for a moment of shrill feedback, then continued, "The winner,

John Brown in his two-wheeler Ford. Might make you think twice about spending all that extra money for a four-wheeler."

• • •

Saturday arrived, sports day for heaps of Kiwis. Steve and I went to Te Awamutu for his club rugby match; Rachel and Kate set off for Rachel's netball game. As usual, from what we gathered, Stephen's team lost and Rachel's team won. After the games, we returned to the farm in time to watch the French-Australia World Cup Rugby test. The family cheered frantically as France defeated the hated Aussies. Stephen, who had sprained an ankle in his game, hobbled out of bed and added his screams to the uproar.

Stephen and Simon, the consummate farmers, guaranteed no rain as we started the pedal north to the Coromandel Peninsula. Predictably, it began to pour ten kilometers out of Te Aroha, so Kate and I pulled in for the night. Fifty kilometers was plenty anyway; with canoeing and visiting in Matamata, we still hadn't biked much in the six weeks since the marathon. We spent the afternoon reading and watching World Cup Rugby. The Kiwi All Blacks continued to ride high, this time humiliating the Welsh in the Cup semifinals.

A hard rain kept us anchored in camp until eleven the next day. A nor'wester battled us all the way to Paeroa, but then a southerly change sent us flying up the Karangahake Gorge to Waihi. We felt excited to finally be at the base of the Coromandel Peninsula. For six months our Kiwi friends had championed its beauty and serenity. The Coromandel became a sanctuary for alternate lifestylers in the sixties and seventies. Much of their spirit was said to remain.

An angry thunderhead accompanied the ferocious winds that pushed us through the gorge. Hard rain pelted down as we landed at the motor camp in Waihi. The sturdy log cabin that housed the camp office doubled as Grandpa Thorn's Restaurant. Eunice and Ashby, the proprietors, graciously invited us to share their home over the restaurant rather than brave the driving storm in our tent. We parked the bikes under an overhang in back and carried the gear upstairs to our room.

Below, Ashby started a pot of fresh ground coffee. Kate and I floated down the stairs towards the intoxicating aroma. New Zealand is a barren wasteland for coffee drinkers. Tea reigns supreme; coffee is almost exclusively of the instant variety. In six months, we had enjoyed fresh coffee only three times. Kate and I both drank a cup, then I proceeded to finish the pot on my own, much to Ashby's amusement.

Along with the restaurant and motor camp, Eunice and Ashby also sold local crafts. Chief amongst their wares were beautiful homespun, hand knit sweaters. As I admired one rugged creation, Eunice said, "I can sell every jersey like that I make. But I've given it up; there's no money to be made. The hours involved are so great that I couldn't charge enough to give myself a good wage. Besides, we're so busy with the restaurant now, I wouldn't have time even if I wanted to make more."

We understood her dilemma. Kate was well into knitting her first jersey and the time involved was great. We, however, had the time.

● ● ●

The morning dawned clear but icy cold. Eunice and Ashby were up early, trundling kids off to school and thinking about the coming night's specialties. We thanked them for their kindness, then bundled ourselves against the chill and started up the Peninsula. On the edge of town we passed the brick remains of the pumphouse for the old Martha Mine.

Gold was discovered on the Coromandel Peninsula in the second half of the nineteenth century. A major field at Waihi rendered over a hundred million dollars of gold and silver during its sixty year lifetime. The Waihi Gold Company recently applied to reopen the former mine, and there is similar talk of reopening mining activities around the Coromandel. Hopeful entrepreneurs see financial opportunity in the match of old mines and new technology. Most locals we met, however, considered "mining" a four letter word. They see the loss of their pristine backdrop and quiet way of life. Signs declared:

"STOP MINING ON THE COROMANDEL!"

and posters urged participation in anti-mining coalition meetings.

Kate and I planned our ride through the Coromandel to be a series of short, enjoyable jaunts. There were several reasons. First, we wanted to have time to hike and explore the bush and coastline. Second, the shortest day of the year was rapidly approaching. Also, it was getting cold. Our frigid departure from Waihi convinced us that riding time would be limited to the warm midday hours.

Finally, and most importantly, we needed a chance to get reacquainted after the tough times in Te Puke. Some hard feelings lingered from our numerous arguments and we stood on shaky ground. Canoeing was a mental high for both of us, but there wasn't much opportunity to think or talk about our relationship. Our departure from Matamata left us alone for the first time since kiwifruit picking.

From Waihi, we pedaled to Whangamata, thirty kilometers north along the east side of the Coromandel Peninsula. Traffic, like everywhere on the Peninsula, was sparse. The road wound up and down through patches of bush and paddock. Every hill crest revealed another postcard view of ocean and coastline. My overwhelming sense of it all, though, was quiet: no cars, no voices, no wind. A bellbird or tui might call out, but even that came infrequently. Tourist season had long since ended and the Peninsula was settling in for the peaceful passage of winter.

We took a room in Whangamata and then headed for the harbor. The tide was so far out that walkers could reach nearby Hauturu Island. Two fishermen in a rusty boat bounced over the waves. The beach stretched endlessly; flat tidal pools mirrored the sunset. Low-angle light caught the excited faces of young surfers riding waves to shore.

The morning ride from Whangamata to Tairua took us inland, over one leg-burning hill. A cold sun arched high into a cloudless sky over the Bay of Plenty. The Peninsula's interior, made up largely of Coromandel State Forest Park, stood tall and dark and deeply bushed. Marijuana, we frequently heard, is grown there.

"Mind where you go walking, mate," one bloke cautioned, "or they'll be after you with machine guns." Hook grass assaulted us a few times, but we never ran across any machine guns.

Kate and I took an exhilarating plunge from the big hill's summit to Tairua and the sea. Tairua Harbour is dominated by Paku Mountain, site of a once heavily-fortified Maori pa.

● ● ●

We were heading for Ferry Landing when Kate spotted the rustic Purangi Winery tucked quietly into a kiwi orchard. Inside, next to the wines, were homespun jerseys, pottery, and honey. Bill, one of the owners, minded the store. Bill proved an interesting study: sheepskin boots, jeans with multi-colored flower patches, plaid flannel shirt, stubbly beard, hair loosely pushed back. He told us that Mrs. Evans knitted up the jerseys off fleeces from her own sheep, that the clay work came from a potter down the road, and that the honey was brought in by the communers from up north.

Purangi Winery makes Coromandel Fruit Wines, largely from kiwifruit grown out back. "We've got two acres," Bill explained. "That supplies us enough fruit for the winery, plus three thousand trays of export."

He moved behind the counter, sat on a stool, and started pulling out wines for us to taste. Bill led us through a myriad of kiwifruit and tamarillo wines and liqueurs, even a mead. Then he guided us around back for a tour. The presses, filters, and fermenters looked unimposing and manageable on such a small scale.

We finally settled on a late harvest kiwifruit wine and got ready to depart. Bill stepped out onto the veranda while we climbed on the bikes. "Where you planning on staying tonight?" he asked.

"We'll just camp somewhere, probably Whitianga," I answered.

"That's only a few kilometers down the road," Bill returned. Then, with a scratch of his head, he said, "Heck, you can stay at my place. Got an old caravan you're welcome to use."

"Really? That'd be great!"

"Just carry on around a couple corners until you see a sign that says 'Large Automobile Pottery.' You're fifty meters too far. Go back and you'll see a Bedford truck with a stuffed gearbox sitting in a greasy drive. That's the place."

The old caravan sat under a dilapidated overhang which was connected to a worn out barn. A rain catch supplied running water via an outside hose. The toilet was a deep long drop; no shelter protected the hole. "Just be sure to cover the loo with the board when you're done," Bill cautioned later. "We don't want to lose anyone."

Kate and I dropped our panniers and gear at the caravan, biked into Ferry Landing to pick up some food, then pedaled out to Shakespeare Cliff for the afternoon. In 1769 Captain Cook named the cliff after a similar white cliff in Dover Harbor. Cook also named Mercury Bay, in commemoration of his observance of the Transit of Mercury.

Back at the caravan, we found a note from Bill inviting us to his house for a visit and some wine. Bill lived a couple hundred meters away at the end of the greasy road. A narrow creek bordered the house on one side, a bushy hillside in back, a small lemon and mandarin orchard in front. The home's large porch faced the orchard and down the valley. On the porch sat a soft, tattered chair; in the chair sat a plump, black chook. Bill waved hello and then pointed us through the bush to his private, forty foot waterfall. A pipe from the top of the falls supplied water to the house.

Inside the house were two cats, two stoves, science fiction books, wine bottles, an unmade bed, gas lanterns, a couch, a chair. A wood stove rendered hot water via natural convection and an insulated storage tank. There was no electricity or phone but there was a twelve volt TV. If the tube aired something Bill wanted to see, he pulled the car up and ran wires in from the battery.

"One thing about visiting a vintner," Bill said after we finished the tour, "he always has plenty of wine." After a couple glasses, Bill invited us to join him for tea. He was having Scotchbroth and asked if we had anything to contribute to the pot. Kumaras and pumpkins, we told him, though neither of us had a clue if those fit into Scotchbroth.

"That'll be beautiful, no worries." We soon found out that, aside from the obligatory barley, Bill's Scotchbroth consisted of anything he fancied tossing in. And foremost on Bill's list of Scotchbroth ingredients was kiwifruit wine. He must have poured three bottles of wine into that big pot over the next hour. The result was mouth watering. "Food here has no variety," Bill said as we all dug in. "Not like you've got in the States, or in Canada where I'm originally from. One time I mixed up a batch of chile con carne and took it to a party. The people here couldn't believe it. They thought it was beautiful."

Excellent Coromandel Kiwifruit Wines preceded, accompanied, and followed the meal. We passed through bottle after bottle with Bill pointing out subtleties along the way. He even dipped into a special bottle he'd been saving for the right occasion. It wasn't necessary; Bill had already done a fine job of proving his contention that the grape is the wrong fruit to make wine from.

"Did a lot of traveling when I was younger," Bill said. By now we were all lounging, Kate in the chair, Bill on the stairs, me on the couch. "S'pose I was quite a bit wilder then. Finally decided to settle down. The Coromandel was brilliant in those days, mostly alternate lifestylers trying to find something for themselves. When I bought this piece of property for three thousand dollars in seventy-two, the locals told me I was being robbed. Now I could probably get two hundred thousand for it."

Bill stood up to uncork another bottle of wine. "When I first started living on this place I was just up here in a tent. Bloke down the road said I better move in with him for the winter. This bloke was rough. He never lived in a house until he was twenty-seven! We ate mutton and potatoes three times a day, every day. Put me off mutton considerably for some time."

We had talked into the dark and could no longer make out each others faces. Bill lit a kerosene lantern; its odd, smoky light hung in the air. Kate asked if he ever considered returning to Canada.

"Been back a couple of times. I love Canada but it's just too damn cold. Always come back here–this time I think it'll be for good. For me, this is home. I feel right here and it fits me. Don't kid yourself, though, New Zealand has some real quirks and problems, especially for someone who's lived in North America."

Kate pulled a blanket over her legs as the night chill set in. "Things can be so far behind here," Bill said, moving to the wood stove. He laid the paper and logs and then continued. "People want to be secluded, left alone, but they're being dragged into the twentieth century. Lots of growing pains. And people are so set in their roles here." Bill lit the paper, then looked back. "I was the first male nurse in New Zealand. That was a tough one for people to handle."

A glow grew from the stove, matching our inner warmth. Bill returned to his seat on the stairs. "I teach some nursing classes now and again. Sometimes I ask the female nurses if they've heard of *Kidnapped, Tom Sawyer, A Tale of Two Cities*. Not one. Some think they may have vaguely heard a bloke named Shakespeare. These girls think that getting beat up by their husband is normal. 'Hey, that's what always happened to mom,' they tell me."

We protested that he must be exaggerating. "I kid you not," Bill said earnestly.

One of the cats hopped up on the couch and settled into my lap. I was happy for the warmth and the pleasant purring. "Laws are crazy here," Bill continued. "Put some wiring in the shed down where the caravan is. Inspector comes out. 'Needs a piece of electrical tape there.' Damn wiring is in half an inch of plastic tubing. 'Nope needs tape.' We stick a ten cent piece of tape on and he OK's it. Brilliant, just brilliant."

The other cat meowed at the door; Bill walked over and let her out. Turning back he said, "I guess one of our biggest problems is so little world news. Anything we do get is slanted. Like what do you Americans really think about nuclear war? I'm not a fanatical antinuke-type, but I'm glad we're not letting your boats dock here. Given the choice, I'd rather not live next to bombs and warheads."

● ● ●

The next morning we crossed the narrow harbor opening between Ferry Landing and Whitianga, the bikes perched precariously atop the small ferry's roof. "She'll be right, mate," the old ferryman assured us. "'aven't lost one yet."

Whitianga, with a population of just over two thousand, is the hub of the central Coromandel Peninsula. Still Whitianga boasts no high rises, no traffic, no noise. There are several pubs, however. We slipped into the Whitianga Hotel pub to watch the first-ever World Cup Rugby finals. The pub bulged with Kiwis excited for a championship. They weren't disappointed as the All Blacks trounced the French. The pub crowd cheered so loudly that one of the few things we heard the announcer say was, "Everything the French throw at the All Blacks gets thrown right back at them...."

Kate and I spent a couple of days in Whitianga, walking, talking, and sorting through our feelings. Our impending jump to Australia gave meaning to time and we began to realize that our year of travel had bounds. Aside from wind and rain, the only stress we faced stemmed from the uncertainty over what awaited us at home. We began to realize that this uncertainty was the source of our problems while picking kiwifruit. We rededicated ourselves to living and learning day by day. The future would take care of itself.

● ● ●

We opted to cross the Coromandel Peninsula on Highway 309. Locals advised against the rugged metal road. One bloke claimed, "I wouldn't want to do it on a push-bike, mate. I 'ate to cross that bloody road in me car." A heavy rain started before we even reached 309, and we covered our gear with garbage sacks. Both Kate and I were thinking the same thing: misery.

But a wonderful thing happened–the sun came out and the temperature rose. The road was curvy, at times washboarded and steep, but pushing the pedals felt good. Rugged bush and open paddocks, both lush and green, guided us through the center of the Peninsula. The sun grew hot and, as we pedaled, we laughed and sang.

Far too soon we were atop the Coromandel Range and ready to descend. Just below the summit came a waterfall, then a stand of monstrous kauri trees. Kauris are remarkable particularly for the breadth; the diameter of one tree in Northland measures more than five meters!

We continued on through open farmland, riding quietly at the base of wild mountains. In the town of Coromandel we purchased some homespun wool for knitting a jersey, then stopped in to the health food store. As we stepped back outside, an old man on a rickety bike pulled up and parked beside us.

"Don't you go gettin' on mine by mistake, mate," he said with a shine in his eye. "She's an English roadster. Got 'er in nineteen hundred and forty-six for six pounds."

We laughed with him, then offered that the bike would probably be worth more than that now as an antique.

He smiled and cocked his grey head to the side. "Yep, I reckon so, but she's not for sale. I ride that ol' girl every day."

South of the town of Coromandel, the road crossed several big hills, then dropped to the ocean and hugged the coast. Shags far outnumbered fishermen on the pebble shores. The sun was a cold, orange ball as we pedaled to the edge of Thames at the Peninsula's base. We had been to Thames our third night in New Zealand, raw and full of excitement. We were certainly seasoned now—ripe some might have said—but no less excited about the beauty and people of New Zealand.

A clear evening sky sapped the earth's heat and we shivered through our coldest night in New Zealand. In the morning, Kate and I hopped around and slapped our hands together as we struggled to break camp. Biking into downtown Thames, we passed construction workers dressed in heavy coveralls, wool jerseys, caps, and gloves. They looked at my bare legs in disbelief. Water puddles along the road were frozen solid. Our eyes watered at the sting of the cold. We stopped for hot tea, then bought me a pair of black sweats pants, my first leg covering in almost seven months.

It was the first morning of winter.

South Island

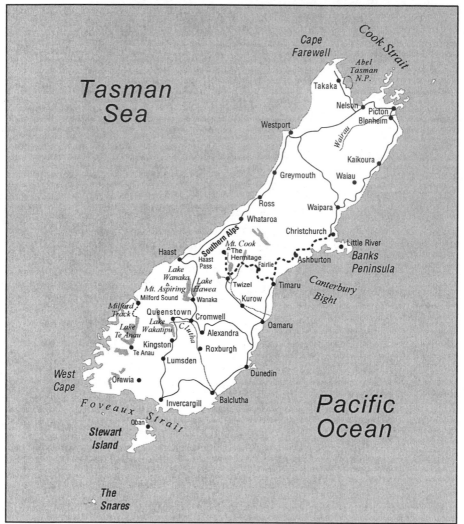

Tasman
Sea

Cape
Farewell

Cook Strait

Abel
Tasman
N.P.

Takaka

Nelson

Picton
Blenheim

Westport

Wairau

Kaikoura

Greymouth

Waiau

Ross

Waipara

Whataroa

Christchurch

Southern Alps

Mt. Cook

The
Hermitage

Little River

Haast

Fairlie

Ashburton

Banks
Peninsula

Haast
Pass

Lake
Wanaka

Twizel

Canterbury
Bight

Mt. Aspiring

Lake
Hawea

Timaru

Milford Sound

Wanaka

Kurow

Milford
Track

Queenstown

Cromwell

Lake
Wakatipu

Oamaru

Lake
Te Anau

Clutha

Alexandra

Kingston

Roxburgh

West
Cape

Te Anau

Lumsden

Orawia

Dunedin

Foveaux Strait

Invercargill

Balclutha

Pacific
Ocean

Oban

Stewart
Island

The
Snares

©1992 MAGELLAN Geographix℠Santa Barbara, CA (800) 929-4627

GOODBYE NEW ZEALAND, PART I

Chapter 16

Warmth and Australia monopolized the conversation as Kate and I pedaled through a couple of easy days to Auckland. Like many Kiwis, we dreamed of holding back the winter for a time on the beaches of New South Wales and Queensland. By a quirk of airline scheduling, our flights took us from Auckland to Christchurch, then Sydney and Brisbane (though we would bike to Brisbane instead), and finally back to Auckland. We decided to make use of the Christchurch flight by visiting the South Island's interior and skiing at Mount Cook. Then bring on Australia and bring on the heat!

We made our way up the west side of the Firth of Thames to Orere Point. A drizzle started as we pulled into a motor camp and put up the tent. The kitchen area was closed for the off-season overhaul, so the manager told us to sit in one of the cabins. Shortly, the drizzle became a torrent.

A few moments later, the manager knocked on the door and poked her head in. "Say love," she said, "why don't you just go 'ead and bunk in 'ere tonight. We can't 'ave you staying outside in this cold, miserable rain." I reached for my wallet but she interrupted me, "No, no. You two are the only bikers we've seen, almost the only visitors of any kind we've 'ad for a month. You just stay 'ere and keep yourselves warm. You know, public relations and all that." We thanked her profusely, then closed the door on the elements. Whoopee! A space heater, a comfortable chair, a light to read by, a roof overhead–could there be anything more to life?

The next morning dawned dimly. Clouds hung low and the rain still felt very close. We pedaled through peaceful hills even though Auckland's sprawl loomed a mere forty kilometers away. At Papakura, the edge of the sprawl, Kate and I hopped the suburban train to the center of Auckland. An icy rain pounded the sidewalks at the railway station. The Kiwi winter was arriving on the North Island with a vengeance.

The local youth hostel was only five or six blocks from the train station, but we still arrived soaked through. It was $10.50NZ each to stay, plus $2.50NZ apiece for sleeping sheets and $1NZ to put the bikes inside for the night–a total of $27NZ($16US), about three times what we'd pay at a motor camp. How they touted these places as "budget accommodations" always escaped me. Free camping, now that's budget.

We got a hold of Fran, our friend from Mount Aspiring Hut, and she rescued us from the hostel for much of the evening. We shared Chinese food and some enjoyable conversation. When I mentioned that our friend Gavin had invited us to the Rotoiti bach again, Fran perked up. "No reason to bus down. I'm driving right past there tomorrow on the way to Kawerau. You can go with me."

The following afternoon Kate and I stored the bikes at Gavin's house in Auckland, then met Fran at the hospital where she worked. We rolled through the dark, south and east to Rotorua, around Lake Rotoiti to Gavin's bach. Gav and his mate Ross, another South African, stepped out onto the porch as Fran pulled away. "Glad you two made it," Gav said. "We knew if there was fishing to be done, you'd find a way to get here, Scott. Never a doubt."

Inside, we caught up on the month since Gavin's big fish, and learned what Ross had been doing since we met Gav and him on the South Island. When I got around to relating my horrific caving story, Gavin, a doctor who was training on the psychiatric ward, sat back and took a puff on his pipe. "You know Scott, that was probably the tougher decision to make: going back. You did right, some people aren't able to admit when they shouldn't do something."

Never has an unsolicited psychiatric evaluation been more readily received.

● ● ●

The routine at the bach was fixed and I knew my part from our first visit. We awoke to a cold morning. Ross threw open the doors so that we could watch dawn form over the lake. The four of us hopped around in our sleeping bags, read, and drank scalding tea.

"Anyone feel like fishing?"

"Naw, let's just relax a bit." We read some more, talked about Gav's dream trip through southern Africa, and drank more tea.

Along about nine o'clock, the books weren't quite as interesting, the tea not quite as tasty. "Anybody feel like fishing?" I asked.

"I s'pose we might give it a try for an hour or two," Gav answered. "What do you think, Ross?"

"Yea, I s'pose we may as well. Scott, are you interested?"

"Well I don't know, this book is pretty good...but I could probably sacrifice. Hey Kate, you want to go?"

Kate looked up from her reading with a wry grin. "You idiots aren't fooling anybody. Why don't you get going? I think I'll just read and knit in front of the space heater today. You three big fakers will be out of here in two minutes."

Kate was almost right. Actually it was only forty-five seconds before we dressed, packed the car (who needs lunch?), and drove off for the Upper Whirinaki, on the eastern edge of Urewara

National Park.

The day's fishing went poorly for the American. Ross picked up a beautiful five or six pound rainbow. Gav took a number of nice trout. The American didn't get a tickle.

The next morning, we again played "Who Wants To Go Fishing?" This day the question required some real thought as a cold drizzle dimpled the lake. I still chomped at the bit to get going, but it took until just past noon for Gavin to say, "Hey Ross, you know we really ought to get Scott a fish, seeing as he was shut out yesterday."

"I suppose it is his last chance to fish before going to Aussie," Ross replied. "What do you say, Kate?"

"Definitely! I don't want to listen to him moan all the way through Australia. Besides, the rain's stopped and I'm ready to get out of the house."

I didn't hear Kate's last sentence; I was already in the car waiting to go.

Since it was late, we decided to head for the Kaituna River, the outlet of Lake Rotoiti. After an hour of precarious fishing above a frothing gorge, I still hadn't had a whiff.

Gav suggested we try the Ngongotaha River, on the far side of Lake Rotorua. The morning rainstorm, he reckoned, might bring big trout out of the lake to spawn. Only a couple hours of light remained and the crew razzed me mercilessly. Gav and Ross gave me the first stretch of nice water, fifty meters from bend to bend. Kate walked along the bank and filled my ears with pearls of fishing wisdom.

The Ngongotaha ran only ten feet wide but was waist deep in the runs. Three-fourths the way along the stretch, I came to a spot where a nice riffle ducked under some overhanging grasses. The indicator dipped. I struck, but the return tug felt weak. "Just a small one," I told Kate. Then the line started heading west as if attached to a submarine. I hung on for dear life and managed to turn the fish just before it reached the corner. That suited the fish fine and it raced by heading east.

"Get down there with it or it'll break the line!" My coach ran along the bank screaming advice. Twice more we went through the upstream-downstream chase. The big trout never came out of the water, but the pull of the rod foretold its size. Huge flashes of white preceded surface swirls as the fish began to tire. Two minutes later I lifted the six pound rainbow skyward. Kate and I whooped as one.

Pictures and a congratulatory beer followed. The razzing started afresh, with Gav commenting, "All I can say is it's a good thing he got that fish. I was really getting sick of his moping around like a whipped puppy."

The needling simply ran off me; I radiated warmth and good humor the rest of the day.

● ● ●

We landed in Christchurch on July 2nd. From the air, the whole of the South Island looked frozen. Icy temperatures precluded enjoyable biking, so we caught a bus for Lake Tekapo, on the eastern side of the Southern Alps.

Inland from Timaru, the bus moved into rolling country, dry like the foothills of the Rockies. Snow began to top the ridges. The further west we drove the more rugged the landscape became, and the lower the snow draped the uplands.

Kate and I stepped down at Lake Tekapo and dropped our gear at the empty hostel. Back outside, we walked along the lakeshore for a couple hours. Lake Tekapo was a jewel, gray-blue from glacial till, surrounded by magnificent white mountains and bathed in cool sunshine.

Later, I left Kate by the hostel fire and went for a run down the Tekapo River. Two boys fished from the Tekapo dam into a pool twenty meters below. The lads screamed with excitement and began to drag a fish skyward. Half way up the dangling fish gave a big shake, then fell back into the water with a splash.

● ● ●

The next morning Kate and I decided to try to hitchhike to Mount Cook. As a couple of free-wheeling bikers, we felt the sting of the $49NZ($30US) bus fare, for two, to Tekapo. We wore every article of clothing we owned to fight the cold morning

The rugged eastern side of the Southern Alps en route to Mt. Cook.

wind. Kate froze up in fifteen minutes; we both became quickly frustrated with hitching. People driving by lifted their noses and looked at us as if we were scum.

We laughed, bemoaned our pitiful state, and decried the evils of hitchhiking. The only recourse was to step into the tearoom for a hot cuppa. So warmed, we made our way back for a final twenty minutes of thumbing before the bus arrived. This time the second car stopped, a 1956 Rover.

Inside the Rover was Duke, a big Doberman with a studded collar, and the driver, a red-eyed Kiwi with greasy hair. The driver made no effort to move Duke, just waved us into the back. As we stepped in, Duke's jaw lowered; drool rolled off his monstrous tongue and his ivory fangs gleamed. Kate and I held our packs protectively in our laps.

The driver was a fanatical Rover loyalist. This was the twenty-second Rover he had owned and he knew every body and every engine ever made. In between telling us about the exhaust system of the fifty-eights and the transmission change in sixty-six, Mr. Rover managed to tell us a little about himself. "Jus' moved down from Kaitaia to Timaru not mor'n a month ago. So bloody cold down 'ere. Never seen the snow. Neither 'as ol'' Duke 'ere, so we reckoned we'd jus' 'ave us a look see. I was at the Chateau one time, but no snow. Spent the 'ole damn day in the pub and 'ad a grand ol'' time."

Not having seen snow meant that Mr. Rover had never driven on snow. Based on his performance on the dry pavement, we looked unlikely to reach Mount Cook. Mr. Rover was a perfect example of why smokers have higher auto insurance rates. Every time he reached for the pack, we veered towards the ditch. Thank God he didn't roll his own. It was the same story when he looked back to talk to us. Kate and I spent a good portion of the ride sucking in our final breaths. Once Mr. Rover chose to ignore a massive bus plowing towards us on a single lane bridge. We screamed and Mr. Rover skidded to a stop, just as the honking bus roared by. Duke never looked up.

The icy section of the road proved mercifully short. Kate and I climbed out at Mount Cook and thanked Mr. Rover for an interesting ride. He fish-tailed off while we wobbled into the hostel. Later, we took a sunset run around town; Mount Cook rewarded us with a cold, imposing facade. Farther along, we found the Rover parked in front of the pub. Duke, waiting patiently, rolled his tongue as we passed.

· · ·

In the morning, we made our way to the Hermitage to have tea and see how the other half lived. The Hermitage is New Zealand's most famous hotel. It was built first in 1884, washed away in 1913, rebuilt, burned to the ground in 1957, and rebuilt again into the present structure. The flags in the lobby gave a clue to the most frequent foreign visitors: American, Japanese, Canadian, Australian, and British.

Kate and I found our way to Alpine Guides by midday, hired some cross country skis, then set out for the Tasman Glacier. Icy conditions prevailed as we skied up the Tasman River. Snow covered peaks, blanketed in clear sky, walled in three sides of the

Sunshine and snow at the terminus of the Tasman Glacier.

board-flat valley. Ahead, the glacier slowly appeared.

We climbed the terminus face and had lunch looking up the immense sweep of ice. Rocks and dirt blanketed the terminus, but higher up the glacier shimmered in stripes of white and blue. The sun glowed brightly and we sloughed off sweaters and gloves. By the time we skied back through the shaded Tasman Valley, however, frigid air had settled over the town.

● ● ●

Departing Mount Cook proved to be another adventure in hitchhiking. Kate and I spent an hour in the cold mountain shade, hopping from foot to foot, unsuccessfully soliciting rides from the four or five cars that passed. Another hitcher gave up and decided to pay the $37.50NZ($22.50US) to get back to Christchurch. We wanted to save the money.

The situation looked hopeless and we grew miserably cold. Kate froze up and moaned, "I can't feel my feet."

"Just a little longer," I said without sympathy. "We'll get a ride. We're not gonna pay to get back to Christchurch."

"Damn it," Kate shot right back, "I don't want to spend seventy-five dollars either, but its going to cost a lot more if I have to have my feet amputated!"

I argued unsuccessfully; we started for the Hermitage and hot tea. Another hitchhiker arrived and filled our spot. Not twenty seconds after we walked away, a car stopped and picked the new hitcher up. He didn't even have a runny nose yet.

Back we went, thumbs extended far out, both disgusted as hell. Amazingly enough, a quiet mountain man picked us up two minutes later. He dropped us at the bottom of Lake Pukaki and a cook from the Hermitage shuttled us from there to Timaru. The cook drove sanely and we were able to enjoy the MacKenzie Country. We'd missed the beauty of the immense highland basin on our harrowing ride with Mr. Rover.

Try as we might, we couldn't get a ride out of Timaru. A short bus trip finally landed us back at Christchurch, where we would catch the morning flight across the Tasman Sea.

● ● ●

The big jet climbed up and over the Southern Alps, then pointed itself towards Australia. Watching New Zealand disappear below us, I thought about how much we'd seen, about how much we still wanted to do. Everyday brought with it a new piece of beauty, another smiling face, another friendly road.

I cringed inwardly then, remembering an American couple that we met along Wellington's Cuba Street Mall. "We just sent the kids off to entertain themselves," the man said. Then, with a not too convincing laugh, he added, "We can't stand the brats anymore."

The man's wife told us they'd been in New Zealand for four days and mentioned what they'd seen and done. "What else would you do?" she asked. "We have six hours tomorrow to see the rest of the country."

Australia

Darwin

Northern
Territory

Cairns

Atherton
Tablelands

Coral
Sea

Great Barrier Reef

Townsville
Prosperine

Western
Australia

Alice Springs

Queensland

Rockhampton

Gympie

Brisbane

Byron Bay

Perth

South
Australia

New South Wales

Port Macquarie
Cessnock

Maitland
Sydney

Victoria

Melbourne

Tasman
Sea

—— Bike Travel
----- Bus/Train

Tasmania

©1992 MAGELLAN GeographixSMSanta Barbara, CA

AUSSIE HOLIDAY

Chapter 17

"Boing, boing, boing."

"What's that?" Kate whispered, shaking me awake.

"Huh?"

"There's something out there." She was sitting up in the dark tent.

Quiet.... "I don't hear anything."

"Shhh, listen."

"To what?"

"Boing, boing." I sat bolt upright.

"That!"

"Boing, boing." The next "boing" sounded like it would land on top of us.

We unzipped the tent and popped our heads out square into the face of a kangaroo. The 'roo twitched its nose, then bent low on its front paws and started to graze. A moment later, the big gray turned, its long tail brushing the tent, and bounced off. Two smaller 'roos, which had been grazing beside the tent, hopped past the door in pursuit of their leader. The sun, a hint on the horizon, silhouetted the departing 'roos. My watch showed six twenty.

*Kangaroo and wallaby sightings are common on
Australia's backroads.*

The kangaroos interrupted our sleep in North Haven, New
South Wales. North Haven is five hundred kilometers north of
Sydney, where we had landed two weeks earlier. The rumors, by
the way, aren't true: to gain entry into Australia we did not have
to smile while eating Vegemite on bread; nor did they issue us ten
thousand flies at customs.

Sydney went by in the blur of a single day. We stayed in the
seedy King's Cross district. No one balked when we carried the
bikes up the two flights of stairs to our room. Kate picked up the
itinerary of a bus tour company and we followed it, on foot, for

eleven hours. The most important discovery of the day was a bicycle touring guide that laid out a ride from Sydney to Brisbane. The Pacific Bicycle Route gave us purpose. We returned to the room leg weary but excited to get back on the bikes and out of the city.

The Pacific Bicycle Route starts in quaint, dusty Windsor. We caught a suburban train there to avoid the hubbub of Sydney traffic. Kate and I planned to continue on as in New Zealand, free camping where practical and paying when a shower sounded good (i.e. most nights). We pedaled out of Windsor to our first Australian motor camp–"caravan park" in Aussie lingo.

"Any cooking facilities?" I asked the camp proprietor.

"Sure, we got barbies."

"Any stoves or ovens?"

"Nope."

"Anyplace to sit indoors?"

"Nope."

"Any light to read by?"

"Nope."

Welcome to motor camping Aussie style. New Zealand motor camps had definitely spoiled us.

Darkness and dew arrived at five thirty. Staying up until nine would mean a new set of flashlight batteries daily. Kate read until seven, then retired. I pulled out my sleeping bag and wool hat, found a post to lean against, and knitted by the light of a street lamp. I had started a jersey of my own while we were on the Coromandel Peninsula. I still fumbled a bit, but was making progress.

The novice knitter's breath fogged the air; dew sparkled in the circle of smoky light around him. Campers peeked through their curtains. One bloke stepped out of his caravan and said, "Hey mate, it's too cold to sleep out there." Mostly the novice shivered through knit-one, purl-one, kept company only by an occasional passing mongrel.

● ● ●

We awoke to find the water in the billy frozen. Kate shivered as she poured our second cups of hot tea, and then lamented,

Pedaling up the Hawkesbury River, N.S.W.

"Where's all that warm Aussie weather we crossed the Tasman for?" After some icy packing, we started for Brisbane, twelve hundred kilometers distant.

As we crossed the Hawkesbury River near Sackville, an elderly couple on the ferry asked where we were going. "North," I replied.

"North?" The old man paused to exchange looks with his wife. "She's a mighty big country, son. There's an awful lot of north and a lot of ways to get there."

Kate and I spent two days working our way up the Hawkesbury Valley. The wide river flowed placidly. Water ski clubs, ski caravan parks, and ski motels were intermittently spaced along the way. Mostly we pedaled through fragrant eucalyptus forest, often along hard dirt roads. Sandstone cliffs towered overhead at the riverbends.

We emerged from the Hawkesbury into dry country filled with fruit orchards and vegetable patches. An election was under way at the intersection which doubles as the town of Mangrove Mountain. Kate stepped into the town hall to ask to use the toilet.

"Ready to vote?" the woman behind the counter asked.

"No, no," Kate replied. "I don't live here."

"Oh, absentee voting. Over here please."

"No, you don't understand...." Kate got the woman straightened out and we were welcomed. The folks running the election even invited us to sleep in the town hall after the voting concluded. We never got the opportunity, however, because a young bloke stepped over and asked if we might join his wife and him for the night.

Phil and Jenny ran a fruit orchard a couple kilometers away. We ate well, then shared some good Aussie wine and enjoyable conversation. Phil and Jenny raved about a place on the coast called Seal Rocks, and assured us we could find warm weather there. Kate and I changed our route on the spot.

We pushed on in the morning across the tree-lined Hunter Range, through heaps of cool sunshine. In Wollombi, we spotted a patch of grass and a pub and decided to call it a day. Aussie pubs, we quickly recognized, could help us beat back the cold and dark of the night.

That evening, a couple greeted us at the door of the local watering hole. Both carried a beer and a big smile. "Saw you pedal in this afternoon," the bloke, Mike, said.

"It's freezin' out there, mate," Jan, the girl chimed in. "C'mon in and warm up." Mike and Jan led us through the crowd to the fire. A couple Victoria Bitters, lots of "Giddays" to Jan and Mike's friends, and a run through of everyone's favorite *Crocodile Dundee* skit followed.

Later, as Kate and I were about to depart, Mike and Jan stopped us. "Where are you staying tonight, anyway?" Jan asked.

"In our tent, over in the park."

"Dinki-di?"

"Huh?" Kate and I both said at once.

Mike stepped in front of us with a melodramatic flourish. "You'll freeze your bloody bums off. No way we're going to let you sleep outside. You're staying with us tonight." The rest of the group added their agreement.

So it was that we rolled up the tent in the middle of the night and loaded the bikes in Mike's car for the thirty kilometer drive to Cessnock. Part way down the road, Mike swerved wildly to avoid a wombat that crossed through our headlights. Braving the cold might have been safer than braving the drive, but we were too happy at the time to consider that.

● ● ●

Kate and I parted ways with the Pacific Bicycle Route, destination Seal Rocks, just past Maitland. Being inlanders, the ocean drew us; the promise of warmer weather didn't hurt either.

We stopped at a grocery shop in Clarence Town for lunch. I laid our muesli bars and fruit juices on the counter and started to pay. The shopkeeper asked were we were headed. "Brisbane," Kate answered, "for starters."

"Brizzie! Fair dinkum? She's a long way, mate." Then, pushing our food and money away, he said, "Here, you take those...go on, take 'em. Anybody push-biking to Brizzie shouldn't ought to pay for nothin'."

The coming days took us through wooded hills to Girvin and then onto the sun splashed meadows near Bulahdelah. The final push to Seal Rocks was our eighth consecutive day of pedaling. We both felt weary, sore, and ready for an easy ride.

The road to the ocean, however, roller coastered over some monstrous hills. Shortly after the turn to Seal Rocks, we ran smack into a wall. Kate dismounted to push her bike. I pedaled to the top of the wall, then made the mistake of stopping and pulling out the camera.

"Don't you dare take my picture!" Kate screamed.

I took the picture anyway. The click of the shutter echoed

"Don't you dare take my picture!" Kate screamed.

I took the picture anyway. The click of the shutter echoed through the forest like a rifle shot. In a single fluid motion, Kate lifted her bike and shot put it into the ditch. Anger, frustration, and aching muscles let loose. "Damn it! It's not like I walk up every hill! I ride and pedal and go hard and all I have for legs is these two wimpy sticks and then you take a picture like I'm walking all the time." She was yelling at me across an empty patch of asphalt. "I do the best I can. Just because I don't have a couple of stumps for legs like you, that's tough!"

Kate plopped angrily down on the edge of the road. I retrieved the water bottle from her discarded bike and sat in the dirt beside her. It was quiet for several moments. Eventually Kate let me put my arm around her, and a few minutes later we were giggling like fools. We definitely needed a day off.

● ● ●

The sun pushed over the horizon right at seven. I was walking along the beach at Seal Rocks, alone with the morning surf. The headland behind me held an immaculate lighthouse and a smattering of sea-worn homes. Jagged rocks defied blue sea off the point. Ahead was a kilometer of untouched beach and, at the end of that, a rugged rock outcropping. I meandered to the beach end, climbed the outcropping to five meters above the ocean, then sat and watched the day find itself.

Pleasant thoughts of two new friends from camp consumed me. Jim and Marie, a couple of vibrant Aussies, had invited us for afternoon tea that soon turned into evening tea, the dinner variety. It was cold and windy sitting outside, Kate in her sleeping bag, me on an overturned rubbish tin. The cold soon drove us into the comfort–ok, it was tight but warm–of Jim and Marie's camper van.

Jim, who had recently retired after 30 years as a primary school principal, told of being a soldier for the British, enforcing the "peace" in Israel. He described marching through the streets, armed but unable to fight unless provoked. "For us it was a joke. We had so little power. But it was no joke if you had a gas bomb rolled into the cafe you were in, like a couple of my mates." Jim also told of a sand hill turned to greenery, the product of enterprising Jewish youth in a kibbutz. We thought of Hanna and Oded from kiwifruit picking.

Jim claimed that Australia was still a small place at heart. "You give me the name and location of an Aussie," he told us, "and within an hour I can find someone who knows the bloke you're looking for."

These two were inspiration to Kate and I; they were having as much fun traveling as a couple of kids. Jim and Marie climbed on our bikes and declared a desire to try some cycle touring of their own. Given their spirit and vitality, we had no doubt that they could and would.

Suddenly, my musing was interrupted. Dead ahead, in the glare of the rising sun, a fin appeared...then nothing. I stared to a spot out of the glare and suddenly three dolphins cut through the surface and blew mist into the air. First a fin, then a blow, then they were gone to appear further along. The dolphins moved easily up the coast and slowly melted into the distance.

I climbed down from the rock outcropping and started walking back to camp. On the opposite end of the beach a purple figure, Kate, came jogging towards me. I paused to wait for her and looked out to the bay. It exploded! Dolphins jumped and raced and frolicked and spouted everywhere; bodies arched through the air and sliced back into the water.

I waved wildly to Kate and we both sprinted full bore for the rock outcropping. The dolphins swam in pods and, miraculously, passed right below us. At our steep angle, looking east into a sun low off the horizon, we could see brilliantly through the water. The dolphins played with the surf, catching waves, using the energy to propel themselves, then ducking out at the last instant before the waves pounded them into shore. The pods moved in perfect formation, sometimes six dolphins abreast. All the while sunlight streamed through the thin waves, back lighting their play.

At length, the last of the pods passed. For another ten minutes, the white froth of racing dolphins continued far up the coast. As

Kate and I climbed down from the rock outcropping, two more dolphins appeared. These two moved slowly–no body surfing or jumps, just the steady progress of a relaxed cruise. We waved and wished the old folks well, then lowered ourselves to the sand and walked back to camp.

● ● ●

We worked our way slowly up the New South Wales coast: Blueys Beach, Tuncurry, Croki, North Haven. Coinciding with our move up the coast came ever increasing temperatures. Even when we woke to a cold morning, the rising sun promised warmth. Nights remained nippy, but they were nothing like the icy evenings of New Zealand or our first week in Australia.

Still, cold is relative. One morning as we sipped scalding tea, a caravaner across from us stepped out his door in obvious misery. He muttered something about the "God awful cold," then started toweling dew off the windscreen of his car. Next he opened the vehicle's bonnet to the morning sun. When he saw our quizzical looks, the man said, "Just want to warm the engine a mite."

As we moved north, Kate and I ran into an unavoidable stretch of the Pacific Highway. The crowded road is the major link between Sydney and Brisbane, yet it has only two lanes and often no shoulder. We were chugging up a hill, riding close against the traffic, when we heard the growl of a big truck struggling to overtake us. Suddenly an enormous trunk flew past, not the kind for storing clothes but the kind for giving showers and picking up peanuts. Another trunk flew by. We raised our sights until they met the soft eyes of two elephants. ELEPHANTS? In Australia? I let out a whoop and pedaled hard to stay up with the flatbed circus truck. The mammoths dwarfed the truck cab, swaying from one foot to another while desperate springs groaned in agony.

It must have been wildlife day. Shortly we departed the Pacific Highway. The hard dirt road that carried us to the sea gave way to deep sand. We wove snake tracks for ten peaceful kilometers. A flash off to the left. "'ROOS!" Two big grays and a joey bounced into the trees. We'd been scoping for kangaroos non-stop for two weeks, but only been successful spotting roadkill.

Kate and I camped in North Haven that night. We faced our door to greet the morning sun and, as it turned out, three early-rising 'roos who almost landed on the tent.

• • •

The first clouds we saw in Australia evolved into a restful rain day in Port MacQuarie. We continued north the next day, pedaling along lonely dirt roads to tiny Crescent Head. Kate and I walked far down the squeaky beach, then returned to climb the hill above town. We sat on the number six teebox of the golf course; there were only six holes. Waves crunched the headland below. Ivory sand, void of any development, traced the ragged outline of the coast as far as the eye could see. It was as if the land and sea had been shattered, and then stuck back together with too much white glue.

We rejoined the Pacific Bicycle Route at Gladstone, followed the coast north for a day, then turned inland. Thirty kilometers of dirt road carried us across a broad range of hills, through warm air and lush forests, past green paddocks filled with the sounds of birds and frogs. A couple of major ups and a doozy down brought us into Bellingen, where a crowded rugby park roared with excitement. Kate and I joined the crowd lining the paddock. A cold Fosters helped quell the weariness of seventy hilly kilometers.

After setting up camp, we showered, climbed into our least-dirty clothes, and walked to the RSL Club. Aside from the pubs, we learned that we were welcome at the local clubs: Athletic, Bowls, Workingman's, whatever. Little more than a signature, an out-of-town address, and some cash got us good food at a good price, a warm spot to sit, friendly company, and light. We usually stretched dinner out for a couple of hours.

From Bellingen, a quiet road wound us through crimson hillsides back to the ocean. A day of heavy rain at Coffs Harbour compelled us into a welcome rest. Even so, eighteen nice days in twenty beat the heck out of our winter batting average in New Zealand.

● ● ●

North of Grafton is almost a hundred kilometers of empty road until Casino. The road rolled over an armada of small hills and Kate started to lag far behind. I pulled off to the side to wait.

Kate pedaled up and climbed stiffly off her bike. She reached for her water bottle with an exaggerated groan, then sucked in her breath with great purpose. "I want to quit biking. I'm tired of it. I'm quitting now." Kate turned to plop down on a rock, but not before I saw the hint of a smile.

"Super, what do you want to do?" I asked. "Buy skateboards?"

She turned back towards me with mischievous eyes. "Sure, that sounds good." Kate's smile got big.

"Great, where are we going to find panniers small enough to fit a skateboard?"

Laughter and lunch brought renewed enthusiasm. As we climbed on the bikes, Kate yelled into the bush, "All right you 'roos, you better get your bums out of the bush and into the open where we can see you!" Twenty minutes farther on, the trees gave way to a large opening with thirty or forty kangaroos variously grazing, playing, and sleeping. Some of the 'roos bounced along through an unperturbed herd of cattle.

"Hey Scott?" Kate asked after we watched the 'roos for a while.

"What?"

"What do you call a baby 'roo ?"

"I don't know Kate, what do you call a baby 'roo?"

"A newy rooey."

Not to be outdone, I countered. "Hey Kate, what do you call three kangaroos in a pot?"

"What?"

"Stewy 'rooey."

"Booey...."

We pulled into Whiporie in high spirits. Whiporie, the only "town" between Grafton and Casino, consists of a service station, a tiny store, and a house–all attached. We asked if we might set up camp by the picnic tables outside; the station owners kindly consented.

Sunset glowed purple and orange over the gold plain west of

A pet wallaby gets a snack near Whiporie, New South Wales.

Whiporie. We made a fire, cooked dinner, and enjoyed the cool night. Later, in the tent, I nudged Kate. "Hey Kate, wake up."

"Huh? What is it?" she stammered, wiping the sleep from her eyes.

"You know what you call a kangaroo who drinks blood and wants to be like Dracula?"

"What?" she asked, a hint of dread in her voice.

"A fanga-kanga!"

"Go to sleep, Scott."

"Good night, honey." Hee hee.

• • •

Kate and I left the Pacific Bicycle Route at Whiporie, this time for good. We crossed through a pleasant mix of rain forest and open cattle country along Bungawalbin Creek. Kangaroos outnumbered cars on the quiet dirt backroad. After thirty-five kilometers, we returned to seal and ate lunch in the center of the road. The pavement radiated heat. We were definitely clawing our way back into summer.

We departed Coraki for the coast on the first day of August, the first day of our ninth month on the road. Six thousand kilometers had passed under our wheels. We'd been pedaling solidly for a month, uninterrupted by visits or fishing, marathons or fruit picking. Both of us felt like bike travelers again.

Our progress north from Lennox Head was slowed when a belt in my front tire snapped, leaving a knot in the tread that "thumped" with every revolution. After eight months of almost perfect performance, my Rockhopper was understandably beginning to fatigue. The bottom bracket needed replacement, and the time for new chainrings, cluster, and chain was near. Kate's Technium continued to perform well, the only exception being a broken shifter which eliminated her lowest gear. We promptly purchased a new tire and had the shifter welded, but left the other problems for later days.

A peaceful dirt road, bounded by bush and untouched ocean front, carried us up the coast from Byron Bay. The seal returned at Wooyung, but traffic remained light. At Kingscliff, however, our peaceful road converged with the Pacific Highway.

For all practical purposes, Kingscliff to Labrador, a stretch of forty or fifty kilometers, is one big town collectively known as the Gold Coast. Without much imagination, the Gold Coast can be thought of as a distant suburb of Brisbane, a hundred kilometers north. By the time we pulled into Tweed Heads and crossed the New South Wales/Queensland border, commercialism and construction dominated the scene.

Kate and I pulled up for a night at Surfer's Paradise, the Waikiki of the Gold Coast. After exploring the haunts of the beautiful people, we stopped at a hole-in-the-wall vegetarian restaurant to mull over our route north. The restaurant was open-air, the night warm. The workers were dressed casually, like they'd just returned from digging in the garden.

A robust woman stepped up to wait on us, saying, "You folks look like bikers."

"We are," Kate replied.

The woman's face lit up. "All right, bikees! I biked from Cairns to Brisbane once by myself–and then back."

"Really? By yourself? That has to be thirty-five hundred kilometers."

"Fair dinkum," she exclaimed with bright eyes. "Greatest thing I ever did. Truckers got to know me and they'd stop and see how I was doing, maybe give me water or some tucker. God, I'd love to be on the road again."

An impatient customer drummed his fingers on the counter. We paid and moved outside to eat. As we were finishing, the woman behind the counter whistled and waved me over. "Hey, I want to shout you cappuccinos and dessert. What'll ya have?"

"Seriously?" I asked.

"You bet. Take your pick."

"You're a star," I told her.

"I'm not the star, mate," she returned. "You're the bikees. You're the stars."

● ● ●

It was mid-afternoon on Friday when Kate and I reached Beenleigh, a suburb of Brisbane. We bought a four liter box of wine to celebrate the end of the first half of our Aussie ride, and the mail that awaited us in Brisbane. We planned to catch the commuter train into the city, thereby avoiding a stressful ride through traffic.

We quickly learned, however, that Brisbane's commuter trains don't allow bikes. That left us forty kilometers of high-tension riding into the city with little time. Missing our mail meant staying in Brisbane until Monday morning. Given the circumstances and the sudden addition of eight pounds of liquid refreshment, what could we do? Drink wine and bike like hell. The wine dulled the crush of horns, yells, and screeching tires. We pedaled fearlessly, reached the post office with time to burn, and then spent two hours pouring over our mail.

The hectic ride into Brisbane convinced us to get out of the city as quickly as possible; we hit the road early the next morning. The ride through Brisbane's northern suburbs, however, rendered further misery. Saturday traffic and construction combined to the detriment of both driver and biker. Cars stacked up and people scowled.

Then a reckless hot rod nearly ended our trip. He was alongside us on a roundabout when he swerved left, rubber screeching. Just at the moment my front tire prepared to disappear into his wheel well, I slammed on the brakes, turned the handlebars ninety degrees, and flew off my bike. The hot rod raced on without a backwards glance. My mouth went dry and I couldn't yell.

• • •

Kate and I departed Caboolture the next morning, anxious to get to the Sunshine Coast and the beautiful weather its name promised. We planned to spend a few days along the Sunshine Coast, take the train north to Proserpine and the Whitsunday Islands, then pedal through North Queensland before returning to New Zealand.

Clouds began to build as we passed the Glass House Mountains. Fifteen kilometers from the Sunshine Coast, we ran headlong into a thunderstorm. We treated ourselves to a caravan at Dickey's Beach, and were rewarded with tumultuous rain pounding on the roof.

We spent five days on the Sunshine Coast. Rain monopolized much of that time. The coast lived up to its name one afternoon when we took a sparkling run through Noosa National Park. A hot sun hung overhead. Intrepid surfers plied the waves off every point. Other surfers, mad-eyed, padded barefoot up the track, boards in hand.

While in Noosa, we had some much needed work done on the bottom brackets of the bikes: lubrication of Kate's, replacement of mine. My bottom bracket continued to click, however, as we pedaled towards Gympie. I later discovered that the shop had installed an improperly sized spindle.

Kate and I caught a train north from Gympie to Proserpine, some nine hundred kilometers. We read, knitted, and sweated as the train and the hours rolled on. The train reached Rockhampton and the Tropic of Capricorn at twilight, then chugged on through the night and pulled into Proserpine at six thirty-five a.m. The air felt warm and thick even at the early morning hour. At long last, no hint of winter lingered.

• • •

The ocean at Airlie Beach, a two hour pedal from Proserpine, was aqua and clear, yet it didn't feel right. Then we realized why: no surf. Thanks to the long train ride, we stood inside the protective envelope of the Great Barrier Reef.

Kate and I spent much of a day looking into camping on the Whitsunday Islands. The major task was to select which of the forty or so islands we wanted to visit, and then find a boat to take us there. We picked WhitSunday Island, which received rave reviews for its expansive beach and lack of people. That meant a trip on the *Apollo*, "One of Australia's Leading Maxi-Yachts." I didn't know what a "maxi-yacht" was, but felt happy that our boat was one of the leaders. The *Apollo* certainly led in price: $40AU($28US) each to get us out to the island, then pick us up four days later.

A heavy morning breeze filled the *Apollo's* sails shortly after we departed Shute Harbor. We rocketed between the islands. Even with the wind, the sea remained remarkably tranquil, thanks to the calming influence of the Great Barrier Reef. The crew dropped the sails as the *Apollo* rounded the corner of WhitSunday Island. That's when Whitehaven Beach first appeared—all six beautiful, white kilometers of it.

We dropped anchor a hundred meters out. A fat, bearded fellow, who had already proved himself the clown of the voyage, prepared to dive in and swim to shore. "What about sharks?" someone asked.

"Don't have to worry about the sharks," the fat man quipped. "Crocs ate 'em all."

After being shuttled to shore, Kate and I lugged our gear far down the beach, found a secluded spot in the trees, and set up camp. Now what? Four days stretched ahead with sun and sand and warm water, snorkel gear and naked bodies and a wine cask.... Let's face it, we were laughing.

We grabbed our sleeping pads and headed for the sand. "My job," Kate said, "is to lay on the beach, read *The Covenant*, and do a little snorkeling. Your job," she pointed accusingly at the sun, "is to keep me warm and happy." For four days the sun did not disappoint.

Most of the day-visitors, including those from the *Apollo*, picked up and started home later in the afternoon. Kate and I watched the sun set over the island, alone but for four or five other tents on six kilometers of beach. A candle lit our small campsite as we worked on dinner and sipped wine. Stars appeared out of the twilight, first one, then thousands.

● ● ●

The cries of ravens and magpies woke us. We lay in the tent, transfixed, as golden morning light poured in the open door. The sun slowly lifted away from nearby Haslewood Island and took control of the morning. By seven thirty, the coolness of the night was gone and we moved out to the sand.

I trotted off for a run down Whitehaven Beach, moving in and out along the water line to cool myself. At the beach end, I rounded the corner to Hiiman Inlet, a shallow blue lagoon with water rushing out. A lone catamaran sat anchored in the lagoon, bow to the current. Bush-clad hills rose up from the island's interior to provide the backdrop. Oblivious to my presence, a nude sunbather draped herself across the catamaran's hull.

Later, we snorkeled off the point on the beach's end. Dull coral beds, four feet deep, soon gave way to brilliant twenty foot columns. Beams of light streamed through the water, revealing small fish of every conceivable color and variety. Willowy white angelfish hovered invisibly over the bottom; only their dark eyes gave them away. A deep recess held a monstrous fish, phosphorescent green with blue spots.

We dedicated the rest of the day, and the days to come, to sun and sand. At sunset each night, we lay close on the beach to ward off the approaching cool. Pinks and oranges glowed over the hills. Wine, dinner, and a dark walk along the beach closed out the days. Nightly, stars flooded the cloudless sky; the Milky Way cut the blackness in two with its ashen glow.

On the evening before we were to depart, I walked alone along the shore's edge, stepping in and out of the water, moving quietly through the darkness. I sensed an eerie presence and shone the flashlight into the gentle surf. A ray paralleled me, two feet from the shore in ten inches of water. The ray followed as I walked, followed as I continued to shine the light. I looked into its eye; it looked back. I stopped, it stopped. Slowly the ray moved off into the dark and the depths. I didn't step into the water again.

● ● ●

The *Apollo* shuttled us back to the mainland. Kate and I pedaled for two hot hours to Proserpine, where we caught the train to Townsville. After a day of rest, we climbed back on the bikes, ready to return to the road in earnest. Our plan was to bike north to Innisfail, turn inland to the Atherton Tablelands, return to the coast at Mossman, then pedal south to Cairns–a total of about nine hundred kilometers. Sometime in the pedal south from Mossman to Cairns, we hoped to take a trip or two out to the Great Barrier Reef.

Kate and I left Townsville around noon. Heavy traffic buffeted us. Hot sun parched the ground and dust swirled into our eyes. Strong winds hindered our progress. From behind, I heard Kate mumbling to herself, "Remember, we are having fun."

A roadhouse at Yabulu provided some much needed lunchtime shade. Before we started again, I stepped into the shower, fully clothed, and soaked myself. The cooling waters evaporated quickly. We sweated through another thirty kilometers and started worrying about making our destination, Crystal Creek Campground, before dark.

The National Park office in Townsville had suggested we stop at the camp, in Mount Spec National Park, because of a superb swimming hole called Paradise Lagoon. Our antennae went up at the mention of a swimming hole. "Any crocs in there?" Kate asked.

"No crocs, least not that I've heard," the woman behind the counter replied. "I reckon they can't get up past the rocks downstream from the swimming hole. Besides, if there are any, they'd likely be freshies."

"Freshies?"

"Fresh water crocs. Freshies won't hurt ya none. It's the salties you got to watch out for." As the woman turned to help someone else, Kate gave me an incredulous look.

Eighty hot kilometers from Townsville, Kate and I were rewarded by a fabulous camp set deep in the woods. Only four of the sixty sites were occupied. And Paradise Lagoon exceeded its billing: cool, clear, deep, and placid. A rock amphitheater dropped into the water on one side, forest gave way to a mountain backdrop on the other. A bubbling stream entered and exited the pool.

"One-two-three-GO!" We plunged in, rejoicing at the chance to soak away the heat and grime and tired muscles of the day. Kate flopped out of the pool shortly, muttering something about not wanting to be croc meat.

We built a friendly fire at nightfall. Toads, bold possums, and huge grasshoppers emerged with the darkness. The crunch of leaves resounded just outside our umbrella of firelight.

At seven the next morning, the sun just peeked over the treetops. We shivered, naked, at the edge of the lagoon, two shameless transients trying to decide how badly we wanted to take an icy wake-up plunge. I dove and instantly became part of the day. Kate cringed and tittered nervously at my whoops.

"One-two-three-GO!" I yelled. No movement.... "C'mon you can do it!" Three times I counted as she tried to will her body into the water. Three times the stubborn thing wouldn't move. "C'mon," I yelled again, "all you have to do is jump."

"I know," Kate anguished, "but I'm going to hate myself in mid-air!"

Again I counted and again she made to jump, only to be held in place by the shore's magnetism. Kate's fourth aborted move to the water was too strong, however, and she lost her balance. Suddenly arms and knees and elbows flew through the air and, rather unceremoniously, Kate plopped into the frigid water.

Lord, what a scream.

● ● ●

In the coming days, we pedaled through hot, desolate countryside to Ingham, then hot fields of sugarcane to Cardwell and Tully. By nine a.m. daily, Kate and I were in sunglasses and white zinc. The transition from New Zealand's cold to the heat of North Queensland seemed to have taken place overnight.

Heavy againsterlies battered us on the ride from Tully to Mission Beach. We set up the tent in some trees just off the sand, then collapsed into the cool ocean waters. At dusk, we retired to a grass park for dinner. Bats the size of small hawks winged through the moonlit sky.

The rugged againsterlies and pleasant campsite convinced us to bunk at Mission Beach for a couple of days. The major event of our stay was the completion, at long last, of my wool jersey–the jersey I originally hoped to finish knitting in time to keep me warm through the cold Kiwi winter. The temperature at Mission Beach hovered around ninety degrees Fahrenheit.

• • •

Month ten began the day Kate and I departed Mission Beach. It was now August 31–three-quarters of a year, seven thousand biking kilometers gone in a heartbeat.

As we crossed into the deep rain forest near Mission Beach, a hand-painted sign announced:

Drive SLOW! Cassowaries on the Road. Please DO NOT Feed!

Cassowaries are big birds that live in the rain forests of North Queensland and New Guinea. They can kill a full-grown person with their powerful legs and sharp claws. Cassowaries can run as fast as thirty miles per hour, even through thick jungle. A number of cassowaries had recently been killed in the area. Though up to six feet tall and a hundred twenty pounds, the big birds prove no match for an automobile.

Kate and I turned into a small clearing in the rain forest, parked the bikes, and started down a track in cautious search of cassowaries. We walked quietly, listening to the sounds of the forest. Suddenly, the track filled with bird. The black-bodied monster recalled an ostrich with its long neck and legs. But its head was red, purple, and blue and topped with a leathery crest.

The cassowary stared at us, unsure of who would vacate the narrow trail first. The stalemate continued for two minutes before the big bird tilted its head quizzically, then turned and started down the track. It crossed a stream, plodded up a switchback, then emerged into the clearing near the bikes.

Two men stood in the clearing, scoping the forest with binoculars. "There's one," one of the men said, as if he'd just spotted a cockatoo. "Wow, look at that!"

The cassowary circled the clearing. "Oh dear!" the second man whined. His voice and movements were distinctly feminine. "Of all the times not to have my camera." Even when the five foot bird approached to within six paces, the birdwatchers continued to follow it through their binoculars.

The cassowary, it became clear, wanted food. Its circles tightened around the men. With the bird only two paces away, they turned tail and beat it twice around their van, the cassowary in hot pursuit. The men alternately laughed and whimpered as they ran. Finally, they scrambled into the van, almost slamming the cassowary's long neck in the door. The door displayed an Audubon Society sticker.

More nervous laughter came from inside as the bird hungrily stalked the van. "Get him some bread or something," the effeminate one called. "Hurry, for goodness sake, or he'll flip the van."

Bread ejected from a crack in the window; fingers dove for safety just in front of the snapping beak. The peace offering promptly disappeared. Then the effeminate one stepped out for a picture, and the bird chased him around the van again. "Oh my, oh my!" the man called as he ran. This time the big bird got one leg and half its body into the van before they managed to close the door.

The men departed. With the entertainment over, the bird turned its considerable attention to Kate. Rising to its full intimidating height, the cassowary glared down at Kate, demanding food. "I d-don't have any," Kate stammered, holding her ground. The oversized feet moved a step closer, the beak only a foot from Kate's face. Kate took a step back and the bird encroached again, this time even closer. Kate stepped back another step, then another, the cassowary always following. Kate bolted. Her dash excited the bird and it pursued closely, beak to bum. They made two loops around the clearing, Kate laughing, the bird deadly serious until it realized no food would be won, and the game ended.

● ● ●

Shortly out of Innisfail, the following day, we turned inland towards the Atherton Tablelands. The road began to climb. We ground up and away from the ocean, through endless fields of sugarcane, and finally pulled into a beautiful campsite in Palmerston National Park.

Our dinner that night was a disaster. We planned a real American meal: hot dogs roasted over the fire. We forgot, however, that our camp was in a rain forest filled with soggy wood. The fire took an hour and a half to start and then burned weakly. One hot dog fell off the stick into the coals, both buns started on fire, the baked beans tipped over, Kate burned her finger....

We ate what little we could salvage, then crawled into the tent and hung out the white flag.

In the morning, we continued on toward the Atherton Tablelands. The biggest climbs of our Aussie visit, climbs reminiscent of New Zealand, stood ahead. We chugged upward through deep rain forest, plummeted to the bottom of a lush river valley, then climbed and climbed and climbed. Eventually the dense rain forest of Palmerston National Park gave way to open, cultivated countryside. By mid-morning, heat gripped the land and we sagged from effort and sweat.

Twenty screaming school kids frolicked in the cold pool under Millaa Millaa Falls as we dismounted the bikes and started shedding clothes. The kids gave us courage we didn't need. We would have immersed if ice cubes bobbed on the surface.

After picking up supplies in Millaa Millaa, we made for Lookout Hill and three kilometers of straight up, gut-check climbing. Halfway through the climb, Kate dropped off her bike and bent over in agony. Spasms shook her body and she moaned in pain.

When the convulsions passed, Kate slowly straightened up, her face ashen. "I'm OK, I guess," she grimaced. "I had these tremendous stomach cramps. I can make it. I just might be a bit slow." We resaddled and continued our onslaught on the hill. High above, a group of people stood at the lookout.

The group, mostly elderly folks, watched as I chugged up the last rise to the lookout. Kate was out of sight around a corner. A small, silvered grandmother stepped forward and asked, "Well, where is she, love? Is she gonna make it?"

"She'll make it all right," I answered. "You can bet on that."

The woman grinned. "She's a real battler, is she?"

"Yep, a real battler."

When Kate pedaled up, the small enclave of people at the lookout started clapping and cheering. The old folks circled around and the silvered woman said, "You better find some shade, love. You'll want a bit of relief after all that work. Come on, dearie," she said pointing to me, "help her along over to that tree." We moved to the grass under the woman's supervision. After assuring herself that all was well, the woman and her group loaded into their van and departed.

Finally, we stood atop the Atherton Tablelands. Mounts Bartle Frere and Bellenden Kerr guarded the ocean front to the east. Nearer stretched a wide expanse of flat farmland, cut by deep gorges and patches of rain forest.

Even though the lookout loomed above anything we could see, the ride to The Crater, our destination, still offered plenty of ups and downs. We pulled into the campground dead tired, put up the tent, then set off down the track. Our walk served two purposes: first, to satisfy our curiosity about The Crater–a devilish volcanic hole in the middle of the rain forest; and second, to better complete the destruction of our bodies before day's end.

Kate's stomach cramps returned in the morning, making the short ride to Malanda miserable. She ached and felt no appetite. We were drinking water from questionable sources in North Queensland and guessed that Kate had picked up a bug along the way.

Aside from Kate's ills, our muscles throbbed because of the endless days of pedaling. We'd averaged five biking days of every six for two months straight. The days we didn't bike, we mostly ran or took long walks, mainly because our bodies craved physical exertion. All that was fine until Kate contracted the bug, which prevented her usual rejuvenation after a night of rest.

• • •

Shortly out of Malanda, we passed a wood mill where a sign lamented:

I'm a Lumberman, not a Tourist Guide!

The Federal Government was spearheading a charge to give the rain forests World Heritage rating, and hence protection from logging. It was a popular idea with the environmentalists, known locally as "Greenies," but not with the loggers, who made up a large part of the working population on the Tablelands. Later, another sign:

Save Our Forests–Plant a Greenie!

It wasn't far past the wood mill that I almost lost Kate. A truck approached on the extremely narrow road, followed closely by an impatient car. I was riding ahead. The car zoomed out to pass, either not knowing or not caring that Kate was behind me. For a terrible moment I frantically looked in my rearview mirror, only to see Kate disappear from view. For fully two seconds there was no Kate, just a car and a truck overwhelming the slim road. I jumped off my bike and turned to witness the carnage. Then suddenly, thankfully, Kate appeared, five feet off the road in the ditch bottom, still riding.

The car and the truck raced on without pause. Kate wobbled up and we held each other in fright and relief. We biked close for the rest of the day.

• • •

As we progressed thru Australia, a closeness had returned in our relationship, as well. The pedal north from Sydney was pure travel: few stops or diversions, rugged daily exertion, a welcome nightly wind down. We had time to talk, to rediscover each other, to dream new dreams. We were together again in spirit, not just body. A friend told us we formed a cohesive team of love and companionship like no couple he'd ever seen.

• • •

Following a local's suggestion, Kate and I stopped on a bridge just outside Kauri to look for platypuses. Just as my high-priced guide said, "This doesn't really look like platy country to me," a platypus surfaced right below us. The midday sun beat straight down into the water, revealing every detail of the singular beast's body: the furry torso, the webbed feet, the hairy tail, the duckbill. The platypus swam, dove, and rooted incessantly. Its webbed front feet spread out like fans to work the mud. The bill followed the rooting and scoured the bottom for food.

After an hour, Kate and I extracted ourselves from the show with a wave goodbye and a word of thanks to the platypus. The platy didn't look up.

We pedaled on to Tinaroo Dam. Sailboats abounded on Lake Tinaroo; rain forest encroached the shoreline. Past the dam, the road turned to gravel. Four rock wallabies, frightened by our appearance, scattered into the brush.

The day ended at Downfall Creek Campground, a peninsula which stretches far out into Lake Tinaroo. After a cooling swim, we set up the tent in the shade of a couple big trees. A pot of billy tea officially kicked off thirty-six hours of much needed rest.

After dinner, Kate and I lay on the grass and watched day turn into night. The lake was glassy and twilight stretched on for an hour. Pelicans dropped through settling mist, then skidded into quiet waters among the skeletons of dead trees. Purple slowly became the color of the night. We watched quietly, listening to the sounds of the forest and water mix.

The jungle laughter of kookaburras woke us in the morning. Not far into the day, two remarkably similar units pulled into the campground. The white Toyota Landcruisers both carried small aluminum boats on top, pulled identical caravans, and housed drivers talking on CB's. The driver in the first Toyota waved to us and hollered cheerfully into the CB mike, "I've just spotted our American friends!"

The twin setups belonged to two friendly couples from Bunbury, Western Australia—Graeme and Helen, and Rob and Sandra. We'd met them, and their kids, in another camp and shared some enchanting conversation, centered largely around crocodiles. The families, who we happily crossed paths with many times in the coming week, were halfway through a tour of Australia. Like many Aussies we met, they claimed a desire to see their own country before heading abroad.

• • •

We camped at Granite Gorge on our last night before dropping off the Atherton Tablelands. A full moon illuminated the sky. Tall boulders cast dark shadows around the tent. Rock wallabies, searching for food, bounced out of the shadows and, more than once, paused in front of our door. Kate never saw the moon or the wallabies. Her stomach bug had returned with a vengeance earlier in the day. She crawled into the tent at four, and wouldn't wake until the following morning.

The plunge off the Tablelands to Mossman and the ocean was glorious. The Cook Highway south of Mossman, on the other hand, offered no shoulder, just an endless stream of heavy trucks with little patience for bikers. The trucks, like us, were bound for Port Douglas, a small town trying to rapidly "upgrade" itself to a big-time resort. The trucks carried giant palm trees, destined to line both sides of the road for five kilometers into Port Douglas. Natural growth, I suppose, would have been too slow.

With no grass available at the local camp, Kate and I checked into a hostel. We booked a scuba diving trip for me on the Great Barrier Reef, my first dive in five years and first ever in the ocean.

I spent the night before the dive reading a scuba manual cover-to-cover in an attempt to numb my nerves with information overload. I was only disturbed once during my study. My traveling compatriot and best pal put her arms around me and whispered, "If I were you and going diving tomorrow, I'd be scared shitless. I'm glad I don't have to be shark bait." Kate kissed me and walked away. I always know where to turn for a confidence boost.

• • •

The dive came off without a hitch. I remembered to open my

tank, and to ascend before the air ran out. I even managed to stay clear of a school of barracuda who rudely chose to hover under the boat. I suppose it didn't hurt that I was teamed with one of the dive instructors.

Kate, who was still green behind the gills, met the dive boat back at Port Douglas. We tried in vain all night to get her stomach right. The folks at the hostel arranged for Kate's gear to be shuttled to Cairns the next morning. She hurt, but wanted to bike down.

In Cairns, we boarded the workers' train for Kuranda, a nearby tourist town on the edge of the Atherton Tablelands. The train climbed through rugged rain forest along the Baron River gorge. We set up camp outside of town, then went for a walk along the river.

Eerie noises accompanied the pitch black walk. I almost climbed into Kate's clothes in mock fright. "Crocs come out of the river you know," I whispered melodramatically.

"No worries, mate," came the giggled reply. "They're just freshies. They won't hurt you none."

● ● ●

We rocketed down from Kuranda the following morning and found a campground in the center of Cairns. Kate and I planned to take another trip to the Great Barrier Reef before calling an end to our days in Aussie and returning to New Zealand. We booked passage aboard the *MV SEASTAR II*, whose flyer bragged, "Ray knows these waters." It was good to know that we wouldn't get lost with Ray, but what really caught our eye was the $91AU($63.70US) price tag—both of us for the price of my first dive.

Ten minutes after we cleared the protection of Cairns Harbor, Kate became seasick. The forecast was for two to three meter swells; in reality, three was the minimum. From seven thirty to ten the boat rocked and tossed as it battled monster waves. Kate and her stomach, meanwhile, carried on their own battle. She threw up repeatedly.

We landed at the rear of the boat in a futile search for the smoothest place to sit. Immediately, an enormous wave crashed over the transom and drenched Kate from head to toe. She looked pale and pathetic. Other passengers stopped and offered help, but the only help would have been to turn the boat around and head back for Cairns.

The sea calmed as we arrived at Hastings Reef and Kate breathed a sigh of relief. I prepared for my dive with the three other divers on board. My partner, Laura, was a new diver who had piled up some experience over the past month while working at a dive shop. "One thing," she told me, "I sometimes get nosebleeds when I dive."

The masses plunged into the water while the divers geared up. "By the way," Ray shouted from the deck of the boat, "there's sharks out there, but they won't worry you any. They're just white tip reef sharks." Thirty snorkelers, bobbing on the surface, gulped as one. As I pulled on my face mask, I wondered at the intelligence of a person, namely me, who would knowingly plunge into shark waters with a nosebleeder.

Laura and I dropped along the descent line. Sunlight filtered down from the surface, but reds and yellows were quickly consumed; everything turned to an eerie blue translucence. We reached the violet bottom at fifty feet and looked up. Fish, big and small, were dark silhouettes swimming above. The dangling legs of the snorkelers seemed distant and detached; the boat rocked above like a toy. Only the sound of the regulator disturbed the quiet.

Without warning, right in front of us, a shark appeared. Laura grabbed my arm and squeezed hard. Now is not the time to spout a nosebleed, I thought. She pulled us together. I saw fear in her eyes—or was I seeing my reflection in her mask?

The shark, a five footer, circled, departed, and returned. I prayed for and spotted a white tip on the shark's dorsal fin. White tip reef sharks are harmless, right Ray? God how I wanted to believe that. But in the next moment the shark coasted overhead and gave us a view of his pearly whites. Funny how much a harmless shark looks like a man-eater when nothing but six feet of unobstructed water separate you.

The shark circled and came straight towards us, then veered off just two arm lengths away. Laura continued her death hold on my bicep, which had long since atrophied from lack of blood. When the shark approached again, Laura climbed right up my back. Later, she would say she was trying to make us look more imposing.

The shark departed and we swam on wondering what could possibly follow such an attention-getter. A look over the shoulder showed the shark's return a minute later. We hovered again until it left. Turning to continue, we ran smack into another shark, this one six feet long and much bigger in girth. His appearance was short but stunning. Looking out from behind the mask, it all seemed unreal, like a movie unfolding on a screen.

When the big shark disappeared, I turned to proceed and slammed right into a rock outcropping. After my heart resumed beating, we swam on.

● ● ●

The bus rolled into Brisbane at six thirty a.m., twenty-four agonizing hours after we departed Cairns. Kate and I picked up some coffee to guide us into the day, then turned our thoughts to New Zealand. Australia had treated us well and given us pleasant memories. But New Zealand, sweet New Zealand! We felt like two kids making their way back home.

North Island

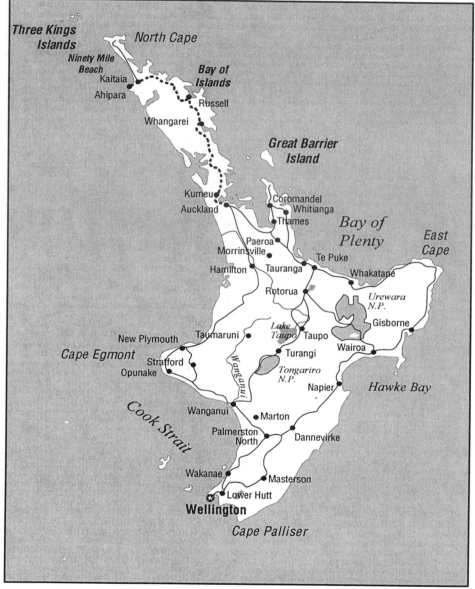

Three Kings Islands

North Cape

Ninety Mile Beach

Kaitaia

Ahipara

Bay of Islands

Russell

Whangarei

Great Barrier Island

Kumeu

Auckland

Coromandel

Whitianga

Thames

Paeroa

Morrinsville

Hamilton

Te Puke

Tauranga

Bay of Plenty

East Cape

Whakatane

Rotorua

Urewara N.P.

Gisborne

Taumaruni

Lake Taupo

Taupo

Wairoa

New Plymouth

Cape Egmont

Stratford

Opunake

Turangi

Tongariro N.P.

Wanganui

Napier

Hawke Bay

Wanganui

Marton

Palmerston North

Dannevirke

Cook Strait

Wakanae

Masterson

Lower Hutt

Wellington

Cape Palliser

©1992 MAGELLAN Geographix SM Santa Barbara, CA (800) 929-4627

KIWI RETURN

Chapter 18

Kate and I rode to the airport through a Brisbane drizzle, then spread out over an entire section of the waiting room. We'd long ago stopped worrying about what anyone thought of two bikers and their gear. There was no wasted motion these days; our packing and preparations were fast and sure.

Twenty mini rugby players surrounded us on the flight across the Tasman Sea to Auckland. They exuded youthful enthusiasm about visiting New Zealand and showing the Kiwis how to play rugby. Their excitement would have been contagious, had we not already had a big dose of our own.

● ● ●

We biked into Auckland in darkness. The moonlit ride felt surreal, like a dreamy step into a familiar past. Could it have really been nine months and seven thousand kilometers since we first arrived in New Zealand?

The dark ride landed us at Ivanhoe Lodge for the night. Zips, dairies, track pants...every nuance of New Zealand flooded back to us and was greeted like a friend. Even the bad things–Watties canned foods, greasy takeaways, Rheineck beer–received bittersweet remembrance.

As always, Kate and I wished to depart Auckland rapidly and get into the country. Our plan was to pedal through Northland, New Zealand's northernmost section, and hopefully minimize the late winter chill.

We hopped a ferry to Davenport, on Auckland's north side, just as a cold morning rain began to fall. The skies cleared soon after we arrived, and we began the pedal up and down through Auckland's north suburbs. Shimmering ocean and green, rolling hills eliminated any sense of city. Locals exuded Kiwi friendliness. Lambs bounced through the grass. The showers returned intermittently all day, but could not dampen our euphoria over being back in New Zealand. For the first time in two weeks, Kate's stomach even felt fine.

After a night in Orewa, we pushed on. Showers continued to fall in the morning, but giant hills provided the real challenge, particularly for me. The drive train on my Rockhopper needed a major overhaul. The Australian spindle change, improperly sized, rendered my Granny gear unusable. Also, my middle chain ring was so worn that the chain slipped right over the teeth. Thus, the big chain ring was pressed into continuous service. The Rockhopper had four gears left, all on the top end. Hills held a whole new challenge.

Kate and I staggered into Warkworth at lunch with a measly twenty-seven kilometers behind us. We turned towards the ocean at Wellsford and followed a heavily graveled back road through lush farm paddocks. A cold rain and heavy againsterlies battered us. But even with the hardships of the day, our New Zealand euphoria persevered.We biked side-by-side, and arrived at

Mangawhai beat but happy.

We found a small motor camp, empty, and snuggled the tent in next to a building for protection. The tent zipper had succumbed to the rigors of the road and we could no longer shut out the elements. Like much of our gear, the tent was simply worn out.

After dinner, Kate and I retired to the rec room to read. The unheated hall was frigid. We huddled together on a torn couch, both in our sleeping bags. Kate shivered and pulled the bag right up to her chin. Only her head was visible. She wouldn't even put her arms out of the bag to hold her book open. I read for a minute, then looked up. Kate's bag had swallowed her, head and all had disappeared. She lay on her back and held her feet high in the air like an inverted cocoon. From within came the sound of hot breath being exhaled.

"What, pray tell, are you doing?" I asked.

"Just trying to warm my feet up," came the muffled reply.

● ● ●

The ride north from Mangawhai continued to be happy. We followed a quiet back road to Waipu Cove. The road paralleled the ocean, then started through the Brynderwyn Hills. Rounding a corner, we ran smack into a solid mass of green. Green dominated the road, green overwhelmed all other sensations, green phosphoresced and sucked us in. It was just another Kiwi hillside, yet so magnificent that we stopped and stared.

The day ended with a strong tailwind pushing us across the flats to Whangarei. Our jovial spirits and good fortune were dampened somewhat the next morning. Icy thunder showers and strong againsterlies blasted us. We hoped to make Russell, some eighty kilometers, but soon realized that we might be forced to stop short. Then a Toyota truck pulling a horse trailer stopped in the road ahead. The driver jumped out and hollered, "How's the wind treating you, mate?"

"Harshly," I replied.

"Wanna throw 'em in the trailer?"

And so we took our fourth and final ride of the year. Steve, the driver, had biked the South Island and thus was sensitive to bikers and the wind. "Had to stop," he said. "Wind's causing me problems just driving." Steve was hauling some ponies to a farm near Russell. One of the ponies found my handlebar grip an enticing treat, but as the grip was already falling apart, I didn't mind.

Kate and I set up camp in Russell and then collapsed. Even with the lift, we'd still done plenty of tough riding for the day. We spent a rest day in Russell, enjoying the sun and calm, and taking some long, thoughtful walks.

Great vistas of ocean and sprawling Northland stretched ahead as we pedaled for Whangaroa. The tiny village clings to bush-laden hills, which in turn drop right into Whangaroa Harbor. A combination hostel/motel sits high on one of those hills. Directly overhead towers St. Paul's Rock. The motel rooms looked great but, with no one else in the hostel, we had our own home. Wistful musings of solitary travelers filled the hostel guest book. Many nights showed no entries. Kate laid her sleeping bag in front of the bay window which overlooked the harbor. I set a pot to boil for tea. It took us a good six or eight seconds to decide that a another day off was in order.

● ● ●

It was a melancholy day as Kate and I pushed off through the hills west of Whangaroa: overcast skies, no wind, cool temperatures. We biked quietly. In the paddocks, cows chewed their cud and watched us pass. One cow, separate from the others, licked her newborn calf. We stopped in the middle of a valley and simply listened. Cows mooed, dogs yelped, the wind moaned. No cars, no human noise disturbed the sense of slowness and peace.

We stopped at Mangonui and picked up some fresh lemon fish for dinner, then biked on to Cooper's Beach. The forty kilometer ride was nothing to brag about, but it seemed enough. We were in a state of winddown, thinking now of savoring our final days in New Zealand, rather than making them tortuous.

In the morning, we meandered towards the end of our

northward journey. Gentle hills rolled into plains and the bush dissipated. Far off to the north, the Aupori Peninsula stretched towards Kerr Point, the northernmost spot in New Zealand. Kate and I, however, turned south at Awanui and pedaled into Kaitaia. We stopped briefly to book reservations for a bus ride back to Auckland, then pushed on for Ahipara and the coast.

Doug and Val, a friendly, sixty-ish couple we met at the kiwifruit orchard, lived in Ahipara, fifteen kilometers west of Kaitaia. They had worked in the she-ed and told us to call in if we ever made it to Northland. Doug is short and fit, with receding silver hair and a handsome face. Val has a pleasant smile, round facial features, and friendly eyes. Doug and Val's house faces directly out on Ninety Mile Beach. They moved us into the bach next door, which they were watching for the neighbors.

After a classic roast lamb dinner, we settled in for a night of conversation and TV. Val showed a video of Ms. Liberty's second unveiling, big and spectacular like so much that is right and wrong with America. The assembled group included David and Denise (Val's twins), Fiona (David's girlfriend), and Monica (Val's mom who was sick and in bed). The family showed great respect to Monica, playing cards and sharing conversation with her. Monica beamed about what wonderful people they were.

● ● ●

Doug pounded on the window at six forty-five the next morning. "Let's go in there! Time for tua tuas." Kate and I knew only two things about tua tuas: that they were like clams, and that collecting them meant getting wet and cold.

Doug rolled his old station wagon out onto Ninety Mile Beach. We drove down the hard-pack surface like the only car on a forty lane highway. David, whose arm carried a tattoo of the Kiwi flag, looked dispassionately out the window. He was not strapped with first-timers enthusiasm. Doug pulled up at "The Spot" and we piled out.

Doug wore a wool hat, a wool jersey, and a pair of shorts, period. He informed us that we'd have to wade through rib-deep water before climbing onto a sand bar full of tua tua beds. Then he grabbed an empty bucket and ran down to the water. Sixty-one? Those legs and that enthusiasm looked like twenty-one. Kate and I exchanged looks as Doug plunged into the cold surf. David followed with a hoot when he hit the water. Oh, was it cold! The first icy step into the ocean rendered pain, the first thigh-topping wave, agony.

On the sandbar, Doug showed us the routine. First we dug our heels into the sand and felt for tua tuas. When we hit a bed, two of us dropped to our knees and started hand- shoveling sand and tua tuas into a chip basket–the kind used in a deep-fryer. Someone else, in turn, dunked the chip basket in the waves to remove the sand. When the chip basket was full, we dumped the cleaned tua tuas into two gallon plastic buckets and shuttled them to shore.

As for the waves? "No worries, mate," Doug shouted. "Just let 'em crash over your back and keep on digging!"

We were quickly soaked from head to toe but the activity and excitement offset the cold. That is until we reassembled in the car and everyone's teeth started chattering. Moments after arriving home, four frozen bodies shivered into four hot showers, then ran headlong into four hot cups of tea.

● ● ●

"Quick, spear it!"

"Damn, missed."

David, Fiona, Denise, Kate, and I stood knee-deep in surf. Denise wore a wetsuit, the rest of us wore warm clothes and sand shoes. It was eleven p.m. and pitch black. Dim lights from homes along the beach wavered like candlelight in the tidal pools.

Denise and I carried shoulder harnesses which contained six volt batteries. We also carried broomstick handles. On the end of each handle, connected by wires to the batteries, was a light bulb. A bent spoon above the bulb reflected the light downward. When held just under the water, the bulb illuminated a three foot circle. The other three carried broomsticks as well, but theirs had been fashioned into spears.

We were hunting for flounder.

We walked five abreast. The others held their spears at the ready as Denise and I moved our lights over the hazy sand bottom. In theory, the late evening hour matched the tide stage that would bring the flounders in. In actuality, we got skunked. Our closest brush with success came when David speared a small sprat. Otherwise, the creatures of the sea remained safe, though in several instances my feet narrowly escaped a painful impaling.

● ● ●

Doug pounded on the window again early the following morning. We were to meet Doug's mate, Ray, and collect tua tuas for a golf club function. David and I rose drowsily, then grabbed some hot coffee to give ourselves a step up on the cold. Kate stayed in bed, not wanting to get too much of a good thing.

We stopped at Ray's special spot. Ray came laden with gear: buckets, a big black tub, a knee length slicker, and, most importantly, a grocery shop wire basket, the perfect sieve for separating large numbers of tua tuas from sand.

As we made for the ocean, the two sixty year olds turned into kids. Frigid waves crashed over us and sapped the heat from our bodies. Yet the old boys laughed, jostled each other, and antagonized the two young softies. Doug and Ray crawled across the tua tua beds with boundless energy. Swamping waves knocked them on their backs, but up they came, sputtering, laughing harder, and ready for more. I held the basket and shuttled buckets in and out to shore with David.

"C'mon Scott, hurry up!" Doug hollered from far out in the surf. I sprinted back from dumping a load and then wondered what the hurry was all about–the tua tuas certainly weren't going anywhere.

"Quick, over here mate. I'm really onto them!"

Soon fourteen buckets stood full. I shivered, soaked through, but the enthusiasm of the two old kids was contagious and the cold didn't bite so deeply this day.

● ● ●

We exchanged addresses and well wishes with Doug and Val before heading for the bus the next day. The bus ride south to Orewa, just north of Auckland, passed quickly. We appreciated the hills and green at a distance, but were not involved with the country we traveled through. Instead, we talked quietly about going home.

Our New Zealand days were numbered.

THE ROAD HOME

Chapter 19

Kate and I packed the gear slowly for our departure from Orewa. Everything slipped easily into familiar nooks and all too soon we were saddled up and on the road. The push to Kumeu, a suburb of Auckland, was to be our last bike ride, the last of the eight thousand kilometers that would pass under our tires. Shortly out of Orewa, the wind belted us head-on, as if registering its opposition to our Kiwi departure. The turn to Coatesville took us off the main road and into a ferocious rain squall. We expected no less on our final day of pedaling.

We rode into Kumeu in the early afternoon and, after getting our bearings, pushed on to Bud and Mary's small farm on the edge of town. We'd been to Kumeu once before, to visit Bud and Mary's daughter, Trish, who we met on Stewart Island. Trish, we knew from an earlier phone call to Mary, had departed on her five year trip around the world. That was the second thing Mary said to us. The first was, "Scott and Katie! You're back from Australia. When will you have a night with us?"

Bud and Mary arrived home just as we coasted into their drive. They greeted us warmly and threw on a pot of tea. Bud has a rectangular face, bushy eyebrows, and a hearty laugh. He habitually ends sentences with "eh?" Mary exudes life. She is shorter than Bud, with dark hair, mischievous eyes, and a ready smile. Both are unpretentious and kind.

Kate and I planned to stay a night in Kumeu, then move into Auckland for a couple of days to prepare for our departure. Bud and Mary, however, would have nothing of it, and told us their home was our home until we left the country. We were happy to oblige, ecstatic might be more accurate. We couldn't think of a better place to end our time in New Zealand.

● ● ●

There were two constants in those final days at Bud and Mary's. First thing every morning, the goats took Kate and I out to the roadside. The goats cropped the grass and, hence, kept the local government happy. The goats, of course, knew little of politics. As the goats saw it, their duty was to make the transit from the goat houses to the road as difficult as possible. They stepped on feet and butted rears. A flushed face, wet gumboots, and an elongated arm were sure signs that the goats had just been taken out.

The second constant was that we always seemed to be moving from one pot of tea to another. Mary fretted over the making of the tea. A carefully tested, time-honored method had to be followed:

1. boil the water
2. prewarm the tea pot with the boiling water
3. add one small scoop of tea per person and one for the pot
4. pour the boiling water over the loose tea
5. spin the pot around three times, then let steep
6. add a splash of milk to the bottom of each cup (proper cups and saucers must be used!)
7. add a small amount of tea to each cup, then pause for the milk to warm...
8. fill the cups (sugar optional)
9. ENJOY!

Mary greeted any deviation from her prescribed method with horror. It took me days to master the technique to her satisfaction.

● ● ●

Kate and I ran an ad in the *New Zealand Herald* to sell the bikes:

HIGH QUALITY US bicycles, Rockhopper mtn bike, $495; Raleigh ultralight tourer, $295. Phone today only.

We derived the asking prices from a split of what bike shops told us they would buy and then resell our bikes for. The prices came out to $305US and $200US, about $100US each less then we'd spent for our bikes new. The incentive to sell the bikes was threefold. They were a year and a half old and in dire need of overhauls. Also, we knew the resale value in New Zealand was likely to be higher than in the States. Finally, a week in the Cook Islands and six weeks touring the Western US separated us from the end of our year. The biggest incentive for selling the bikes was to avoid transporting them through those times.

We joked about being up at six thirty to get the early callers, but secretly hoped that someone, anyone, would call. At eight thirty, we got our first, and as it turned out, only call. The caller owned a triathalon shop and, after a short discussion, offered to buy the bikes outright, sight unseen.

We cleaned up the bikes and Bud ran me into Auckland. The buyer was good to his word and, with less than a thirty second inspection, he wrote out a check. As he scribbled out the sum, a customer walked in and asked about some bikes. "They just came in," our buyer said.

By the time we got back to Bud and Mary's, I felt naked. We had no wheels, no way to get anywhere, no freedom. It was the start of a constant feeling of loneliness that tugged at Kate and I in the coming weeks. Where were the bikes? Our bodies craved exercise and we answered by setting ourselves on a rigorous running and walking schedule. Still, every time it rained Kate asked if the bikes were under cover...then laughed...then fell silent.

● ● ●

It rained the morning we departed Bud and Mary's. It continued to rain as we rode the bus to the airport, and as we waited through the evening for our flight.

The airport was empty save for a janitor or two when our flight finally boarded. Kate and I stepped quietly through customs and then settled into our seats. Outside it was dark and drizzling.

Our plane departed at midnight. Tears fell and two stomachs knotted as the wheels lost contact with the ground. We held each other tight and remembered Mary's parting words earlier that day, "I'll not be sad. You'll be back–it suits you here."

The lights of Auckland slowly faded. Farther along the coast other lights, in small clusters, showed dimly. We looked down and wondered if one might be the town of Russell, then remembered that day three weeks earlier....

The morning sun belied the fact that our rest day in Russell was to be a special day. In the three weeks we spent Northland, this was the only day that the sun shone throughout. We took a pleasant walk along the waterfront. Two old men leaned against a white picket fence, talking and watching.

Kate and I walked south, away from town, then circled back over the intervening hill. As we walked, we talked about leaving New Zealand. It was an increasingly pervasive thought, one that saddened us greatly. So much about New Zealand felt right: the beauty of the country, the friendliness of the people, the relaxed pace of life, the ties that people still hold to the land. Life in New Zealand is simple, naively so some might argue, but nonetheless genuine and real.

As happened often in the final weeks of our journey, Kate and I also talked about our future. We were scared. Yet we felt a confidence we didn't know at the start of our Kiwi travels. Most importantly, we felt the strength of growing together, closer.

On the walk back to our broken-zippered home, I told Kate, "I have some important things to do today." It was the same thing I told her when I shaved that morning, and when I had her cut my hair. We sat at the tent for a while, then climbed up Flagstaff Hill to watch the sun set. We laughed, joked, slapped hands. Four quail scurried into the bush on the hilltop. I piggybacked Kate across the clearing to the flagpole. A plaque told that the flagpole had been erected and torn down numerous times as Maori and

English struggled to form a partnership.

Kate and I sat in the grass beside the flagpole to watch the sunset. The breeze was cool, the sun warm and increasingly golden. A fishing boat left a slow V in the shining water far below. The sun dropped a notch lower, coloring the clouds.

I proposed; Kate accepted. Simple as that. We held each other through the sunset's final moments, alternately laughing and crying. Later we walked down through the bush, and then back to camp. All night we exchanged glances and smiles, like little kids with a secret that everyone would surely want to know.

THE END

Bicycle Adventure Resources

Whether you choose to strike out on your own or join a group, the following resources may be of help in planning your journey.

Bicycle Tour Operators

The following companies offer a selection of organized tours spanning the globe. No endorsement, expressed or implied, is made for the services that are provided.

Adventure Cycling
POB 8308-M2,Missoula, MT   59807 406-721-1776
Bicycle Adventures
Dept L POB 7875 Olympia   WA   98507 360-786-9661
Bike and Cruise Tours
2130 NE Hogan Dr   Gresham, OR 97030 503-667-4053
Brooks Country Cycling
140 W 83rd   New York   NY   10024 800-284-8954
Classic Adventures
POB 153   Hamlin   NY   14464 800-777-8090
Cycle America
POB 485   Cannon Falls MN   55009 800-245-3263
Cycle Venture
2517 Wilhaven Dr, Cumberland, Ontario,
CANADA K4C 1M7   613-833-3343
Dynamo Dave's Discover Tours
85-30 121 St Kew Gardens NY   11415 800-646-9260
Easy Rider Tours
POB 228-B   Newburyport MA   01950 800-488-8332
Elphinstone Mtn Bike Tours
General Delivery, Roberts Creek   B.C.
Canada V0N2W0   604-886-3627
Escape the City Streets
POB 50262   Henderson   NV   89016 800-596-byke
ExperiencePlus! Specialty Tours Inc.
1925 Wallenberg Dr, Ft.Collins CO 80526 800-685-4565

Forum Travel International
91 Gregory #21,Pleasant Hill, CA   94523 510-671-2900
Fred Time
6823 Gaston Ave, Dallas   TX   75214 800-208-1590
Freewheeling Adventures
RR#1,Hubbards,Nova Scotia,CAN B0J1T0 902-857-3600
Gerhard's Bicycle Odysseys
POB 757   Portland   OR   97207 503-223-2402
Mountain and River Adventures
POB 858   Kernville   CA   93238 800-861-6553
Nichols Expeditions
497 N Main   Moab   UT   84532 800-648-8488
Off-Roads Plus
703 Pier Ave Suite B203
 Hermosa Beach   CA   90254 800-788-7587
Outpost Wildnerness Adventure
POB 511   Hunt   TX   78024 210-238-4383
Paragon Guides, Inc.
POB 130D   Vail   CO   81658 970-926-5299
Planet Earth Adventures
POB 49525   Austin   TX   78765 512-467-1602
Roads Less Traveled
POB 8187-E4 Longmont   CO   80501 800-488-8483
Scenic Cycling Adventures
17021 Abuelitos
Fountain Valley, CA   92708 800-413-8432
Thierry Tours
POB 8015   New York   NY   10150 800-742-3872
TK&A
200 Lk Washington Blvd Suite 101
Seattle WA   98122 800-433-0528
True Wheel Tours
POB 366E, Long Lake, NY   12847 518-624-2056
Ultimate Bicycle Tours
1123 #1 Los Palos   Salinas, CA   93901 800-337-tour
WorldCycling
112 Prospect St, Stamford   CT   06901 800-225-2380

Books

New Zealand by Bike by Bruce Ringer
Mountaineers Books ISBN 0-89886-409-7

Bicycle Touring in Australia by Leigh Hemmings
Mountaineers Books ISBN 0-89886-302-3

Tramping in New Zealand by Jim DuFresne
Lonely Planet Books ISBN 0-908086-33-4

The Pacific Bicycle Route
Published by Bicycle Australia
POB K499 Haymarket, New South Wales

New Zealand Embassy

37 Observatory Circle NW
Washington, D.C. 20008
Telephone: 202-328-4848
http://www.emb.com/nzemb/

Internet Resources

Here's a great spot to point your Web browser for
New Zealand information:
http://www.nz.com

Kiwi-isms

Here is a list of commonly used words and phrases that will make your trip a bit easier. Kiwi colloquialisms on the left are matched with the American version on the right.

bach	vacation cottage
billy	teapot
biscuits	cookies
boot	trunk
chips	French fries

dairy	covenience store
fortnight	two weeks
greasy	slippery
half-six	6:30
hire	rent

jersey	sweater
longdrop	outhouse
metal road	gravel road
nappies	diapers
paddock	pasture

pinched, nicked	stolen
pissed	drunk
pozzi	position
pudding	any type of dessert
Saturday week	next Saturday

shout	buy for another
stone	14 pounds
stuffed	ruined
ta	thank you
tea	dinner